Achieving QTS
Teaching Citizenship in Primary Schools

Achieving QTS

Teaching Citizenship
in Primary Schools

Edited by Hilary Claire

Learning Matters

First published in 2004 by Learning Matters Ltd.

British Library Cataloguing in Publication Data
A CIP record for this book is available from the British Library.

ISBN 1 844450 10 4

Cover design by Topics – The Creative Partnership
Project management by Deer Park Productions
Typeset by PDQ Typesetting, Newcastle under Lyme
Printed and bound by Bell & Bain Ltd, Glasgow

Learning Matters Ltd
33 Southernhay East
Exeter EX1 1NX
Tel: 01392 215560
Email: info@learningmatters.co.uk
www.learningmatters.co.uk

CONTENTS

EDITOR

HILARY CLAIRE

Hilary Claire was brought up in South Africa, which has made her very sensitive to issues of democracy, social justice and identity. After her undergraduate degree in history and politics, she trained as an Early Years and primary teacher. She was a class teacher for several years and then moved into research and teacher education. She teaches history and citizenship on the primary ITE courses at London Metropolitan University. She is the author of books and articles on pedagogy and curriculum development in both primary history and Citizenship Education and is currently the coordinator of the Primary Network for the Advancement of Citizenship (PENAC).

CHAPTER 6: GEOGRAPHY, GLOBAL CITIZENSHIP AND CITIZENSHIP EDUCATION

JULIA TANNER

Julia Tanner is a Principal Lecturer in Education at Leeds Metropolitan University, where she is responsible for leading Teacher CPD programmes in the School of Education and Professional Training. She was previously a primary and middle school teacher, and has a particular interest in geography and its contribution to a broad and balanced primary curriculum. Julia is a trustee of the World Studies Trust, which works with student teachers, schools and teacher educators to promote a global dimension in the school and ITE curriculum.

CHAPTER 8: RELIGIOUS EDUCATION AND CITIZENSHIP EDUCATION

LINDA WHITWORTH

Linda Whitworth teaches religious education and citizenship on the Primary ITE courses at Middlesex University. Before moving into ITE she taught Religious Education at secondary and primary levels, and now tutors students on school experience. She is currently involved in developing a PGCE secondary course in citizenship. Her particular interests are in researching ways of developing pupils' understanding of religious identity and developing cross-curricular investigations of community in the primary curriculum.

This book is intended for primary student teachers, but will be useful to NQTs (Newly Qualified Teachers) and established teachers wishing to clarify their understanding of Citizenship Education.

The national scene and status of Citizenship Education in primary schools

In England, Citizenship Education, linked in the primary sector with PSHE, was introduced as a non-statutory subject with the publication of the *National Curriculum Handbook* for primary teachers in 1999. Citizenship Education in primary schools in Scotland has an overlapping but slightly different focus, with less emphasis on PSHE and more on children participating responsibly in political, economic, social and cultural life.[1] In Wales, PSHE is also a separate area of study, and citizenship comes under the broad heading 'Education for Sustainable Development and Global Citizenship',[2] much of which overlaps with the recommendations in this book, and in the NC Framework.

It is important to remember that not only is Citizenship Education (which we will abbreviate to CE in this book) relatively new in primary schools, but, unlike numeracy and literacy, there has been virtually no INSET for practising teachers, and within teacher education the training in CE so far has been patchy. The result is that some students will find excellent practice in schools, often led by a knowledgeable and committed teacher or manager. But others going into their practice schools fired up with enthusiasm can find that they are pioneers, needing to break new ground. As a student, this situation can be liberating, but of course, how much you can do as an innovator will depend hugely on how receptive the environment is to your ideas, and how much support you get.

The QCA is currently developing end of key stage attainment targets for PSHE intended to help teachers assess achievement, and consider progression. For the primary sector, where PSHE and CE are set out in a combined framework in the *National Curriculum Handbook*, CE will have its own statement separated from the PSHE aspects. Exemplification of standards, which is also in the pipeline, will do much to sharpen the focus on CE concepts and clarify what these are.

Although CE is non-statutory, there is nevertheless a requirement to record and report on children's learning in the annual reports that go to parents and carers. Moreover, school OFSTED inspections do focus on CE, and expect to see general assessment of progress. They will note good practice and identify areas for development.[3] Within ITE, OFSTED inspectors also look at how citizenship is being addressed through courses, asking to see the documentation, even if they do not observe taught sessions in the primary sector.

Students, tutors, mentors, teachers

We hope that this book will be useful to all the people involved in CE in the Primary sector, from students entering the profession, to those supervising them and those receiving them into their schools. On the whole the material is addressed directly to students. Tutors running courses or sessions, mentors and supervisors may also find the material is helpful for examples or discussion, and we envisage that some activities can be used for staffroom INSET for qualified teachers and non-teaching staff.

The structure of each chapter in this book

Each chapter starts with a short introduction to its main concepts and finishes with a summary of what you have learned. In each chapter you will find a variety of classroom stories or case studies, followed normally by a short commentary, to help you consider concepts and ideas in action. Along with diagrams which summarise ideas, these provide accessible models for students, and opportunities for group reflection and discussion. In addition, there is a variety of activities which you can either do on your own, or in a group. In the spirit of active, participative citizenship, you are regularly asked to think about your own response to ideas, rather than just accept what the authors or someone else has said. Many of the activities can be used with groups of students or for INSET with teachers.

The overall structure of the book

The chapters in Part I deal with the main concepts and issues about CE and are best worked through sequentially. There are plenty of activities and some case studies in Part I. Citizenship Education through the humanities is the main focus of Part 2. You can read the chapters in Part 2 in any order, according to your interest in a specific theme or curriculum area.

Part I

Chapter I starts by considering what we mean by democracy, and what it means to educate children for democracy or to 'do democracy'. We examine the basic concepts of CE through activities which you may be able to replicate with your own class.

Chapter 2 explores values which underpin the National Curriculum itself, the PSHE/Cit Ed guidelines and the processes and issues of democratic practice.

Chapter 3 is about developing active work with pupils, or 'doing democracy'. You will explore self-esteem and identity, classroom ethos, skills and understanding which support political literacy, thinking skills, debating and persuasive advocacy, and Philosophy for Children.

Chapter 4 provides a variety of strategies for students and teachers to deal with controversial issues in the classroom, including drama techniques. You will also consider the importance of some understanding of economics to help children make sense of the political world in which they are growing up.

Part 2

Part 2 builds on and refers back to Part 1, through the humanities. We haven't been able to cover every other curriculum area, but hope that these chapters will stimulate your own creativity in other subjects. Some activities do refer to work in literacy or maths and we hope that you will see opportunities yourself to develop citizenship through these two core subjects.

Chapter 5 – Stand-alone and cross-curricular work uses case studies where the work generated from children's own concerns, or was introduced by teachers to develop children's understanding or attitudes.

Chapter 6 – Citizenship through geography and global citizenship, written by Julia Tanner, explains how geography supports Citizenship Education through its approaches and its content. There are several case studies from primary schools to exemplify how children can address citizenship, and in particular the global dimension, through the statutory geography curriculum.

Chapter 7 – Citizenship through history uses case studies and classroom stories to show how the history curriculum and its distinctive concepts link and develop knowledge and understanding, attitudes and skills in CE.

Chapter 8 – Religious education and Citizenship Education, written by Linda Whitworth, considers the important links in pedagogy between the two subjects, and explores some of the ways in which RE can take on issues of identity, community and respect.

Resources

The final section of the book provides suggestions for where to find out more, either for classroom activities, or to develop understanding at adult level. It is organised alphabetically, under sub-headings, and includes adult resources, material for use in classrooms, websites and organisations.

The standards for QTS

Citizenship is a theme which addresses all the Standards for QTS. It would be repetitive and not very helpful to list every Standard addressed in each chapter, since every chapter provides concepts, ideas and support which provide evidence for the Standards, if implemented through your practice. Broadly speaking, you will find that Chapter 2 explicitly addresses S1 – the Professional Values and Practice Standards. S2, Knowledge and Understanding for Citizenship, is covered through discussion of the main concepts in Chapter 2 but followed through in every subsequent chapter. S3.1, Teaching: Planning and Classroom Management, is not restricted to any specific chapter. The classroom stories and the discussion throughout the book are relevant to this particular standard, as is the general discussion about classroom ethos and the role of the teacher addressed in Chapters 3 and 4.

Monitoring, Assessment and Recording (S3.2)

This aspect of the standards is discussed briefly in Chapters 3 and 5, but the state of assessment with respect to PSHE/Cit Ed in primary schools when this book went to press (mid-2004) means that we were unwilling to offer definitive guidance. OFSTED advises teachers to 'make your own judgements on the extent to which pupils' attainment, attitudes, values and personal development compare with those that you would normally expect'. There is considerable debate in the compulsory Secondary sector about assessment, with self-evaluation, profiles and portfolios coming high on the list of appropriate methods. Their approaches provide a useful starting point for primary practitioners.[4]

Notes

1 See **www.ltscotland.org.uk/citizenship** for the requirements and excellent examples of practice in the Scottish setting.
2 See **www.cewc-cymru.org.uk**
3 See OFSTED, 2004, *Inspecting subjects 3–11: guidance for inspectors and schools*.
4 See Jerome, L. et al, 2004, *The Citizenship Coordinator's Handbook*, Nelson Thornes, and Jerome, L. *Planning assessment for Citizenship Education: workshop booklet*: **www.citized/info/articles.shtml**

1 WHAT IS CITIZENSHIP EDUCATION ALL ABOUT IN THE EARLY YEARS AND PRIMARY SCHOOL?

What will you learn about in this chapter?

- *what 'Citizenship Education' is all about*
- *where the ideas come from – a broad sweep*
- *why the government has decided that children need to be taught 'citizenship' in primary schools*
- *why we talk about Citizenship Education as 'education for democracy' and what this means*
- *what is in the National Curriculum*

This chapter explains the background to Citizenship Education in the National Curriculum and will help you get to grips with some of its concepts and approaches. It's an important chapter, laying the foundations for what follows in the rest of Part I and in Part 2. For the most part we will shorten Citizenship Education to CE. Some of the concepts in the box above are the same that you might raise within your staff-room or student group, as part of a collaborative approach to understanding and implementing the new guidelines. Some are the seeds of thinking that you might want to share with your own pupils. If you are trying to come to grips with CE yourself, why not start with this brainstorm.

Activity 1

What do you think makes 'a good citizen' and what do you consider Citizenship Education should be about? Brainstorm some of your ideas about adult citizenship and we can work back from there, following the spiral curriculum back to its source.

This is what a group of my own students came up with about adult citizenship. At first they hesitated, then found that one idea quickly sparked off another. How does your brainstorm compare?

- **Knowing about the political system – how it works and how to work within it yourself.**
- **Sharing a view about the importance of democracy and using democratic approaches to express your views and needs in society.**
- **Understanding that there is more than one point of view about different issues and that a democracy recognises this and has legitimate ways for people to express their differences.**

- Knowing how to make your views known and having a commitment to taking part in ensuring a just society.
- Being committed to searching for peaceful ways to resolve conflict.
- Knowing about the legal system – what your rights are and how to exercise them.
- Understanding and practising all the social issues about being part of a law-abiding community – being a considerate neighbour, not wilfully breaking the law, etc.
- Identity issues – feeling that 'you count', that your own identity and culture are recognised and respected, just as you recognise and respect others' identity and culture.
- Feeling that you belong and have some allegiance to the various concentric circles in society – your own local group, a wider national group, global commitment.
- Having a strong sense of justice and morality underpinning the way society is organised and which you can ascribe to.
- Caring about the environment and being prepared to take a part in protecting it.
- Caring about the lives of people in other communities, including those very different from yourself.
- Understanding that in an increasingly globalised world, the old barriers between 'us and them' no longer make sense, politically, economically or morally.
- Human rights education.

We could have gone on and on … it's quite a personal list reflecting the people who were there and you may not agree with everything. That is fine, since agreeing to disagree is essential to citizenship. We agreed that we could broadly group our ideas under a number of headings and then group the issues with the appropriate concept.

These seemed to fit under:

- Rights
- Responsibilities
- Identity
- Values
- Political literacy (I provided this term as the students were not familiar with it)

Children's concepts – thinking about learning objectives

Perhaps you have also developed a brainstorm about how CE might apply to children. If so, you will have started on important thinking about your planning and teaching. As with all other subjects, you must plan for CE using *learning objectives* which will have outcomes that you can evaluate. Figures 1.1 and 1.2 will start you off in thinking about concepts and approaches which will become learning objectives in your planning.

Spend a moment or two thinking about the different issues and approaches and whether they also fit into categories that mirror the adult concepts above – for example, are some about how children behave to one another and the kinds of responsibilities they might take on, some about public/social behaviour in the wider community (all *responsibilities*), some about learning to speak for themselves *(political literacy)*? Figure 1.1 shows some of the ideas that came from a group of students for you to compare.

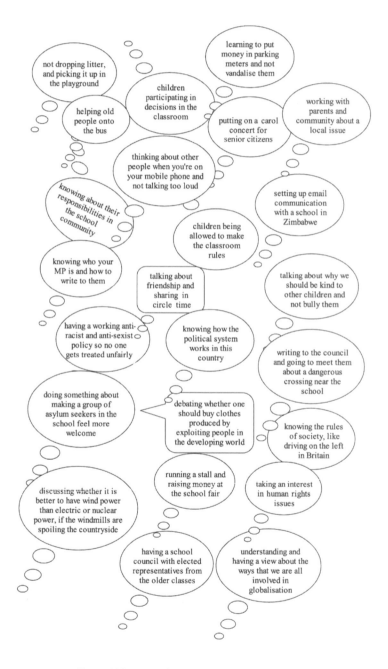

Figure 1.1 Issues and approaches for children in CE

In Figure 1.2 the main concepts which we identified for 'the good adult citizen' are shown as ovals. Then each has a series of rectangles which belong with it, with diamond shapes which give examples of that issue. Some have been left empty, for you to put in your own ideas. Add more ovals, rectangles and diamonds to fit your own 'map' of citizenship concepts and discuss it with a colleague. Consider how this diagram accords with your ideas for developing citizenship education with children.

Why citizenship and where does it come from?

In this next section we will discuss some theoretical ideas about CE, what is in the various official documents and legislation, and then put our ideas together in diagrammatic form to help make sense of ideas and connections. It is important to establish straight away that because citizenship is about the way ordinary people are involved in the governance of society, there is no way to avoid its political nature. Politics is about power – who has it and how it is maintained and exercised. Some primary teachers are worried that this is not the business of schools, and that 'politics has no place in education'. In the sense that indoctrination to one way of thinking has no place in education, they are right. However, as we shall see in this chapter and subsequently, CE is not about indoctrination at all. It is about preparing children appropriately with the knowledge, skills, understanding and values that they will need to function as fully fledged members of society and empowering them to be members of their society now. *What we want is for children to be able to 'do democracy'.*

Democracy

There are a variety of ways to organise the political management of society, ranging from military dictatorships to theocracies (where a religious elite is in control), autocracies and oligarchies (an elite or small group, but not necessarily religious) and democracy. Democracy itself has a number of variations, from socialist-inspired systems to those that are more conservative, but within these variations the following principles of governance apply:

- **Full adult suffrage – that is, all adults have the vote.**
- **Representation of voters through regular elections in which different parties set out their programmes.**
- **Representatives govern with the consent of the people who elected them.**
- **Taxation to fund public projects.**
- **Responsibility and accountability of the elected governing group to the electorate.**

As we shall see, there are other important characteristics of democratic society. A long and sometimes thorny history lies behind the development of democracy in Britain, but democracy is not in dispute as the chosen form of governance now. It is important to have some clarity about democracy because, in England, CE is quite explicitly called 'Education for Democracy'. This means that we will be developing children's understanding of democracy, ensuring that they experience democracy at first hand through the ethos of the school, and through giving them opportunities to

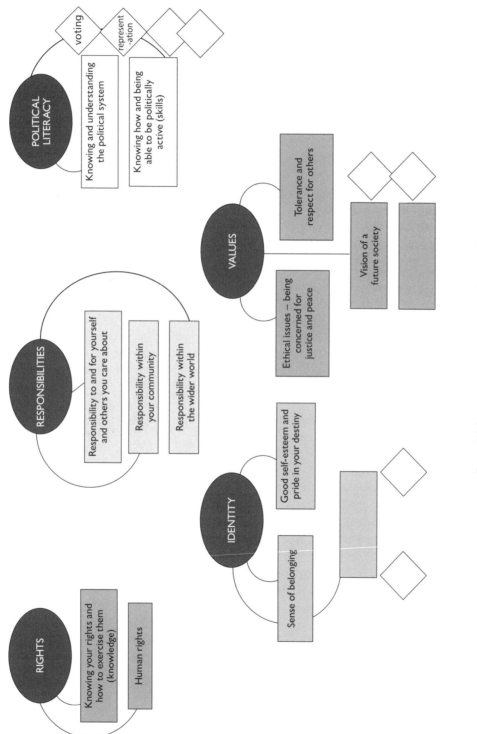

Figure I.2 Some important concepts in being a citizen

practise democracy within the classroom and school. In this book we will talk about children 'doing democracy' to remind us that it is active and encompasses the important ideas of 'having a voice', participation and empowerment.

Rights and responsibilities

Ideas about citizenship date back to the early Greek city states. Although we talk about Athens as the cradle of democracy, it wasn't a democracy in the sense that we now understand this, since a great many people did not have the right to participate in decision making (all women, all slaves and some men were excluded). Nevertheless, the notion has lasted that democracy gives people certain rights balanced by a variety of duties or responsibilities, and that in turn, the governing group has a variety of responsibilities towards the populace and is accountable to them. Although early Greek concepts have been critiqued and significantly developed over the centuries by political philosophers, we have distilled out the concepts of **rights and responsibilities** at the heart of democratic societies. As far as 'rights' go, the American Declaration of Independence is explicit that humans have a right to safety and happiness. It states that

> We hold these truths to be self-evident, that all men [sic] are created equal, that they are endowed by their Creator with certain unalienable Rights, that among these are Life, Liberty, and the pursuit of Happiness. That to secure these rights, Governments are instituted among Men, deriving their just powers from the consent of the governed, that whenever any Form of Government becomes destructive of these ends, it is the Right of the People to alter or to abolish it, and to institute new Government, laying its foundation on such principles and organizing its powers in such form, as to them shall seem most likely to effect their Safety and Happiness ...

The women's suffrage movements and the American Civil Rights movement of the 1960s called on these precepts to justify their campaigns.

In the modern world there is a continuum of beliefs and values about rights and responsibilities. Some people emphasise people's rights and are less concerned about responsibilities, and some put more emphasis on responsibilities. Rights range from personal rights through to human rights for people we don't personally know. Responsibilities range from our own personal responsibility to ourselves and people immediately round us, to those far away whom we may never meet. The Universal Declaration of Human Rights provides an overarching statement for international as well as national or local situations. We will return to a discussion of human rights in Chapter 2.

Education for democracy

There is much more one could say about what citizenship means in the historical and theoretical senses, but this book will concentrate on ideas of citizenship which relate to education for democracy. This is the phrase used to frame CE in schools, and explains why CE appeared in the National Curriculum in 1999. The idea that children needed to understand about their future roles, their rights and responsibilities in society is not new. The original National Curriculum documents (1989) contained the now familiar phrases 'broad balanced curriculum' and 'entitlement', and as part of this, eight booklets of cross-curricular guidance were produced, covering issues such as multiculturalism, environmental education, health education and economic and careers education. NCC No. 8, *Citizenship* (1990), was among them. Much of the content of these non-statutory booklets eventually got recycled into the new Citizenship Curriculum for the Secondary sector, and the PSHE/Citizenship Guidelines in Primary.

In 1997 there was a general election in the UK and Labour came in, triumphantly riding on its slogan 'Education, education, education'. The new Labour government, and particularly David Blunkett, then Secretary of State for Education, was extremely concerned that the population generally, and young people in particular, were apathetic, ignorant and cynical about public duties and responsibilities, as evidenced by low levels of participation in elections and public life. One of the first publications of the new government, the White Paper 'Excellence in Schools' (1997) contained proposals about strengthening education for citizenship and the teaching of democracy in schools. David Blunkett appointed Professor Bernard Crick to head an Advisory Group on Citizenship and a year later their report *Education for citizenship and the teaching of democracy in schools* (QCA, 1998) appeared. Systematic citizenship education, the report said, was an entitlement which could no longer be left to chance. The aim is

> no less than a change in the political culture of this country, both nationally and locally: for people to think of themselves as active citizens, willing, able and equipped to have an influence in public life. We should not, must not, dare not be complacent about the health and future of British democracy. Unless we become a nation of engaged citizens, our democracy is not secure. (Crick, 1998, pp.7–8).

So, education for citizenship became an entitlement, *a question of social and moral responsibility*, a matter of the health of the nation, in which community involvement and political literacy were fundamental. The following quotation indicates how political apathy and morals were linked:

> Active citizens are as political as they are moral; moral sensibility derives in part from political understanding; political apathy spawns moral apathy. (QCA, 2000, p.10)

We'll start by considering what underlies democracy in a multicultural society because this will help us think about what children will need to learn about and be able to do as part of their Citizenship Education.

Activity 2

Diamond ranking exercise to help you think about democracy

There are nine concepts listed below. Copy them onto slips of paper. Feel free to substitute your own ideas for any of them, but you need to work with nine concepts. With a colleague/friend, do a diamond ranking exercise in which you decide between you which (in your view) is the most important idea for democracy, which are the next two most important ideas, then three, then two again, ending up with the one which you think is less important than the others. It's not a competition, nor a 'right/wrong answer' exercise; merely a game to get you thinking about the respective ideas. You can easily play an adapted version with the children in your class.

- *Tolerance and respect for others*
- *Strong opinions about issues and a clear programme*
- *Willingness to allow others their point of view*
- *Everyone has the right to vote*
- *Notions of being fair to a minority*
- *The majority decides*
- *A strong/charismatic leader to hold the factions together*
- *Regular elections so that the voters can change the group in power*
- *Voters feeling it is worth voting*

In this form, the activity is probably too hard, even for KS2 children. However, you can adapt it using easier and more concrete examples which the children can discuss and rank, and then share. There are no right answers.

Activity 3

For you to try with children – a poster about democracy

An alternative way to help children think about the concept of democracy is through making a poster. First talk about what we would want to see in a democracy, and what would be undemocratic. Then allow them to cut images from magazines, take headlines from newspapers and draw or paint their own images to represent their ideas. Build in a session where they present their posters to each other and discuss their representations. Use this opportunity to assess their understanding at this stage, and consider what you need to develop, according to their age.

Authenticity and Citizenship Education

'Authenticity' is an important principle which will run through this book, meaning that, as far as possible, we will be developing children's understanding of citizenship and of their role and responsibilities within the local and wider communities, within real contexts. If we want to empower children, and develop their sense of agency, they need opportunities to work with genuine situations, and debate and influence genuine issues.

The Crick Report and the CE curriculum

The Crick Report became virtually the blueprint for the compulsory KS3 and 4 curriculum, and the framework underpinning the KSI and 2 non-statutory guidelines.

The Crick Report has three strands which are quite clearly present in the Secondary citizenship curriculum and evident in the non-statutory guidelines for the Primary sector:

- **Political literacy:** knowledge and understanding about becoming informed citizens: this includes how the political system works in Britain, and developing skills of enquiry and communication which will make citizens effective in the life of the nation.

- **Social and moral responsibility:** self-confidence and developing socially and morally responsible behaviour both in and beyond the classroom, towards people in authority and each other; considering problems in society originating in political, spiritual, moral, social and cultural differences; understanding and empathising with other points of view/experiences than one's own; expressing personal opinions

- **Community involvement:** developing skills of participation and responsible action in school and community; learning about the role of community and voluntary groups, the media, European and global issues.

Though the Crick Report included notions of combating racism, and developing under-standing of Human Rights, some people (myself included) feel this was rather marginal (see Osler, 2000b, chapters 1 and 2). We discuss the relationship of racism and citizenship later in this chapter and return to the issues in subsequent chapters.

Values education in citizenship

The Crick Report talked about 'values and dispositions'. 'Values' are included at the beginning and at the end of the National Curriculum document. 'Values' underpin concepts such as human rights or taking responsibility for the welfare of others. We saw that political apathy was linked with the morality of young people, who were seen as *wrong* in not recognising their obligations to be involved in political action. As you will appreciate, our concern with 'authenticity' has a bearing on countering such apathy. During the 1990s, there was a certain amount of moral panic about apparent deterioration in moral standards in the young, with the notorious Bulger case, involving the murder of a toddler by two ten-year-olds often quoted as the horrible proof. SCAA (the Schools' Curriculum and Assessment Authority, the predecessor of the QCA) organised a 'National Forum for Values in Education and the Community'. Its remit was to discover whether there was a set of values upon which everyone in society could agree and to decide how best to support schools in promoting pupils' spiritual, moral, social and cultural development. Their deliberations and consultations resulted in the Values statement on pages 147–9 of the *National Curriculum Handbook*.

Values are always part of any person's attitudes and actions, but to be so explicit about values education as part of Citizenship Education was new. This has not been without problems. Chapter 2 is devoted to more discussion about values in CE. For the moment it will be enough just to introduce values as a 'nesting circle' for all our actions and beliefs.

The Race Relations Amendment Act (RRAA) (2000) – identity, diversity and anti-racism

The RRAA took the recommendations of the Macpherson Inquiry into the death of Stephen Lawrence a step further than the earlier legislation[1] and made teachers responsible for proactive work in the curriculum towards inclusion of minority cultures, and reduction of racial tension and prejudice. This means that we must pay more than lip service to a wider inclusive curriculum and be ready to challenge racism and eurocentrism. Moreover, the discredited idea that 'There is no problem here'[2] because there are very few children of minority heritage in a particular community simply won't wash in a multicultural society and globalised world. In fact, there is evidence that children who have little contact with people from different ethnicities may be more, rather than less, prejudiced.[3] Research from the 1970s onwards has shown that racism among children is a bit like an iceberg: they learn the politically correct things to say in front of people they think will pull them up. But beneath this 'tip' can be a huge mass of prejudice and ignorance, which they may well reveal in other situations where they feel they are not being 'policed'. This throws into stark relief our responsibility as teachers. Are we happy with politically correct but dishonest responses to 'please us', or do we feel we need to recognise and try to deal with the iceberg below the surface? As with many of the ideas in this book, you will not all respond in the same way.

Audrey Osler explains how racism undermines democracy, and why it is essential to challenge it if one wishes for a functional and just democracy.

> Racism restricts citizenship rights of minorities and undermines principles of democracy. Understanding of racism, the ways in which it serves to undermine democracy, and skills to challenge this anti-democratic force are therefore essential features of any education programme which seeks to promote the political literacy of citizens. (Osler, 2000a)

It follows that mere tolerance of diversity will not be sufficient to ensure the rights of minority groups to citizenship. In order to appreciate when racism is at the heart of some problem, teachers will themselves need understanding about institutional factors and sensitivity to the subtext of what is going on. As well as wishing to deal with individually prejudiced acts, it will be important for teachers themselves to have analysed and understood what institutional racism means. To challenge racism, as the Macpherson Report requires, will then follow. Which issues they explore and challenge with children will depend on their pupils' age and maturity. This is a theme that we return to in Chapters 4 and 5, in the light of the children's revelations about their experience of racism. You will find useful references in the Bibliography to follow up these themes.

Identity and self-esteem

The ideas which we have introduced about rights, responsibilities and values, including those of mutual respect and tolerance, all form part of the growing network that will make up our understanding of CE.

There are two more concepts which we now need to explore. They are linked to each other and the ideas we have just been discussing, they appear in much of the literature on citizenship, and thread implicitly or explicitly through the official documents.

Identity and citizenship – the notion of belonging

The Crick Report recognised that issues of identity are central to citizenship. It was concerned that national identity had become 'dangerously fragmented', and that our plural society has not been able to establish a secure, cohesive multicultural citizenship in which minorities and diversity are tolerated and respected. Citizenship doesn't make sense except in terms of a wider community, since you can't be a citizen all on your own without a community to which you belong. Most people who research and write about identity focus on questions like 'Who am I? What can I do? Where do I belong? What do I believe in? What is my history?' The idea of belonging and being part of a longer history is very important. Belonging implies that you feel accepted as part of the community, that your concerns are recognised, you feel allegiance, possibly pride, in your membership of the community, but also you have the right to criticise and suggest changes *as an insider*. Historical identity means that the history of your community is recognised and not denied – however uncomfortable that might be for some people – and that it is included in the 'official story' about a nation. The Parekh Report (2000) pointed out that many white people assume that whiteness is a condition of a British identity and do not include others in their view of who is a citizen. A recent project with primary children in Bournemouth has corroborated this.[4] But many citizens in Britain are not white; they belong here, but that they are *made to feel* that they don't belong.

Your identity as someone who 'belongs' as a citizen has a flip side. You have reciprocal responsibilities, you agree to give something back, not just take, you agree to obey the law, and take responsibility for your actions in the wider community, because you realise that the whole is only as strong as its parts, and you identify yourself as one of those parts. Because not everyone acknowledges the different identities of citizens in this country, the concept of identity relates to challenging racism, which in turn relates to the health of a just democracy.

Multiple identities

The Parekh Report (*The Future of Multi-Ethnic Britain*, 2000) discussed the important concept of multiple identities. Parekh noted that

> *Citizens are not only individuals, but also members of particular religious, ethnic, cultural and regional communities ... Britain is both a community of citizens and a community of communities ... Every society must find a way both to nurture diversity and foster a common sense of belonging and a shared identity. (Parekh, 2000, pp. viii – ix)*

This idea is extremely interesting because it suggests how we can *become inclusive*, build bridges between people, and also recognise our connections and responsibilities in wider communities, including the global community. Many people (including many white people) have personal, political and economic connections with a wider world, which may be neither white nor British. This does not stop any of us having an allegiance to Britain, but enriches our identities and underpins global identity. Parekh uses the riveting phrase 'cross cultural navigators' to express the qualities of people growing up in a plural society. It is not about a 'melting pot' in which we lose our sense of identity, but a way to consider our links, help us recognise and tolerate differences, and move away from the idea that a citizen of Britain is always a certain colour, culture, religion and so on. Increasingly, too, since Britain became an official member of the European Union, a European identity is one we need to consider, not just a national identity.

Activity 4

Spend a moment, now, thinking about your own multiple identities

I have thought about my own and started off with ... white woman, wife, mother, grandmother, grandchild of Russian Jewish immigrants who fled from pogroms; raised in South Africa, lived and worked in England for most of my life; teacher and writer; immediate connections through my upbringing and my family with Dominica in the Caribbean, Canada, South Africa, France, West Africa, New Zealand, Guatemala; loves music and gardening.

When individuals have done this, the next step is for the student group to learn about each other and consider the overlaps between their own and others' sense of who they are. Personalise the activity as appropriate for the group. Ask them to move around – physically – to form small groups following your instructions. Find someone in the whole group who shares at least one of your identities (e.g. thinks of themselves as musical). Keep changing the categories, so that people are constantly in a group with different (perhaps unexpected) others. Ask people in the group to suggest categories. Afterwards, sit in a circle and discuss what has come from the activity in terms of self and mutual understanding about identity.

Commentary

A group of my own students did the following activity. First they thought about their own individual identities, then in small groups chose three categories from their long lists and mapped the results. With these adults, personal characteristics like 'resilience' and 'independence' were important parts of their identity. Ethnicity, for some religion, and family relationships (e.g. mother, sister) were also important. This is a good activity to do with children (including quite young ones) to show how we are all linked in different ways. With children, start by calling out a category such as 'supports Man. U or Arsenal', 'has a relative in the Southern Hemisphere', 'likes watching birds', 'enjoys swimming', 'eats fish and chips' or 'likes curry'. Afterwards talk about all the different people who were at some point in the same group as each other and how we are linked. You can adapt and simplify the procedure which showed multiple identities using Venn diagrams. While you will want to emphasise the children's personal and individual identities, which they may express through art, poetry, music or dance, the important concept here is how identities overlap.

Self-esteem and citizenship – another critical concept: 'I matter, I count; you matter, you count'

Those little phrases sum up why high self-esteem is so important to CE and links with the concept of 'identity' above. It's about believing in yourself, in your value, in there being some purpose in saying what you think or feel, because others will listen and care. It's about valuing others and their rights as well as your own.

Self-esteem is central to the PSHE/Citizenship non-statutory guidelines for the Primary phase. It's an important element of the Foundation Guidance and though it hasn't been given the same explicit status in KS3 and 4 (where PSHE is separate from citizenship) in many resources it is recognised as integral to citizenship.

Why is this? People tend to take the value of good self-esteem for granted, but its relationship to CE bears some examination, starting with what we mean by self-esteem. Self-esteem is a combination of how we value aspects of our own person, and our recognition that other people also make judgements about us. So people with high self-esteem typically feel loved and valued by those they care about, but are also aware if some people dislike or disrespect them.[5] For children this can be harder to take than for adults. But with either group, knowing that other people whose views you value have a low opinion of you, can affect your self-esteem.

There is considerable psychological research with people from the youngest to the oldest, about the qualities of people who are broad-minded and tolerant. This demonstrates that open-mindedness about diversity, tolerance and respect for others correlates with a person's own self-esteem. In other words, people who feel good about themselves, with a strong sense of who they are and what they can do, are *less likely* to be resentful, envious, judgemental about difference and intolerant, than those who are unhappy, feel that the world has not done right by them and that others somehow have a better deal.[6] Think about some of the pupils you have come to know and whether this fits. It certainly matches with the well-known phenomenon of those who feel victimised and marginalised, scapegoating another group for their problems.

The idea of the 'good citizen'

In the first activity in this chapter, you thought about the notion of 'a good citizen'. We have covered most of the concepts we summarised in Figure 1.2, except for one which is crucial noted in the second box under Political Literacy. Briefly, the good citizen is an *active citizen*. She or he does more than know about society and its working, what the law is, and his or her rights. S/he exercises her or his responsibilities towards herself and others by doing something. S/he is concerned with justice and the values underpinning society, takes an active interest, tries to get involved, is prepared to try to change things.

The Crick Report (1998) has a number of interesting ideas about why teaching our pupils to be *active citizens* matters for the health of society generally. Much of this connects with and develops the ideas we have already introduced about political literacy, social and moral responsibility, community involvement, self-esteem and confidence.

Empowerment – Pupils have an entitlement that will empower them to participate in society effectively as active, informed, critical and responsible citizens. Pupils should have the opportunities for exercising responsibilities, taking initiatives and to be consulted realistically. (Crick, 1998, pp.9 and 25)

Influence – Society needs an active and political literate citizenry convinced that they can influence government and community affairs at all levels. (Crick, 1998, p.9).

Voluntary action – Volunteering and community involvement are necessary conditions of civil society and democracy (but not sufficient in themselves). (Crick, 1998, p.10)

Independence of thought – Good citizens reflect, enquire and debate issues.

The example in the Crick Report itself is from a Year 3 class who wrote to their council about the state of their local park, describing the litter, graffiti, dog mess and broken play equipment. They made suggestions about how they would like to help to put it right. Representatives from the council visited the class and discussed how to take things forward. Eventually, as a result of the children's initiative, a local residents' association was set up which took responsibility for monitoring and helping to care for the park. (Crick, 1998, p.26)

In Chapter 3 we will explore active citizenship in more depth, and look at the conditions in a school itself, which make this kind of active approach possible and workable. Now, having put the last piece of the jigsaw in place, let's take a look at where we are. Below are the concepts we have introduced and discussed so far. Remember that they are not just the building blocks for CE but are the concepts and approaches that will form the learning objectives for your planning. Fig. 1.3 summarises these ideas.

Rights – which, as we will explore later, include personal rights and human rights.

Responsibilities – starting with yourself and moving through the immediate community, out to a wider world, including global and environmental responsibilities.

Political literacy – understanding ideas about democracy, how democracies work, and learning what you need to do to be part of a democratic society.

Social and moral responsibility – mostly included in the two concepts above, but going wider to include developing ethical understanding.

Values – which justify and explain why and whether we value actions and ideas in society, and which move us beyond selfish concerns to those which go wider.

Challenging racism – acknowledging that racism undermines citizenship.

Identity and multiple identities – a sense of self and belonging, and understanding how identity underpins your connection to smaller and larger groups in society.

Self-esteem – understanding how high self-esteem connects to your ability to recognise and tolerate diversity, but also having the confidence and courage to 'be yourself' and engage with issues.

Active citizenship – being prepared to engage with, debate and reflect on issues, and follow through by trying to do something about them.

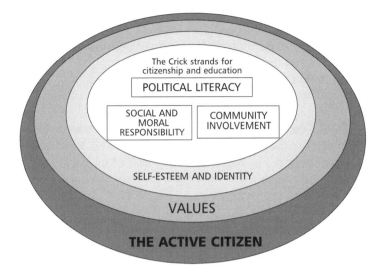

Figure 1.3 A representation of how concepts of citizenship 'nest' in identity and self-esteem, broader values and the notion of active citizenship

What does the National Curriculum say about Citizenship Education in primary schools?

Now that we have explored the ideas that underpin CE, we are ready to focus on what the non-statutory guidelines for Key Stages 1 and 2 have to say. It's important to remember that 'non-statutory' means just that. We are offered a framework, but we are not expected to implement a prescriptive curriculum without regard to the issues and concerns of our own pupils and our own communities. Crick and all subsequent advice have emphasised that we have responsibility to think through what we need to do and work with, in our own settings. Because CE needs to be relevant to children's own lives, we have a set of concepts, skills and attitudes, but not a prescribed content, which will be taught in every school in England.

It is really important to grasp the opportunity that this freedom gives us as teachers to be creative, and to work with issues that our pupils generate themselves, that emerge from what is happening in the outside world at any particular time. We hope our pupils will think creatively about the society they live in; as teachers, we need to take a creative approach to the curriculum we offer them.

Why are PSHE and Citizenship Education combined in the Primary Guidelines?

The headings for Key Stages 1 and 2 PSHE/Citizenship are:

1. Developing confidence and responsibility and making the most of their abilities
2. Preparing to play an active role as citizens
3. Developing a healthy, safer lifestyle
4. Developing good relationships and respecting the differences between people.

In KS3 and 4, PSME – Personal, Social and Moral Education – is separated from citizenship, though in practice many secondary schools run them all together. In primary, health education is included with personal and social education, the word 'Moral' doesn't appear in the title, and the whole lot is covered in the same section in the non-statutory guidelines.

Though there are concepts from citizenship that are NOT part of PSE (for example, voting, democracy, knowing about power or economics), values, self-esteem, identity, and social and moral development fall within both PSE *and* citizenship. This has caused some confusion and uncertainty among primary teachers. Numbers 1, 3 and 4 above are familiar enough. Traditionally, in the primary and early years we have seen ourselves as teachers of 'the whole child' with responsibility for personal, social and moral development inseparable from cognitive development. We know what health education is – no problems there. But active citizenship in primary schools – what kind of animal is that?

We will go through the four main headings from the PSHE/Citizenship Guidelines and think through what these mean in terms of the citizenship model we have already set up.

1. Developing confidence and responsibility and making the most of their abilities

The first key idea here is that high self-esteem and personal confidence underpin acting in a responsible way, and positive responses to other people. We need to think through the links between these qualities and citizenship. The bedrock of belief in human rights is that each human being is unique and has equal worth. This starts with a sense of personal worth and self-understanding which children will build on as they develop empathy and understanding for others. Someone who has the confidence – often the courage – to do something in the wider world needs a strong sense of themself. Much work on self-esteem and self expression is already happening in primary schools, and feels quite familiar. Identity work can happen through literacy, art, history, geography, music, dance, PE, circle time … Remember our discussion earlier about multiple identities and the various characteristics which contribute to our identity, and appreciation of others' identity.

The second key idea is that *doing* something to participate in decisions and actions, plan and develop projects or make a stand about something (being an active citizen) requires a child to have some skills and aptitudes. I will come back to these ideas in Chapter 3.

2. Preparing to play an active role as citizens

Broadly, this strand can be summarised as:

attitudes – having sufficient concern about situations to want to get involved; having care and compassion about people, animals, the environment, including global issues;

skills – e.g. researching or debating controversial issues; resolving difficulties;

knowledge and understanding – mainly 'political literacy': how laws are made and changed, how democracy works, roles of community, voluntary and pressure groups, diversity in society and the downside of community or individual hostility, e.g. racism or bullying, conflicting interests;

empathy – using your imagination to understand others' experience.

This section of the guidelines forms the basis of Chapter 3, so we will move on.

3. Developing a healthy, safer lifestyle

At one level, such matters are very individual, and you might be wondering about its relevance to our concerns, since citizenship is about relationships of individuals to others in society, not individuals in isolation. However, as the above paragraphs implied, you start with the individual and then consider the broader context.

Good self-esteem is related to having a sense of what is right for you, and what you need, and not being tossed this way and that by every pressure that comes your way. At the same time that children start to understand about healthy eating and a healthy way of life, drug and alcohol abuse, exercise and rest, and living in a safe environment (physically and emotionally) for themselves and their peers, they will be developing a sense of 'the right environment' for themselves – and for other people – in which to grow up safe and healthy. They will need research skills to find out more about what is good for them, and what isn't. Along with the ability to put together a case about staying healthy and safe, research skills are part of Citizenship Education. As part of understanding about a healthy, safe lifestyle, children might start to learn how they are being manipulated to buy unhealthy food, or participate in unhealthy behaviour, and how to guard against it.

The introduction of *value judgements* about what one 'ought' to do (not smoke and so on) – called 'normative thinking' – implies that one should be discussing the underlying values. Citizenship again! We said that children will be thinking about healthy, safe life-styles for others, as well as themselves. This might mean learning about children in other communities in Britain or the wider world which are falling short of what we would want for ourselves. For example, they might consider children who don't have safe places or the opportunity to play, eat healthily or rest, or who have to work long hours in unhealthy conditions, perhaps to produce goods which we consume in the wealthier West. You will find that much of this relates to human rights education and that you can move from 'keeping safe and healthy myself' to wider citizenship issues in the community and even the world.

All this leads logically towards understanding how to protest or draw attention to things going wrong and being able to state a case for improvements. We might want to *do something* about situations that fall short of the ideal. For example, children might want to do something about unsafe traffic, about pollution which affects their health, adverts which encourage them to eat unhealthy food or drink alcohol and so on. And so they quickly move from individual work about (say) the amount of sugar in fizzy drinks, E numbers in packaged foods, or how to stay safe from abusive adults, to what they *can do* about protecting their own health and safety. From there, the springboard takes them into concerns about, for example, children being forced to work long hours in other countries, or with insufficient food to grow up healthy.

4. Developing good relationships and respecting the differences between people

This section of the guidelines talks about children understanding about diversity in society, seeing things from other people's point of view and realising the consequences of racism, bullying and aggressive behaviour. There's a statement about understanding about the ways in which people are similar or different, and being prepared to challenge stereotypes. You will also appreciate the links with identity and self-esteem that we outlined in (I) above.

Activity 5

Considering and critiquing sections 2 and 4 of the Primary Guidelines

Look at sections 2 and 4 of the guidelines in your own National Curriculum document, for Key Stage 2 preferably, which has more detail.

- *how would you like to add to and develop this section?*
- *what would you like to emphasise?*

Commentary

I would want to change some of the more neutral verbs in this passage to much more active and positive ones, which match up with the notion of the active citizen that Crick talked about. For instance:

The original is '*realise* the consequences of anti-social and aggressive behaviours, such as bullying and racism, on individuals and communities'.

My stronger version would be '*realise and debate what they will do about* the consequences…, *followed by taking some real action*'.

In section 2 of the NC Guidelines I would put more emphasis on human rights. For example, in section 4, I would like to move from '*ask for help*' in (g) to considering what children can themselves do to support individuals' families or groups needing support, e.g. refugees, or children in other countries who are being exploited. I think this is more in the spirit of 'active citizenship'.

Activity 6

Reflecting on what you have learned so far

Now is the moment to think back to the way you defined citizenship for adults and what you thought CE should entail for children.

- *How have your ideas developed?*
- *Have some of your ideas been confirmed or challenged?*
- *Were there things missing in the guidelines which you had expected to be there?*
- *Were there ideas which you hadn't expected? What were they?*

If you are working in a group, you might like to discuss this with others.

Summary

This chapter started with theoretical ideas about rights and responsibilities in a democracy, and how these related to CE. We considered the main concepts of CE that come from the Crick Report; acknowledged that values underpinned the views of a democratic society that we would like to inhabit; acknowledged the importance and relevance of the Race Relations Amendment Act in CE; explored notions of identity and self-esteem; and emphasised the importance of active citizenship. Lastly, in the light of this broad conceptual framework, we considered what the NC Guidelines say to us about CE in the Primary sector.

The concepts we covered were:

- **Democracy**
- **Rights and responsibilities**
- **Political literacy**
- **Social and moral responsibility**
- **Challenging racism**
- **Values**
- **Self-esteem and identity, including multiple identities**
- **Active citizenship.**

These are the building blocks for CE and will structure the way we set out learning objectives for CE in our planning for class work.

Notes

1 The Race Relations Amendment Act (2000) extended the Race Relations Act (1976), which provided protection from race discrimination in the fields of employment, education, training, housing, and the provision of goods, facilities and services.

2   See Chris Gaine's book *Still no problem here* for evidence of this blinkered attitude.

3   **www.guardian.co.uk/racism/Story/0,2763,439683,00.html**   'The   most dangerous areas for ethnic minorities are also those where there are the smallest communities. Northumbria tops the list, but is closely followed by Devon and Cornwall and south Wales, where racial crimes affect one in 15 and one in 16 respectively. Other race crime hotspots are Norfolk, Avon and Somerset, Durham and Cumbria. Between them, the top 10 worst constabularies in England and Wales for racist incidents are home to just 5 per cent of the total ethnic minority population. By contrast it is the urban centres – London, Greater Manchester, West Yorkshire and Leicestershire – which appear to be the safest. Racist incidents affected just one in 200 of the ethnic minority population in the West Midlands, according to statistics.'

4   Unpublished report from Peter Barton and Norman Schamroth, 2004, 'Dealing with Differences – valuing diversity: tackling racism through story, drama and video in mainly white primary schools.'

5   The psychologist Carl Rogers wrote about the importance of significant others in developing self-esteem.

6   See **www.self-esteem-nase.org** for American research about this issue.

2 VALUES AND CITIZENSHIP EDUCATION

What will you learn about in this chapter?

- why 'values' are part of Citizenship Education
- what we mean by values and how they relate to behaviour and decisions which are connected with CE
- our own value systems and how these relate to our professional role
- which values official groups have identified as particularly associated with CE
- why the interpretation of some values is quite problematic and controversial in practice

In Chapter I we introduced the idea that values underpin both societal choices about how the country is governed through democratic principles and processes, and also the way CE is interpreted officially and at the local level in classrooms and schools.

Some definitions to keep us clear about meanings

Some definitions may help us to get a better sense of how values, morals, actions and behaviour relate to one another. These connections answer the question about why we have a responsibility to develop children's values and morals and encourage certain qualities, as part of CE. The definitions come from Halstead and Taylor (2000). You will probably notice some overlaps.

Values – principles and fundamental convictions which act as general guides to behaviour; enduring beliefs about what is worthwhile; ideals for which one strives; standards by which particular beliefs and actions are judged to be good or desirable. *Examples: love, fairness, equality, freedom, justice, happiness, security, peace of mind, truth.*

Attitudes – acquired tendencies or predispositions to make judgements and behave in a predictable manner. *Examples: openness, tolerance, respect, acceptance, freedom from prejudice.*

Personal qualities – personal attributes, dispositions or characteristics. *Examples: honesty, generosity, courage, confidence, self-esteem, care and concern for others, truthfulness, responsibility, loyalty, compassion, self-discipline, integrity, politeness, sensitivity to others.*

Moral development – acquiring a set of beliefs and values relating to what is right and wrong, which guides intentions, attitudes and behaviour towards oneself, other people, one's own society and others, and the environment, and developing the disposition to act in accordance with such beliefs and values.

If you turn back to Figure 1.3 in Chapter 1, you'll see that all the concepts of CE were set out as 'nesting' within a wider circle called 'Values', which itself nested in a circle called 'The active citizen'. This may at first glance seem unproblematic. *Of course*, you may be thinking, behaviour, attitudes and action are determined by our values. Even the idea of a 'good citizen' is value-laden! People will think some actions are evidence of good citizenship, while others will not put the same ones at a premium. For example, some students in a group recently thought that the right to be 'passive' was an important value, while others valued 'active engagement' very highly. Values are reflected in behaviour and attitudes. A *value* such as respect for other people's humanity, leads to *attitudes* of tolerance, while failure to hold this value can lead to *attitudes* of hostility and *behaviour* such as discrimination, even abuse. Ask yourself if these are evidence of 'good' or 'bad' citizenship. *Pro-social* values like believing in the rule of law, lead to people behaving appropriately towards one another in public places – generally viewed as 'good citizenship'. For the moment, we'll leave that discussion there, but we will be coming back to it. We also need to remember that citizenship in the Primary phase has been linked with personal and social education, which itself rests on a number of value judgements about appropriate attitudes and behaviour.

The Professional Standards for QTS

The Professional Standards are a good starting point for this chapter because they make clear that a number of values lie beneath the way we need to behave as professionals. In Table 2.1 I have chosen statements which explicitly mention pupils' behaviour or are based on value judgements underpinning the teacher's actions. As the paragraphs above suggested, behaviour and actions can always be traced back to values, even though this may not be explicit. Often, we take actions or decisions for granted and we can be quite surprised if someone asks us to justify them in terms of our values, and give 'higher-order' reasons. When we are asked to do this, we draw on our ethical position about what is right or wrong. For some, notions of right and wrong are based on a religious or philosophical position such as 'it is always wrong to kill', or 'the holy book I believe in has given me guiding rules which I will always follow'. This is often called 'absolutism'. Others use 'consequentialist' reasoning to help them decide what is right or wrong. This means they are thinking about the consequences of some action, rather than calling on a rule which applies in all circumstances. Others may favour 'the golden rule' (do unto others as you would have them do unto you) or 'utilitarianism', which suggests one should think of the greatest good for the greatest number (though this leaves open the question about what to do about minority rights). So you can see that in a multifaith, multicultural society, the idea that everyone will share the same values or moral principles will be problematic.

In selecting some statements from the QTS requirements for you to consider in Table 2.1, I have tried to analyse the underlying values about education, teaching, and the kind of personal qualities in our pupils which we hope to encourage. I have deliberately problematised some of the interpretations of the statements so that you will be encouraged to think more deeply about your own interpretations. The final boxes are empty, for you to complete. As you read, decide whether you agree with me and, if not, what values you would say underlie the statements. If you would have selected different statements from the Standards, what values would you say underlie them?

Statement from the QTS Standards	An interpretation of the underlying values	What does this mean to you, and questions raised
I. **Professional Values and Practice** (the heading for the first set of Standards).	Teachers themselves need to have a set of explicit values which underpin their practice.	*Do all teachers have to have the same set of values?*
I.I They have high expectations of all pupils, respect their social, cultural, linguistic, religious and ethnic backgrounds, and are committed to raising their educational achievement.	Teachers should VALUE ALL PUPILS EQUALLY, RESPECT them for who they are and respect their DIVERSITY. Teachers need to believe that all their pupils are worthy of their highest commitment and attention; everyone's potential must be developed.	*Presumably this doesn't mean 'anything goes'! There must be an assumption here that all cultures and backgrounds share common principles which everyone can endorse. It must mean that there are not some children who are 'more worthy' of our commitment than others.*
I.2 They treat pupils consistently with respect and consideration, and are concerned for their development as learners.	In addition to the above, teachers must be FAIR and SENSITIVE TO FEELINGS and do their best for each child's learning.	*What if being 'fair', 'sensitive' and 'supportive' to one group seems to discriminate against another group? For example, 'good girls' are often put in a position of supporting challenging boys. Is this fair on the girls?*
I.3. They demonstrate and promote the positive values, attitudes and behaviour that they expect from their pupils.	Teachers SHOULD MODEL AND INFLUENCE children's BEHAVIOUR AND VALUES and VALUE HIGH STANDARDS OF BEHAVIOUR.	*How can I be sure I'm not imposing my cultural values on other children, unintentionally? What does this mean in practice?*
2.2 They know and understand the Values, Aims and Purposes and the General Teaching Requirements set out in the *National Curriculum Handbook*. They are familiar with the PoS for Citizenship and the NC framework for PSHE.	Teachers have a DUTY to work within the broad philosophy of the education profession and to TAKE RESPONSIBILITY for children's social, moral, personal and health development, not just their cognitive development.	*Does 'knowing and understanding' mean you have to agree with everything? Presumably, to achieve QTS you must undertake not to undermine the values, aims and purposes.*
3.1.2 and 3.1.3 … take account of and support pupils' varying needs, so that girls and boys from all ethnic groups can make good progress … take account of pupils' interests, language and cultural backgrounds.	PUPILS ARE INDIVIDUALS and their individuality, diversity and individual needs must be recognised and supported.	*Isn't there something missing here? people are part of social groups, not just individuals. What about social context and social and ethnic groupings? Sometimes there are clashes between different interests and cultural backgrounds. What then?*
3.3.3 … employ interactive teaching methods and collaborative group work … promote active and independent learning that enables pupils to think for themselves, plan and manage their own learning.	LEARNING TO WORK TOGETHER IS A GOOD THING (note that competition is NOT being advocated here). We value ACTIVE INDEPENDENT MINDS (not automatons, or 'sheep').	*Is collaborative work better in all circumstances? A lot of classrooms are quite competitive. How do I cope with an 'independent mind' that challenges me and my authority?*
3.3.9 They set high expectations for pupils' behaviour and establish a clear framework for classroom discipline … Promote self-control and independence.	We expect good behaviour, but based on SELF-CONTROL and INDEPENDENCE, not fear or behaving well because some else says you must.	*Much behaviour management that you see in classrooms doesn't seem to promote self-control and independence but is geared towards extrinsic rewards (doing things to get a star or sticker). Is this alright?*
3.3.12 … encourage pupils to learn independently.	Another statement putting value on INDEPENDENT THOUGHT.	
3.3.13 They work collaboratively with specialist teachers and other colleagues.	We value SHARING EXPERTISE and COLLABORATION in the interests of our pupils.	
3.3.14 They recognise and respond effectively to equal-opportunities issues … including by challenging stereotyped views, challenging bullying or harassment	EQUALITY OF OPPORTUNITY as a value. CHALLENGING TRANSGRESSION of EQUAL OPPORTUNITIES is THE RIGHT THING TO DO.	

Table 2.I Interpreting the Professional Standards for QTS

Commentary

You will recognise lots of the capitalised words in Table 2.1 from Chapter 1. Words like RESPECT, RESPONSIBILITY, DUTY, DIVERSITY and EQUALITY have come up before. Some, however, didn't appear in our earlier explorations of CE.

The National Curriculum Statement of Aims, Values and Purposes of Education (AVPS: National Curriculum, pp.10–13)

The AVPS at the beginning of the National Curriculum document establishes the broad context for state education. It came about because many people in education had noted that there wasn't anything in the earlier version of the National Curriculum which set the objectives of the various Programmes of Study into a broader framework about the meaning and purposes of education. The Dearing Committee, which reviewed the National Curriculum in 1999, responded to this by providing a wider philosophical context. The interesting thing is that the AVPS is not just relevant to CE, covering several of its concepts, but actually offers a stronger philosophical foundation to CE than the guidelines themselves which we described in Chapter 1.

I have grouped the ideas in the AVPS under headings, but you should read it for yourself and see if you might have used different categories. This will give you a chance to revise and consolidate some of the ideas in Chapter 1 and see how they have been set in a broader context of educational aims.

Values

The AVPS starts by stating that 'students need the opportunity to become articulate in values, including the democratic values of our society' (HMI 1641, 2003, p.12).

Values, according to the AVPS:

- **influence and reflect both the values of society and the kind of society we want**
- **influence equality of opportunity, a healthy and just democracy, productive economy and sustainable development**
- **lead to us valuing ourselves and diversity in society**
- **reaffirm virtues of truth, justice, honesty, trust and sense of duty**
- **develop principles for distinguishing between right and wrong**
- **help pupils become responsible and caring citizens capable of contributing to the development of a just society**
- **promote equal opportunities and enable pupils to challenge discrimination and stereotyping**
- **help pupils understand their responsibilities and rights.**

Active engagement with change and contemporary issues

Specifically
- **respond positively to the opportunities and challenges of a changing world**
- **engage with economic, social and cultural change, including globalisation of economics and society**
- **respond personally to a range of experiences and ideas**
- **cope with change and adversity**

Curriculum issues

- **The curriculum must be responsive to changes in society and economy – society only flourishes if it adapts to the demands and needs of the time**
- **Provide opportunities for children to become creative, innovative, enterprising and capable of leadership in their future lives as workers and citizens**

Critical and creative thinking and problem solving

- **Enable pupils to think creatively and critically, solve problems and make a difference for the better**
- **Help them make informed judgements and independent decisions**

Individual and community identity and involvement

- **Promote self-esteem, respect for themselves and others**
- **Collaborate with families and local communities**
- **Contribute to pupils' sense of identity through knowledge about heritages of Britain's diverse society and the local, national and global dimensions of their lives**

Some of you might find it easier to take in these ideas by means of a diagram. I have started it off, with a short commentary, for you to complete yourself (Figure 2.1)

The Values Statement at the end of the National Curriculum

The AVPS statement at the beginning of the National Curriculum document, and the Values Statement at the end, 'top and tail' the government's advice and requirements for state education. The Values Statement differs from the AVPS in that it is advisory and not statutory, but the mere fact that it has been included gives it status and force. As we explained in Chapter 1, the statement came from a forum set up by SCAA (the predecessor to QCA) in 1996, following concern expressed by many teachers, governors and parents that children's spiritual, moral, social and cultural development was being neglected, at the expense of their academic development. The forum described these values as an ideal, something we try or would like to live up to. We don't always manage to live up to values, but that doesn't stop us expressing our commitment to them. The problem comes at a different level – how to put

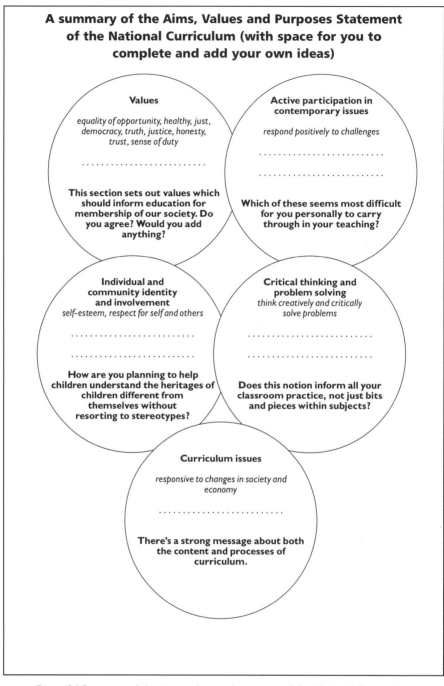

A summary of the Aims, Values and Purposes Statement of the National Curriculum (with space for you to complete and add your own ideas)

Values

equality of opportunity, healthy, just, democracy, truth, justice, honesty, trust, sense of duty

. . . .

This section sets out values which should inform education for membership of our society. Do you agree? Would you add anything?

Active participation in contemporary issues

respond positively to challenges

. . . .

. . . .

Which of these seems most difficult for you personally to carry through in your teaching?

Individual and community identity and involvement
self-esteem, respect for self and others

. . . .

. . . .

How are you planning to help children understand the heritages of children different from themselves without resorting to stereotypes?

Critical thinking and problem solving
think creatively and critically solve problems

. . . .

. . . .

Does this notion inform all your classroom practice, not just bits and pieces within subjects?

Curriculum issues

responsive to changes in society and economy

. . . .

There's a strong message about both the content and processes of curriculum.

Figure 2.1 Summary of the aims, values and purposes of the National Curriculum

abstract values into practice – and may lead to conflict between people who profess the same values. For example, someone might use 'respect' to justify allowing people to wear any clothes that they like, while others might use 'respect' to justify intervening with what people are wearing, on the grounds that they are offending some other people.

After much deliberation the forum came up with a set of values which they claimed everyone would agree to, irrespective of race, ethnic group, religion, age, gender or class, and a MORI poll quite soon after confirmed that at least the majority of people who were asked did agree with them. The forum made it clear that it was not necessary to agree on the source or authority for such values. In other words, people didn't have to share religious beliefs, and secondly, and importantly, that agreement about the values is *compatible with different interpretations and applications* of the values. In other words, they both acknowledged and sidestepped the controversies inherent in their list. They included such values as Friendship, Justice, Freedom, Truth, Self-respect and Respect for the Environment. These were organised under four headings, each of which had a number of subheadings:

- **The self – we value ourselves as unique human beings capable of spiritual, moral, intellectual and physical growth and development.**
- **Relationships – we value others for themselves, not only for what they have or what they can do for us. We value relationships as fundamental to the development and fulfilment of ourselves and others, and to the good of the community.**
- **Society – we value truth, freedom, justice, human rights, the rule of law and collective effort for the common good. In particular, we value families as sources of love and support for all their members, and as the basis of a society in which people care for others.**
- **The environment – we value the environment, both natural and shaped by humanity as the basis of life and a source of wonder and inspiration.**

The subheadings provide a kind of blueprint for behaviour and actions, such as '*show others that they are valued*' or '*work cooperatively*' which are both under 'relationships'; '*respect religious and cultural diversity*' under society; and '*understand our responsibilities for other species*' under the environment. You need to look at them for yourself, since we don't have space to reproduce them all here but you might like to reflect on the inherent problems with 'respect religious and cultural diversity'. Does this mean (to use historical examples) respecting torture of religious dissidents in the sixteenth century, cultural practices such as clitorectomy (cutting or sewing girls' genitalia), or imprisoning or giving electric-shock treatment to homosexuals?

The publication of the Values Statement was not met with universal acclaim. In fact, a great many people reacted very negatively, saying that the whole exercise actually avoided the real areas of dissent and controversy in society, and thus was not helpful. Some said that the statement was bland and self-evident – a bit like saying you were in favour of motherhood or apple-pie. Some people, such as the philosopher Mary Midgley, pointed out that unthinking moral conformity to various values is actually very difficult in contemporary society.[1] The idea that morality might be relative or dependent on the consequences of actions, rather than absolute, has been mooted, but others strongly disagree with this. Others try to justify the rightness or wrongness of certain values on traditional grounds, and this gets one into conflict too.

Nevertheless, the forum was probably right in thinking that establishing a common code of values was helpful in a democracy – even if very difficult – so that one could debate and make judgements about the right and the wrong thing to do, and have some basis for developing children's ethics and morality. As we shall see later in this chapter, however, many people feel that there are already two important statements of values and attendant actions which have worldwide ratification, namely the Universal Declaration of Human Rights and the Convention on the Rights of the Child.

The QCA Guidance for PSHE/Citizenship for KSl and 2

About the same time that Curriculum 2000 came out, the QCA also published a little booklet of initial guidance on PSHE/Citizenship for KSl and 2 (QCA, 2000). (It may help you differentiate between the QCA and NC to remember that the QCA produced 'guid*ance*' and the NC material is called 'guide*lines*'.) The guidance contextualised PSHE/Citizenship within the broad educational aims which had been set out in the AVPS, namely

- **provide opportunities for all pupils to learn and achieve;**
- **promote children's spiritual, moral, social and cultural development;**
- **prepare all pupils for the opportunities, responsibilities and experiences of life.**

This booklet also discussed aspects which were not included in the Crick Report and not spelled out in any detail in the National Curriculum Guidelines, for example whole-school approaches, school-improvement models and curriculum planning. It offered sources of guidance and support for implementing the Framework. We will return to those in Chapter 3, but for the moment, having noted that they are included here alongside issues of moral development, we'll put them on one side.

The QCA guidance booklet implicitly draws on value-laden concepts covering community relationships, equality of opportunity, children's wellbeing, independence and attainment. It emphasises that CE and PSHE would

- **help schools relate positively to their neighbourhoods and local communities;**
- **promote equal opportunities for all;**
- **make children more secure, motivated, confident and independent learners; and thus,**
- **raise standards of achievement.**

Now we have a wider context in which to think about CE. Along with the statement that developing children's self-esteem and sense of identity would contribute to secure/motivated/confident/independent learners, some new ideas have been introduced. CE is not just about children learning how to be good citizens in their own communities, and preparing for a future adult citizenship role, but also about how the whole school functions, the relationship of the school to its neighbourhood and its part in raising achievement. This last idea has its roots in school effectiveness theory, which suggests that 'effective' schools are well run, democratically managed, and encourage collaboration within the school and with the community.

What does the Crick Report say about Values and Citizenship?

In Figure 1.3 on page 19 of Chapter 1 we set out a series of ovals, with the last one labelled 'Values'. Figure 1.2 on page 9 gave a little more detail about what this meant. The Crick Report said 'Social and Moral Responsibility... both in and beyond the classroom, both towards those in authority and towards each other ... is an essential precondition for citizenship.' (p.40). The Report talks about 'values and dispositions'. 'Dispositions' is an interesting word suggesting inclinations and attitudes, and also suggesting that neither need to be fixed in concrete, but might be amenable to open-minded reflection and possibly change.

> *Pupils should be encouraged to recognise, reflect and act upon the values and dispositions which are appropriate to citizenship education. They should be helped to reflect on and recognise values and dispositions which underlie their attitudes and actions as individuals and as members of groups or communities. This is vital in developing pupils into active citizens who have positive attitudes to themselves as individuals and in their relationship with others. (p.41)*

The Crick Report then sets out a long list of values and dispositions which should underpin citizenship education (p.44).

Activity 1

What do some abstract concepts mean in practice?

Rather than ask you to agree or disagree with these, try to translate these abstract phrases into something concrete and meaningful in the primary school context. Copy the list on the left and leave off the column in italics. Then try to provide your own suggestions. Afterwards, you can compare your ideas with mine. I have written from a child's perspective but please don't feel bound by my suggestions and do consider them as an adult rather than a child if you prefer. It's an activity which would be sensible to do in a larger group, perhaps dividing the statements up so that small groups take 4 or 5 each, and shares their ideas later with the main group.

Essential element from the Crick Report	Translated into something real for primary children
Concern for the common good	Deciding on what we can do about a playground problem which affects us all.
Belief in human dignity and equality	Being ready to give the same time and attention to an elderly person who doesn't speak your language, as to your best friend.
Concern to resolve conflicts	Trying to find out what lies at the bottom of two children's ongoing hostility; trying to work through a conflict peaceably, instead of hitting, ostracising or bullying.

Disposition to work with and for others with sympathetic understanding	Agree to have someone in your football team who is not your friend and help her, even if she's not that good.
Be ready to act responsibly – care for others and oneself	Volunteer to be a 'buddy' to children who are having a hard time in the playground.
Think about consequences of actions on others and take responsibility for unforeseen or unfortunate consequences	Your ideas.
Practise tolerance	Your ideas.
Judge and act by a moral code	Take the chance of getting into trouble, and don't let someone get away with bullying just because he's bigger than you.
Courage to defend a point of view	Don't fall in with the 'in crowd'. If you think some rap lyrics are sexist, say so, and why, even if it makes you unpopular.
Be open to changing your opinions and attitudes in the light of discussion and evidence	Saying, 'Sorry I was wrong', when you find out that the majority of Asian people in Britain don't support Al-Qaida.
Take individual initiative and effort	Finding out about conditions for battery chickens and talking to your parents about not buying them any more.
Civility and respect for the rule of law	Keeping to the rule about walking on the left when you go up the stairs to your classroom and not pushing.
Determination to act justly	Stand up for your friend who is being wrongly accused.
Commitment to equal opportunities and gender equality	Challenge someone who is being rude and unfair about asylum seekers. Stand up for the rights of boys to learn ballet and girls to play rugby if they want to.
Commitment to active citizenship	Write to UNICEF when you find out about conditions of child workers in a developing country, asking what you could do.
Commitment to voluntary service	When you get home from school, visiting your elderly next-door neighbour who has broken her ankle, just to give her some company.
Concern for human rights	Being prepared to learn about the conditions of workers who make the 'brand named' clothes you wear, and stop hassling your parents to buy you the latest thing when you find out what's going on.
Concern for the environment	Finding out about how global warming is affected by some products we use, taking an assembly about this, and discussing with your parents about buying alternative products.

Commentary

Did the exercise become easier as you went on? Probably, too, you found that several of the concepts overlapped with each other. Probably, you also found that you disagreed with the ideas that I suggested. If so, you have hit on a very important point, which we will be elaborating on later: that although there are indeed many values that we share when we express them in the abstract, there is not always agreement about how to put them into practice. There is another important and noteworthy characteristic of the values and dispositions, and that is that none is a normative statement telling you how you 'ought to behave', such as 'you should always obey your parents', or 'you should never drop litter'. Rather, in line with the idea of 'dispositions', children are asked to show 'concern about' or 'commitment to' various principles like justice, equality, the environment or open-mindedness. The effect of this is to provide a very inclusive set of ideas, with which few would argue. At the same time, the possibility of grave disagreements about how to carry out the commitments or concerns, which can be highly contentious, is set to one side.

Recognising emotional investment in values and attitudes

There is another important point about values, attitudes and the behaviour that goes with them. Because our value systems are at the core of our sense of identity, we mostly have an extremely strong emotional attachment to them. We can become very upset if we find ourselves up against people who don't understand or share our values, because we may feel that our very core is under attack. This has important consequences for CE, since in a democratic society we are both trying to make space for people to express their different identities and values, but also trying to find ways to live tolerantly and respectfully with diversity. We need to recognise that controversies and conflicts can arise when people don't share values. An important part of our role as educators for citizenship will be to help our pupils deal with such conflicts in a rational and peaceful manner, in which their feelings don't run away with them. 'Emotional Literacy'(EL) is a reasonably new concept about recognising and articulating one's feelings. This helpfully suggests that though some people may be more attuned to their own and others' feelings (i.e. strong on both intrapersonal and interpersonal intelligence – two of Howard Gardner's multiple intelligences), EL is also a skill and characteristic which can be learned and developed. Some claims for EL seem excessive – that it can sort out all the problems of the world – but helping children deal with their feelings of anger, fear or negativity, and learn to trust in their peers and adults, can all be part of their ability to handle conflicts and difficulties in their own lives. Joe's story in Chapter 3 refers to emotional literacy and there are resources at the end of this book.

Universal Declaration of Human Rights and the Convention on the Rights of the Child

Some people believe that although the Values Statement contains some useful material that needed spelling out (particularly about environmental concerns), the most basic statements of values and commitments which should underpin CE are already contained in the UN Declaration of Human Rights (1948) and the Convention on the Rights of the Child (1989).[2] In this view, there really was no need for a restatement of values specifically for England. The UN Children's Rights Convention emphasises the importance of eradicating inequalities, exploitation, discrimination, abuse and neglect, listening to and empowering children, and working in their best interests to ensure their health, education and safety. Neither the Declaration nor the Convention make reference to environmental issues, and we shouldn't forget that these are now also critical to citizenship locally and globally.

The Preamble to the Human Rights Declaration sets the 30 Articles by which humanity shall live in this introductory context:

> *Whereas recognition of the inherent dignity and of the equal and inalienable rights of all members of the human family is the foundation of freedom, justice and peace in the world.*

> *Whereas disregard and contempt for human rights have resulted in barbarous acts which have outraged the conscience of mankind and the advent of a world in which human beings shall enjoy freedom of speech and belief, and freedom from fear and want has been proclaimed as the highest aspiration of the common people.*

> *Whereas it is essential, if man is not to be compelled to have recourse, as a last resort, to rebellion against tyranny and oppression, that human rights should be protected by the rule of law.*

In thinking about values underpinning human rights, it is helpful and realistic to remember the context of dispute and difficulty in which the Declaration was promulgated in 1948 in the wake of the Second World War. Furthermore, as we know from bitter experience, ever since the Declaration was drawn up, human rights have continued to be ignored and abused. However, for many people, the Declaration, along with the Convention on the Rights of the Child, provides a set of ideals and values against which we can try to make our own decisions about what to do, and judge the actions of others. But like the Values Statement, the Declaration and the Convention don't solve the problems of different interpretations or conflicts arising where one value is set against another one. All this is of the utmost relevance to CE.

How teachers influence the developing values and attitudes of our pupils

This is what someone with long experience in classroom research had to say:

> *I can think of no other social arrangement, save parenting of course, in which the modelling component plays as large and pervasive a role as it does in teaching.* (Jackson, 1992, p.404)

Children don't always or necessarily learn and internalise concepts merely through being told, especially if the subject is behaviour and appropriate moral values. There is research evidence that moral understanding emerges in the first years of life, and that adults contribute by helping young children understand their own feelings and realise why some actions are right or wrong by getting them to think about consequences and other people's feelings, and encouraging them to learn to share and cooperate, help others and resolve conflicts peacefully. In addition, children are influenced by other people's example, by imitating what they have seen or experienced (including television and stories), and through the opportunity to discuss ideas with their peers and with adults.

Research with children and expert advice indicates how teachers can provide a positive influence in children's moral development, helping them develop trust, respect and sensitivity for others, and appreciate the importance of honesty and responsibility. Not surprisingly, children are most likely to be influenced by teachers whom they respect and like, showing that establishing warm, positive and secure relationships between children and teachers is important not just for providing a supportive learning environment for other classroom work, but is part of the hidden curriculum of values education. Children pick up messages about tolerance, fairness, being reasonable, gentle, caring, compassionate and courteous from the way their teachers behave with them, and to other children and adults. They may summarise their view of a teacher in the short phrase 'kind and nice' but these judgements can encapsulate a whole variety of important qualities which the children are experiencing first hand and learning to emulate.

In the next chapter we will go more deeply into the ways in which the classroom and school environment nurture the values and characteristics that will go towards developing good citizens. For now, we will stay with teachers' own values.

Our role in educating pupils in values – exploring our own value systems

The QTS Standards with which we introduced this chapter require student teachers to 'demonstrate and promote the positive values, attitudes and behaviour that they expect from their pupils' (1.3). The next statement relates to the ability to understand parents' (you should include carers') rights and responsibilities, recognise their roles in pupils' learning and, as professionals, be able to communicate sensitively and effectively with them.

This is what Halstead and Taylor (2000) had to say about this challenge:

> Teachers need to be clear about their own values and attitudes in order to be aware of their practices and to reflect critically on their role as values educators. This is all the more important given the difficulties schools face, being required to pay attention to pupils' SMSC (Social, Moral, Spiritual and Cultural) Development within a minimum and imprecisely specified framework, whilst operating in a liberal pluralistic society, with little consensus on values issues and remaining sensitive to the values and attitudes of parents and local communities. (p.15)

If we are not clear in our minds about our own values, how we interpret them and how they connect up, we will have difficulty with fulfilling this aspect of the QTS Standards, and difficulties with Citizenship Education. When we get into the classroom or school setting, we may find that values and their interpretation differ between our pupils, between their families and the school, or even between ourselves and some of our colleagues.

Values, actions and conflicts

Activity 2

Your own actions, decisions and values

In the first column of the grid opposite there are a number of actions and decisions that someone, including a child, might take or be asked to take. All the actions or decisions relate in some way to the concepts of CE. In the middle and right-hand columns are possible differences in the values and responses that these actions might evoke, or be based upon. The idea of this activity is to identify how we still find ourselves disagreeing about certain actions, even though we may share a variety of basic values, because we may interpret the implementation of these values differently. Where there are conflicting values, we may decide that one value overrides another.

You may not agree with the suggestions in the middle and right-hand columns, and as I emphasised in Chapter 1, that is fine, because CE is not about forcing ideas on other people, but acknowledging that we do have different viewpoints, and should be given a chance to discuss them. First, discuss or think about the middle and right-hand columns in the light of the 'action or decision' and consider which of the statements you might agree with. Then, continue the table, putting actions or decisions that are meaningful to you on the left, and considering the underlying values on the right. If you are doing this with other people, you might find it interesting and helpful to compare your tables, or do them together. I think you'll notice not just that sometimes your values disagree, but that sometimes there is a conflict of values within the decision/action itself.

An action or decision	The underpinning values	An alternative value or interpretation
Allow a child to argue with you.	Everyone, including children, has a right to have their view respected and heard.	There are occasions when children must learn to accept the authority of older people.
Stop someone pushing in front, in a queue.	Orderly behaviour and fairness, not overridden by physical strength.	An extremely urgent matter has arisen, needing a person to get home as fast as possible. This overrides rules about taking your turn.
Telling Michael to go and sit outside the head's door and miss PE, because of his bad behaviour.	Obedience to the teacher and punishment for bad behaviour; not allowing other children to suffer for one child's misdemeanours.	Michael has a right to his PE lessons and is losing his entitlement to full education.
Mum tells Shireen to hit back if that boy next door has a go at her and calls her names.	Standing up for yourself is the way to achieve justice.	Two wrongs don't make a right. Violence doesn't solve anything.
Insisting that Tommy share the Lego set with Shazia.	Equality for girls means they must have equal access to all the toys.	Tommy is autistic and his needs have, on this occasion, to be put higher than Shazia's rights.
Trying to explain to Jo's mother why you allow him to dress up in girl's clothes in the role play area.	Equality for boys means they must have equal access to all resources, even if parents don't agree.	It is not right to go against parental wishes; gender equality doesn't mean 'gender bending'.
Writing letters to the council protesting about a new club which is very noisy late at night.	One group's rights to noise shouldn't interfere with another group's rights to peace and quiet.	This is about cultural difference – people have a right to their culture. The majority should be more tolerant and accepting.
Telling a white lie to stop someone's feelings being hurt.	Valuing people's feelings over telling the truth.	It is never right to lie.
Deciding not to tell your teacher that Siobhan cheated in the maths test.	Loyalty to your friend is better than honesty in some situations.	Honesty is always the best policy.
Paying your taxes.	Society depends on obedience to the law.	Only just laws should be obeyed. If I had been alive in Gandhi's time, I would have joined his protests against various taxes.
Protesting about the death penalty for a murderer.	Valuing human life above everything.	The stability of society depends on clear deterrents; the victims must have justice.
Supporting someone who is asking for voluntary euthanasia.	Someone has the right to decide that their own life is no longer worth living.	It is never right to take life.
Refusing to take up arms.	I am not a pacifist, but I refuse to fight an unjust war.	Individuals can't go against the national interest in this way.
A National Front march through a certain area should be banned.	Citizens have the right to be protected against the abuse (even if non-physical) of any group.	It is fundamental to a democracy that people have the right to express their views.
Muslims should be allowed to wear hijab (headscarves) in school, Rastas to wear locks and woollen caps, Sikhs to wear ceremonial objects.	It is the right of any group to express their religious identity and obey the rules of their religion.	In a multiethnic/multicultural society signs of religious difference are divisive (NB at the time of writing, the French government had banned all symbols of religious identity in schools).
National Health treatment should be available for everybody, regardless of cost.	*Fill this one in yourself.*	
Space for your own examples		

Commentary

This activity should have helped you realise how important values are in trying to implement a peaceful, just democracy which recognises different rights, responsibilities and identities. However, as you read through the grid, and thought about the examples offered, and your own responses, you probably concluded that there can be very different views about actions and their justifications. You will also have appreciated that these divergences in interpretation of values can't be avoided in a pluralist, multicultural society. People are not all clones of each other, and there are many legitimate areas of difference. In other words, one of our values – to respect diversity – may itself lead to situations where values, attitudes and behaviour are not in harmony. Moreover, merely stating that we believe in values like truth, justice or respect won't make the disagreements go away.

This activity was intended to help with a number of different ideas:

- **Attitudes, behaviour and decisions, both in private and public lives, depend on our value system and beliefs about what is right and wrong.**
- **Implicitly and largely without us thinking about them, we draw on our value system all the time for actions and decisions.**
- **Some actions and decisions are *not problematic* for us – they don't involve conflicting values.**
- **Some actions and decisions are quite problematic, and involve us weighing up the strength and the consequences of some action in the light of our own values, i.e. there may be conflicts *within ourself* about values.**
- **Some actions and decisions involve conflicting values *between* people.**
- **Some values are about *outcomes* and some are about *processes*. For instance, some people believe the ends justify the means, and some do not.**
- **Anything else that occurred to you about the links between values and behaviour.**

Activity 3

Where do we stand?

Here is one more activity to consolidate the idea that deciding on the 'right thing to do' and 'appropriate values' may be more complicated than we reckoned. Think about the underlying values in the following scenarios, and consider where you stand, marking yourself on a scale of 1–5 (where 1 is absolutely disagree, and 5 totally agree). If you can, compare your rating of each item within a small group, being ready to listen to everyone's viewpoint and register the different values and reasons that people offered. See if you can identify whether you are using 'absolutist' principles (that is, drawing on rules, perhaps provided through a religious source, which cannot be 'bent' to suit the circumstances) or consequentialist or utilitarian arguments to justify your position.

i) *'Swampy' and his friends' non-violent protest against the building of a new highway in an area of natural beauty in Devon. This included burrowing underground where the bulldozers would dig, and trying to prevent the road-builders cutting down trees.*

ii) Peasants in famine-ridden Ethiopia being prevented from leaving the land and moving into Addis Ababa by their government, on the grounds that there is no work in the towns and they will swiftly become a destitute, landless population.

iii) The appeal by Ms X to the High Court in 2001. Although she had not lost her mental faculties, injured in an accident, she was faced with living the rest of her natural life inside a machine which breathed for her. She asked for her machine to be turned off, an appeal which was granted in an historic court case.

iv) The illegal actions of 'animal rights' activists to prevent medical research being done on animals before trialling research on humans.

v) When Nelson Mandela decided to move from constitutional protests against the apartheid government of South Africa, and advocate armed struggle, he faced a possible death sentence, which would have left his small children without a father. As it was, he was imprisoned for 27 years and they all grew up without him.

vi) The current Egyptian government has decided not to prosecute taxi drivers whose cars emit noxious fumes, because to take these cars off the road would hugely increase unemployment and poverty.

Commentary

The last activity should have brought home to you not just that values can cause conflict, but that dealing with differences in values is part and parcel of learning to be a citizen. In Chapter 4, we will look at various strategies to help children deal with conflicts between values, attitudes and beliefs in a peaceful, reasonable way.

Children's values, parents' values and where do teachers stand?

Next we are going to move from exploring the possibility of conflict between adult values and think how the pupils in our classrooms may also reflect such diversity of values and viewpoints. Our role as teachers is 'to develop appropriate values and morals', but, as this chapter has demonstrated, this is not as simple as it might seem. Pupils get their values from a great many sources not within our control. On top of this, there is possible difficulty for us as teachers, in that we are enjoined to respect and value parents, at the same time as realising that some of the values and attitudes that we may be worried about in children reflect parental or community values.

Activity 4

Thinking about underlying values expressed by children or their parents

The scenarios below come from real incidents in schools round the country. Your task is to identify the underlying values and issues in each, if possible working in groups. Don't worry about what you might want to do about the situations described with respect to the children – Chapter 4 is designed to help you with that.

Scenario 1
Kate was doing School Experience in a Year 2 class and the RE curriculum she was following said she should be teaching about Islam. There were three practising Muslim children in the class, but the rest were of different faiths (mainly, but not all, Christian) or no professed faith. She decided to arrange a visit to the local mosque, and spoke to the head who was in favour but said she would need to send a letter home asking permission for this outing. Kate was shocked to receive back 11 letters from parents strongly objecting to their children making this visit.

To give you some help, this first scenario seems to be about the students' (and the school's) desire to take a multi-faith approach to RE, and the existence of hostility to Islam and/or to Muslim people in the parent community.

Scenario 2
Jennifer was in a Year 6 class for her School Experience. On the Monday after a school social evening, a group of children in her class started giggling about Jake and making very camp gestures behind his back. Then someone stuck a notice on his back (which of course he couldn't see) reading 'I'm a poofter'.

Scenario 3
Faith was in a Year 5 class. No one had told her that Tom's family consisted of two lesbian mothers: he called both by their first names. This emerged incidentally when Faith had the children making mother's day cards. Tom told her that he was going to make two, one for Barbara and one for Kirsty. He also mentioned that he didn't have a daddy. Thinking that she was helping him understand the biological facts of life, Faith said gently 'Everyone has a daddy, even if they don't know who he was. It's how babies get made.' 'Well I don't, and I wasn't made like that,' said Tom emphatically and clearly. 'Barbara and Kirsty have told me that I was made in a test tube.' Faith herself didn't know how to react personally, but she was also aware that some children were whispering about this.

Scenario 4
Kevin was a mature student. He was on playground duty with his class teacher when he overheard a small group of Year 5 girls from his class taunting Aysha with the words, 'Your Mum's so tight she never buys you new things, she gets your clothes from the dustbin by the charity shop. I saw this old tramp, he looks just like you, he's your Dad.' Kevin knew that Aysha's mother was having an extremely difficult time, and that the school was trying to intervene to get her rehoused, away from a violent husband. He felt he should do more than just tell the girls to stop being abusive, and comfort Aysha. He felt the girls were lacking compassion and that their attitudes to poverty were very worrying.

Have you any scenarios to share that indicate worrying values, clashes in values and dilemmas that the teacher or adult concerned might find him/herself facing?

Few would claim to have the definitive answer to these controversial scenarios. However, like much of the material in this chapter, the intention has been to help you realise that you need to clarify your own values about issues before you can feel confident about how you might intervene or lead discussions with children.

Summary

Before we move on to Chapter 3, which is about 'active citizenship', let's look back on the ideas that this chapter has introduced and debated. As you read through this summary, you might like to think about personal issues that the chapter stirred you to consider, how you felt about this (the emotionally laden aspect of values) and what you feel you have learned personally through the material introduced here.

- **The relationship between values education and Citizenship Education, how they link to issues of identity and PSHE, and how they provide a framework within which Citizenship Education itself can be developed.**
- **The Values Statement, and the Aims, Values and Purposes Statement in the National Curriculum and how they connect to CE.**
- **Your own values, and where there might be potentially contentious issues in the way people implement their values through their attitudes and actions.**
- **Your reactions to some controversial, thought-provoking scenarios from the classroom.**

Activity 5

What is problematic to me personally?

Before you move on, you might like to consolidate your thinking with the following activity. Photocopy the statements that follow, and add several more on blank slips of paper that represent your reaction to the chapter. Cut out the statements and sort them into those whose implications you find most problematic personally, and those you find least problematic. If possible, discuss with someone else why you sorted them that way, and share your ideas.

- *Our actions and behaviour are underpinned by our value systems, even if we don't often have to spell them out explicitly. Values may be 'absolutist', 'consequentialist' or based on 'golden rules', and we need to live with this diversity.*

- *Children are learning values and attitudes all the time – from home, from the media, from each other – as well as being influenced by teachers.*

- *Even if people share values, such as truth, justice or freedom, they may interpret what you do to achieve these ideals very differently.*

- *In a democracy we have to find ways to reconcile our different values and interpretations of values, without coming to blows. However, there are some values people might be asked to fight and die for.*

- *In practice, we may find that there are conflicts between our own values in deciding what to do about something – for instance, whether to respect parental values even if we don't share them.*

- *There are times when children express values that we might find unacceptable, because they are (for example) racist, sexist or disrespectful of other people's humanity. If this happens we need to be clear about our own position and what we want to do.*

- *Values are not just held as cognitive concepts. They are part of our personal identity, and we may have extremely strong emotional investment in some of our values.*

In this chapter we have not tried to emphasise learning objectives. However, you may want to consider which values you would hope to develop as part of your planning for CE. Are they inclusive? Do human rights figure? What about conflicting values?

Notes

1 Midgley in Smith and Standish, 1997.
2 You can find the Convention of the Rights of the Child on the following sites. The Unicef site has a useful commentary. **www.unicef.org/crc/crc.htm**; **www.unhchr.ch/html/menu3/b/k2crc.htm.**

What will you learn about in this chapter?

- *a democratic classroom within a whole school ethos which supports, encourages and provides opportunities for children to practise democracy*
- *the importance of high self-esteem and work on identity*
- *specific skills of thinking, researching, acting and reflecting to support CE*
- *strategies coming from philosophy for children and 'communities of enquiry'*
- *school and class councils, and school parliaments to learn skills of debate, advocacy and persuasion*

Introduction

Chapters 1 and 2 set out the framework for Citizenship Education. In the first chapter you thought about what democracy entails, and the concepts of citizenship in a democratic society. In the second, you explored some of the values which underpin citizenship in a democracy, including those that are far from straightforward, and where putting them into practice can lead to controversy.

This chapter aims to help you with perhaps the most distinctive feature of CE – that children can be 'active citizens' now, as well as learn to develop and practise the skills, values and attitudes that will prepare them to function effectively in a democracy, in the future.

Chapter 1 contextualised CE in the notion of learning to 'do democracy'. An activity asking you to do a diamond ranking exercise set out some of the distinguishing features of a democracy. A straightforward way to help you think about democratic societies is to compare them with *un*democratic systems. However, it's not just a question of knowledge about the system and the rights and responsibilities that make democracy work; it's about ordinary people having skills and attitudes which mean they *can and will participate* where this is possible. As Crick and others have warned, and as we know from history all over the world and throughout the ages, where people don't – or are unable to – exercise their democratic rights and responsibilities, a country can slide into autocracy and tyranny.

Active citizenship: what does this mean in a primary classroom?

The Crick Report includes a paragraph which has become virtually a mantra in CE:

> we aim at no less than a change in the political culture of this country, both nationally and locally: for people to think of themselves as active citizens, willing, able and equipped to

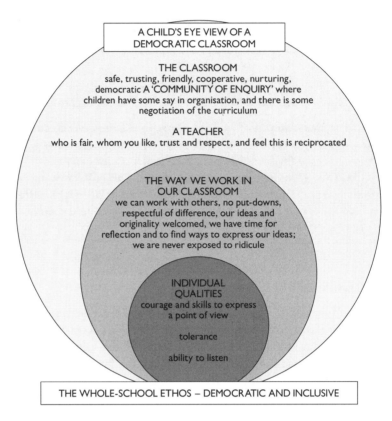

Figure 3.1 Nesting circles for a democratic classroom

have an influence in public life and with the critical capacities to weigh evidence before speaking and acting; to build on and to extend radically to young people the best in existing traditions of community involvement and public service, and to make them confident in finding new forms of involvement and action among themselves ... we should not, must not, dare not be complacent about the health and future of British democracy. Unless we become a nation of engaged citizens, our democracy is not secure. (Crick, 1998, 1.5, pp.7–8)

Our task in this chapter will be to try to translate the ideas in that paragraph into manageable and relevant practice in the primary school.

Learning outcomes and accountability

The idea of defined learning outcomes will be familiar to you from other curriculum areas. As you know, the system which ensures accountability and standards in schools is inspection through OFSTED. The inspectors work within a framework which clearly identifies various aspects of school life. Increasingly, they will be looking for evidence that Citizenship Education has been properly thought through, with learning outcomes which are transparent to the children, to senior management in the school, and to themselves. Learning outcomes can be summarised in terms of specific knowledge, but also as the acquisition of skills and attitudes. We are going to concentrate on all three in this chapter, trying to keep clarity about how these become learning objectives, and hence outcomes, in your planning. Although at the time of going to press, an Attainment Target for Citizenship and exemplification of standards were not yet available, they are the logical concomitant of learning outcomes and accountability. Keep your eyes open for these, which are coming from the QCA shortly.

Nurturing active citizenship in a democratic classroom

Active citizenship will be a sickly specimen if it is not growing in the fertile ground of democratic classroom practice and ethos. It is not just that children will be the first to note the mismatch between what we ask them to do, and what we do ourselves! Let's for a moment consider what it takes to be able to debate important issues, put forward a point of view which may conflict with someone else's and discuss pros and cons of sometimes passionately felt positions. Figure 3.1 on page 46 shows a 'child's eye view' of a classroom in which s/he is able to develop the essential skills and qualities for CE.

Whole-school ethos

This book does not have the space to explore in depth the wider issues about whole school ethos, in which individual teachers and classrooms function. But just as children need an individually nurturing classroom, their teachers need to work in a broader supportive context, which does not set up conflicting messages between different adults, or for children. Policies for behaviour management, anti-bullying, equal opportunities and parental liaison will all contribute to whole-school ethos, though how they are put into practice will be crucial. The involvement of non-teaching staff is also important, especially as so much of school life for children revolves around playtimes, lunch times and moving around the school generally. In Chapter 5 you will read about an NQT who had some influence on that wider context, starting with her own classroom (see Paula's story), but for the moment we will stick with individual classrooms and some ideas about possibilities in the early years of your professional career.

The importance of classroom ethos in fostering democracy – the teacher's role

We'll start with the largest ring in Figure 3.1 in which the others nest – the classroom ethos – and work inwards. For a moment take yourself back to your own childhood. Can you remember the primary school teacher who made you feel that your ideas and opinions were worthwhile, who valued you as an individual, not just an anonymous cog in the busily turning wheel of classroom life; the one in whose class you really felt you were learning and growing? Can you remember what that classroom was like – what happened to your written work, or your art, how you were organised for lessons? Were there times when the class relaxed and laughed together with the teacher, and you talked about things that you, rather than the teacher, had chosen, in a safe environment? And the flip side — those teachers for whom you were either invisible, or naughty, or dim, who made you feel that the classroom was somehow not yours but theirs; where there was seldom collaboration, and competition to be 'best' often led to put-downs or humiliation of individuals? I can remember one of the most ordered classes in which I spent a primary year. We were certainly well disciplined; in fact we might as well have been in the army! But we didn't learn anything about participation in decisions, collaboration or expressing our points of view. Each of you will have your own mental picture of positive teaching environments, but there will be some common features, which add up to an ethos:

- **which is respectful;**
- **in which individuals feel valued;**
- **which empowers and encourages children to venture their ideas without feeling at risk, and to take ownership of what they learn;**
- **where children collaborate and work to improve their personal targets rather than feel that at every turn their success is measured against that of others (and they are often found wanting in consequence).**

Now let's take our minds back to the very first pages of this book, in which we considered what democracy means and what it might mean to 'do democracy'. In contrast to apathy and cynicism, we talked about participating, 'having a voice', feeling empowered and part of the system. It will be plain to you that for children to 'do democracy' will depend on creating a classroom community in which democratic practices flourish, as much as on children's personal skills and attitudes.

The following two classroom stories show how two teachers set about creating that supportive community.

Classroom story

Joe and Year 6: building self-esteem and trust to underpin a democratic classroom

I was new to the school and inherited a really challenging Year 6 class. I wanted to have a democratic classroom but knew that it had to rest on better self-esteem and trust between the kids, and that had to be my first objective. Their previous teacher had had them all in rows facing forward, and ruled with a rod of iron. Before term began I'd organised the tables in groups and brought in a carpet but these simple organisational features didn't seem to be working. I decided to ask the children how they would like the classroom and they said (to my dismay) that they preferred how 'sir' last year had arranged them so they didn't get distracted by anyone and get into trouble. I felt that this reflected the competitive and rather authoritarian culture of my predecessor and suggested a compromise — a large horseshoe in which we could all see each other and the board. I put the carpet in the middle, with a 'wait and see' attitude towards using it. It took me quite a while to establish my authority. The kids were suspicious and resentful of me, very competitive, wouldn't (couldn't?) collaborate and were quite spiteful to each other. I decided that the first thing I would tackle was the animosity and competitive atmosphere and I introduced a simple activity I'd seen during school experience.

A large display board was given over to making 'shields of friendship'. I printed everyone's name on pieces of card, and every other day or so, I'd get a child to take one of the names out of a hat. This would be stapled to the display board. The child would be asked to go outside, and with me presiding and scribing, the children had to volunteer something good about the person. I had to teach them how to do this initially, by coaxing and modelling the sorts of things they could say, such as 'Ayo was really helpful to me at lunch time' or 'Joshua is a great person to have in your football team'. Then the child would be called back in, we'd read all the nice things that had been said about them, and they would make their own shield incorporating all this. I decided that each child would make her/his own shield because I'd remembered reading about the idea of 'positive self-talk' at uni, and that self-esteem was related to knowing you were valued by significant others. I also had been impressed by some research I read that low self-esteem could be correlated with being resentful, intolerant and closed-minded.[1]

Perhaps because everyone knew their turn would come, they got more into the spirit of this and more positive about each other. It didn't solve all my problems, but I think it contributed to creating a more positive mood. Another thing that worked well was a 'dear Aunty Aggie' box. Anyone could put in a letter to Aunty Aggie, anonymously, with some problem. I typed these on the computer so you couldn't recognise the handwriting and handed them to groups, who had to come up with suggestions which we shared. This seemed to encourage 'emotional literacy' and trust.[2] The other thing I did was to encourage and value more creative work, such as art, music, drama. A lot of the kids with the lowest self-esteem, and more likely to be anti-social, found academic work and endless writing just set them up for failure, but could shine in other areas. Drama was particularly good for role-playing scenarios where children had fallen foul of one another, and modelling alternative ways to react. We role-played some of the 'Aunty Aggie' problems, and the kids' own solutions. Gradually, particularly through drama, I was able to introduce more collaboration, and as long as I considered the group dynamics carefully, I felt I was getting somewhere. This was a foundation for starting to introduce discussions about issues in Circle Time. I started bringing in headlines from newspapers about current affairs and we'd have quite structured discussion time, using the rules of P4C which I'd learned about at college. It's only halfway through the spring term now, and we're all getting stuck into SATs preparation, but I do feel I've made a lot of headway towards my goal of a more democratic classroom ethos.

A checklist for Joe – how well did he meet his learning objectives?

CE learning objective	Comments
Encourage collaboration	
Build self-esteem and mutual respect	
Encourage emotional literacy	
Put more value on the arts to ensure all children's talents are recognised and valued	
Deal with difficulties in the class through role play	
Introduce structured discussions of topical issues in Circle Time	

Thinking about the ethos of Joe's classroom and where next?

I. BREAKING THE NEGATIVITY THROUGH GAMES AND SMALL ACTIVITIES

Joe recognised that he couldn't develop the kind of open-minded debate that he wanted in his classroom while children were so negative and unpleasant towards each other. As well as the particular activities described above, he made a regular practice of spending 5–10 minutes each day on games to build listening skills, like 'mirroring' which he introduced through PE. Children were in pairs and took turns to be the person outside or inside 'the mirror', and had to reflect exactly what the other did physically. From mime, Joe moved to using words. In pairs, children took turns to speak for one minute about a subject which Joe introduced, such as 'what I saw on my way to school this morning', which the other had to repeat back to the satisfaction of their partner.

2. DEVELOPING THE CHILDREN'S ABILITY TO COLLABORATE

Joe also planned for increasing amounts of collaborative work, starting with small group sequences in PE. In music and art and design he also planned collaborative work which would relate to the Greek myth that they were reading (Persephone is kidnapped and taken to the Underworld), and their work in history on Ancient Greece. He talked about composers who specialised in film or television music and gave small groups of children a set of instruments, requiring them to develop short compositions to represent specific moments in the story. These would also be developed through drama. He decided that the children could make a large frieze of the story, and had children working in small groups planning different sections, to represent the sequence of the story. Children could make or paint different parts of the scenes individually (for example, flowers on the hillside, Hades' chariot, Persephone eating the pomegranate seeds) and they would be cut out and stuck onto the large collage, so that eventually each of their ideas would be represented. A small 'committee' took responsibility for the totality of the design, but the rest of the class had a say using the technique of 'forum theatre' (see p.79 Chapter 4).

3. WORKING TOWARDS DEBATING ISSUES FROM DIFFERENT PERSPECTIVES

Joe planned to move towards simulation games where different children took roles where they would work together. Some ideas are discussed further on in this chapter and in the following one.

Classroom story

Natalie and Year 1: empowering children and negotiating the curriculum

My first job, straight out of uni, was in a Year 1 class. I was trained for Early Years and I understand about child-initiated activities. I was convinced that a democratic classroom was essential for children to develop their full potential, and I was fortunate because most children had come up from a wonderful nursery, which fostered their individuality and initiative but also collaboration.

For example, they had been given a choice about what their role-play corner would be when the 'restaurant' was dismantled, and had been involved in its transformation into 'the wild things house'. At the beginning of the new term, I did the usual things like create a list of class rules together with the children, giving over more than one Circle Time so that we could carefully discuss the pros and cons of different rules, and decide jointly how we would deal with transgressions. I used Circle Time for discussions about the sort of class we'd like to spend our time in and so forth – quite conventional stuff really. I was keen to foster a cooperative 'we are a class together' ethos, rather than go for competitive or individual reward systems. I had a large jar with water in, and some rather beautiful large shells and stones that I'd collected on my travels. Every time any child, or a group, or the whole class did something really good, I would put a shell or a stone into the jar and make quite a big thing of the person or group who'd earned it (taking care of course to reward children for things like trying hard, or keeping to their own targets for work or behaviour and so on) or saying how pleased I was with the whole class. Because the stones and shells were big, treats came round about every three weeks when the jar was full. We had a good discussion about possible treats, and the children were really sensible about things that were unrealistic. We created a list of treats to include different children's ideas and worked through it. It included things like having a video at story time, having extra outdoor play, doing painting in the morning instead of literacy!

My next step was a bit more radical. By now we were coming to the end of the spring term and I wanted to see how far we could negotiate the curriculum for the summer, together. Our history project was 'Ourselves', and before I did any planning I asked the children what sorts of things they'd like to learn and find out about. I did a brainstorm on sugar paper of their ideas. Though some of it was predictable (like what toys we like, and what we were like when we were babies) there were things that I probably wouldn't have thought of. For instance, three girls wanted to do something about the places their parents had come from (in the Caribbean) and another group wanted to make a chart of the things the whole class were most interested in. One boy wanted to find out more about Druids, because he'd heard his parents talking about the midsummer festival at Stonehenge. Three of his best friends worked with him. I was surprised when my mentor said that I was operating a 'negotiated curriculum'. I hadn't known that what I was doing had a special name!

A check list for Natalie – how well did she meet her learning objectives?

Learning objective	Comments
Negotiate class rules and how to deal with transgressions	
Set up rewards system which builds sense of class as a community	
Involve children in deciding what 'treats' they would earn	
Include children in planning for new topic and allow them to negotiate some ideas they want to learn about	

Thinking about the ethos of Natalie's classroom and where next?

I. MOVING THE CHILDREN ON FROM BEING ABLE TO COLLABORATE AND TAKE INITIATIVES, TO SOME NEGOTIATION OF TEACHING AND LEARNING

Natalie had learned about 'communities of enquiry' in her final year at university as part of her module on Philosophy for Children (discussed later in this chapter). Though she was not ready to try P4C, she was trying to establish a classroom in which there was negotiation of the curriculum with the children, rather than an entirely top-down approach. She decided that history was a good place to start, since it is an enquiry-based subject, where the curriculum is less prescribed than in some other areas. 'Big questions' and 'little questions' are the starting points for history, and she encouraged the children to be part of setting them both, and then follow through with their own research. Her next step would be to introduce P4C formally in Circle Time, probably using a picture book, such as *Not Now Bernard*, along the lines of the advice given in 'Storywise'.[3]

Activity 1

How far does your own classroom or EY setting offer a democratic environment for citizenship skills to develop? Rather than feed you all the concepts you need to consider, you might do this in a small group, listing the concepts on one side of the page, and skills on the other. Don't forget equal-opportunities issues to do with gender, 'race'/ethnicity, learning needs, class, and physical or other (dis)abilities.

2. GROUND RULES FOR A DEMOCRATIC CLASSROOM

You could work on this with your class. They'd need an introductory input about what democracy means (remember the adage – any child who can remember 'triceratops' can remember the word 'democracy'!) You'll need to simplify the ideas according to the age of your children, and the outline at the beginning of Chapter I will help you.

Take some time and don't necessarily try to do everything in one go, because you are aiming for more than deciding on the 'classroom rules', which tend to say things like 'wait your turn, don't push, listen to the teacher, do your best work' and so on. All of these are important and in the philosophical jargon 'necessary', but they are not 'sufficient'. In other words, you will need to dig deeper with the children, to get them to consider not just the kind of 'community' they want to work in, but how it can be achieved through people recognising the different rights and responsibilities of all concerned. Though majorities get to make the laws in democracies, minority rights are very important. You can help your class think about what to do to protect minorities. Children should be involved not just in setting the ground rules, but also in decisions about what to do about breaking the rules. Remember, too, that one of the distinguishing features of democracy is that 'the people' (your class) can review the rules and come to a decision to change them, and so they might be involved in discussion about how the ground rules are working in practice, and not just 'told' by a higher authority that they are being good or bad.

How self-esteem and identity issues relate to active citizenship

In Chapter I we looked at how PSHE and CE had been linked in the Primary Guidelines, and how self-esteem and identity formed the foundation for CE. Natalie and Joe, in the stories above, had both thought about improving self-esteem and the identity of the class as a community. Chapter I discussed important considerations about personal and cultural identity, which would help all children to feel included and that they belonged, and also enhance understanding, tolerance and mutual respect for diversity.

There are already a great many resources designed to help you with this kind of work, listed in the reference section at the back. In broad terms, these resources cluster round

- *developing personal self-esteem*, which is often about what to do in Circle Time and is really **PSE**. Examples are 'All about me' (in *Let's Make a Difference*, JCRE, 1999); Circle Time ideas from Borba, Bliss or Mosley.
- *curriculum work* which is designed to develop identity and mutual understanding through acknowledging different groups' history, culture and community, often called 'multicultural education'. The vehicles can be art, music, cooking and festivals, drama, poetry and literature, religious education, history, geography, PE (through dance and games). Some ideas for this way of working are given in Part 2 of this book.
- *work about group identity in a multicultural society*. This goes beyond work on cultural and religious differences in identity, described above, and looks for opportunities to emphasise links and similarities, rather than differences.

Activity 2

Our group identities

In Chapter 1 you looked at your own 'multiple identities'. The following activity takes that idea into the classroom, to encourage feelings of 'we' rather than 'us and them' through emphasising the characteristics we share, as part of our multiple identities.

The teacher asks one child for her favourite music (author/food/place to go on holiday etc.) and then asks everyone who shares this either to go into a huddle with her or to put up their hands. Try to include some of the events and customs that are often presented as defining difference rather than similarity. For instance, everyone who celebrated a wedding in their family (never mind if the rituals are different), or who gives a baby a special welcome or name. As you become more sure of your group, and that you won't inadvertently be causing offence or embarrassment, you can move into more sensitive preferences or attributes. These can include those issues which can lead to some people feeling excluded from the national identity, rather than having their qualities valued and acknowledged as part of a plural society. For example, 'can speak a language other than English'; 'has family or friends living in another country' (you may want to be specific); 'has visited family or friends in other countries or lived in another country'.

Another version involving quite a lot of bustle and noise (so don't try it with a class with whom you are still feeling your way!) has one person (the teacher or a child) calling out a category, such as 'music', 'favourite spectator sport', 'favourite author'. Each person decides on their personal preference and then has to find someone or a group who share this.

Here is a similar activity, which you could try before the one above with children, or with the younger ones. They sit in a circle, and you go around whispering in their ear 'horse, sheep, cat, dog'. (Don't use pig or cow – some children could be offended on religious grounds, and anyway, to call someone a cow or a pig can be insulting.) Then bang your drum or tambourine: the children jump up making their animal noise and try to find other animals like them, where they huddle together. You can change this several times so that they regroup.

KSI/2 PSHE/Citizenship Guidelines: Preparing to play an active role as citizens

What better place to start than with the requirements and recommendations of the National Curriculum! For convenience, I am going to refer to the KS2 guidelines, which both repeat and take further what is in KSI. KSI people should keep their guidelines in front of them, and put brackets round the parts that are not relevant to them, though it is always useful to keep the next stage in mind, both in order to know how to challenge more able children's thinking, and also so that you can consider transition.

Figure 3.2 shows the skills and understanding children need to be active citizens. There are three thin rectangles which have shading – *Thinking skills* which are quite generic, *Skills for functioning in the wider political domain* which relate more closely to CE, and *Having a vision of a 'good' society and wanting to actively create this*. The last one, which will entail imagination, not just skill, is important in translating Crick's ideas about active, participative citizenship into reality. Citizenship Education is not necessarily just to learn to fit with the status quo. Unless children are developing values, thinking skills and a vision of a future society as part of a 'jigsaw of learning', their education to be active citizens is likely to be quite limited.

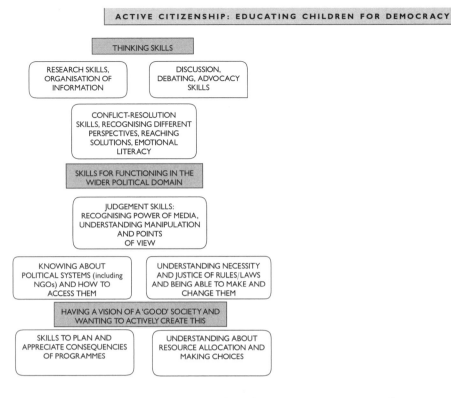

Figure 3.2 Skills and understanding children will need in order to be active citizens

Activity 3

'Thinking skills' are right at the top of the skills that children need for active citizenship. Figure 3.2 suggests what some of these skills might be, but begs the question about why they would be necessary. Why do you think CE and in particular active citizenship might rely heavily on thinking skills? If you are in a group, brainstorm your ideas and compare and add to Figure 3.3, the start of a brainstorm which comes from a group of primary student teachers.

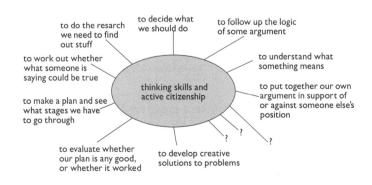

Figure 3.3 Why do we need thinking skills in active citizenship?

Commentary

Every area of the curriculum develops thinking skills in one way or another, whether it is mathematics, science, literacy, art, music, PE, history or ICT. Science and mathematics, for example, develop powers of logic and rational thought, proof, generalisation and problem-solving. History relies on evidence-based induction and deduction to try to explain change in society, and also relies on imaginative, empathetic thinking. Literacy develops a variety of thinking skills, including logic and explanation, understanding rules and irregularities in language, and like the creative arts, also emphasises creative thinking. PE, for example a team game, can involve thinking through the consequences of some actions, or evaluating prior actions and altering one's strategies. In addition to developing thinking skills which are transferable through the subject areas, there are possibilities for concentrating on thinking skills in their own right. These are discussed below.

Philosophy for Children (P4C), communities of enquiry, critical thinking skills

Natalie's story introduced an important idea – the classroom as a 'community of enquiry' – explaining that this was a concept from Philosophy for (or with) Children. This section starts with two extracts to help you think about the relevance of the thinking skills developed through P4C. The first extract comes from St Matthew's and Overslade Church site, and shows how quite young children were encouraged to discuss important ethical issues using the methods of P4C.

> 'Who made God?' 'Why did God make Adam and Eve if he knew they were going to be bad?' 'Where did badness start?' These were all questions asked in a class of 7-year-olds recently. Developing the skills to think well is actually part of our school curriculum in the UK. Teachers in schools today should be helping children to learn to ask questions, to process information, to reason, to enquire, to evaluate information and to think creatively. Teachers are encouraged to make their classrooms into a *community of enquiry*. Those 7-year-old children were being encouraged to learn by exploring issues with their questions. A very healthy approach to discovery and learning! Yet sometimes in churches (not in St Matthew's and Overslade, I hasten to add!) we are discouraged from asking questions. This may be because it threatens the leaders, or it is seen as rebellious and lacking in submission to the leaders, or because it is interpreted that we are having doubts in our faith.
> Source: **www.stmatthews.org.uk/Devotional/2003/1003/101003.htm.**

The second extract comes from one of the principal organisations involved with P4C in Britain, Dialogueworks, which has published material you can use directly in your classroom. Like the statement from St Matthew's, this second extract emphasises how P4C develops children's ethical thinking, and their ability to articulate values, as well as helping them think logically, express themselves convincingly and keep open minds.

> **Classroom philosophy improves the quality of thinking!**
> Philosophy – with its emphasis on careful thinking and openness to ideas – enriches the experience of classroom dialogue. Any discussion about **morality**, **citizenship**, **values**, **actions**, and concepts such as **friendship**, **beauty** or **freedom** will be poorer without a philosophical dimension.
> Source: **www.dialogueworks.co.uk/indexedu.html**

The ability to *think critically and put together reasoned arguments* is essential to CE. Philosophy for Children is one of the most important and exciting developments in developing children's power of critical, rational thought: it comes from a programme originally developed by Professor Matthew Lipman in the USA, who showed that children as young as 6 could become proficient at debating quite abstract ideas about ethics and justice, and is increasingly practised in Britain and all over the world. One of its central ideas is that the classroom should become *a community of enquiry*. In P4C it has quite a specific meaning, not only offering a particular strategy through which children can learn to explore and debate issues, but is a powerful metaphor for a classroom in which people learn together – the teacher included. A community of enquiry depends on everyone acknowledging that they do want and need to learn. But it also depends on a theory of learning which comes from social constructivism: namely that people learn from each other, through talking about their ideas, and following through on issues they're interested in. In a community of enquiry, the participants are prepared to be provisional and tentative about their ideas, open-minded, willing to listen and to change their minds on the basis of good arguments and convincing evidence. In a community of enquiry, the responsibility for what is learned is not just the teacher's province, but where possible is shared with children. Given the requirements of the National Curriculum, it would be unrealistic and utopian to abandon all one's planning, but within this there are possibilities which some teachers successfully exploit to give pupils a voice in planning. Natalie's was one example. Some teachers allow children to choose which people and issues they will work on (within a given framework) in history and geography, whose curricula are less prescriptive than some teachers imagine. The literacy strategy does not have to be interpreted in the inflexible way that happened sometimes when it was first introduced, as *Excellence and Enjoyment* (DfES, 2003) and the current proposals for Language across the Curriculum, both emphasise. This means you *and the children* might discuss which texts you study. Speaking and listening and the general recommendations about report writing, non-fiction or fiction, poetry, and so on, actually allow you quite a lot of flexibility, which you could share with your class. In a book about citizenship, there is not space to go into all the possibilities within different subjects for giving children some say in what they learn, but you will find examples from some subjects in Part 2. Meanwhile, I'd like to plant the idea of communities of enquiry in your mind as a way to enhance democratic practices. As we reiterate throughout this book, children need to be educated *for* democracy through *living in and participating in* a democratic environment. Incidentally, you might be interested to know that a secondary school went a long way along this road. The teachers decided to ask the children *how* they would like to learn, and rethought their teaching and learning strategies in the light of what the children said (reported by Citizenship Foundation, 2004).

Resources for P4C in the primary school include picture books and texts which are interesting and accessible to children. They start by raising questions themselves about the text or the illustrations. The teacher facilitates their exploration of ideas, without dominating. This process has two important consequences for CE: the first is that children learn a procedure for debate, including disagreement, which is carefully managed, and depends on logic and evidence. The second is that the actual subject matter which follows from their own questions regularly moves into citizenship areas that we have already identified in our first two chapters, namely rights, responsibilities, identity and values.

In Britain, the main forum for P4C is an organisation called 'Sapere'. Here is an extract from its website, to give you a flavour of the approach and relevance to CE.

Philosophical enquiry aims to help children develop the basic skills and dispositions that will enable them to contribute to a pluralistic society. It can boost children's self-esteem and intellectual confidence. It aims to create a caring classroom situation where children

- **learn to listen to and respect each other**
- **make links between matters of personal concern such as love, growing up, friendship, bullying and fairness, and more general philosophical issues such as change, personal identity, free will, space, time and truth**
- **are encouraged to challenge and explore the beliefs and values of others, and to develop their own views**
- **experience quiet moments of thinking and reflection**
- **learn to be clear in their thinking and to make responsible and more deliberate judgements**
- **learn to be more thoughtful by basing their decisions and actions on reasons.**

Philosophy and moral education

Philosophical enquiry initiates children into public discussion of values and morality. It encourages them to make judgements but also to consider what making a moral judgement really involves and what it means to be reasonable. But good discussion is not just a talking shop. It has its own moral culture. It initiates us into a special way of acting together, cultivating dispositions and virtues of conduct such as respect for others, sincerity and open-mindedness.

A world of difference

There are many differences that separate people. Philosophical enquiry with children aims to promote a dialogue across differences and the communicative virtues that make understanding possible. The community of enquiry provides a public forum where children and adults can talk together without displacing differences like those of class, sex and culture. Children are encouraged to find their own path to meaning via discussion with others. (**www.sapere.net**)

We highly recommend P4C as part of Citizenship Education (as well as in its own right). P4C helps children to think through their values in a structured framework, and develops their powers of logic, advocacy, discussion and debate. It is a powerful tool for helping children deal rationally with difference and conflict. It is a vehicle for children to set their own agenda, and then debate their views and the consequences of various positions. To find out more, look at the reference section at the end of this book.

Research skills

Earlier in this chapter we mentioned that CE might be taught through other subject areas, be cross-curricular or might 'stand alone'. All are worthwhile and legitimate, as Part 2 of this book explores further. Research skills are actually generic and cross-curricular, and your class will be practising and developing them throughout the curriculum, using resources such as the internet, non-fiction, pictures and newspaper reports, material from organisations, etc. Authentic research for a purpose will be built into your history, geography and design technology planning, and your children may well use research in other subject areas. For CE, research skills will involve finding relevant information about an issue, organising and selecting material to support a position, or refute one. You will need to develop the professional skill to recognise subject-based opportunities for research to support CE as well as plan for research in support of 'stand-alone' CE work.

Persuasion, advocacy and debate

P4C is one important way to help children with these skills, but we can go further. Broadly speaking, democratic practice depends on people being able to

- **make their own wishes and views known;**
- **critically evaluate programmes on offer;**
- **offer a programme to try to attract support;**
- **recognise alternative positions and either incorporate them, change one's own position, or have very good arguments to refute them.**

All these will be important tools in a pupil's repertoire as an active citizen, and they are the sorts of skills that they need to learn and practise in school.

Here are some real examples from primary schools to help you consider how you might build in opportunities to develop these skills in your classroom.

Classroom story

Reza and Year 4: a debate in literacy time, drawing on ICT and geography

Reza saw that there were opportunities in the non-fiction section of the literacy strategy to bring in newspaper articles and to write newspaper-style reports. She brought in a headline with its picture of protesters who had dug themselves into an abandoned slate quarry in the Derbyshire Peak District, to prevent its development for sandstone production. First the children read different reports about the quarry development and identified the protesters', the landowner's and the developing company's perspectives. They had a look at the Campaign to Protect Rural England's website. Then, having helped them locate issues and websites, Reza asked them to do some research on the net about other campaigns involving the natural environment and its development. She remembered doing an activity in uni and brought in material about 'Swampy' in Devon who with his followers had dug himself in to try to prevent a motorway development.[4] Another group researched the campaign by Arundhati Roy at the end of 1999 on behalf of millions of Indians who would be displaced by the Narmada Dam project. Following the model of the 'Swampy' activity, each group used a writing frame to set out their findings in terms of 'two (or more) sides to the story'. Given the chance to choose, they decided they would like to debate the Narmada Dam story. Reza allocated them into two groups – the pros and the cons – using the material already put together by the 'Dam research group'. With herself as the chair, the class ran a proper debate and voted. They voted to have the dam stopped. Reza told them that in reality it was going ahead, and that Arundhati Roy had been put on trial, and sentenced to one day's symbolic imprisonment; then a loud cheer went up!

Commentary – Evaluating learning

We have said that we need to establish CE-related learning objectives and look for learning outcomes which allow us to evaluate the value and the success of our work. Reza identified the following learning objectives for citizenship in the work, all coming from the CE guidelines. (You will be able to check the literacy, geography and IT objectives yourselves.)

1. Research, discuss and debate topical issues, problems and events.
2. Discuss laws and the morality of breaking the law.
3. Realise that there are different kinds of responsibilities in the community and that they can conflict.
4. Reflect on moral and cultural issues, using imagination to understand others' experience.
5. Resolve differences by looking at alternatives, making decisions and explaining choices.
6. Recognise role of pressure groups.
7. Learn that resources can be allocated in different ways with economic choices which affect communities and the sustainability of the environment.
8. Learn how the media present information.

The difficult part is not identifying these objectives, but knowing how to assess the extent to which children have achieved them. To ensure that we are 'on target' with outcomes, we need to look for evidence of children's understanding and learning. This could come from statements they make, or written work, or something about their drama, or the debating points they raise and their ability to deal with the issues. 'Norm referencing' rather than 'criterion referenced evaluation' would be necessary. This means considering the evidence that seems most sophisticated and appropriate in the group you're working with, and using this as the 'gold standard'. This is the best you can hope for at this point. Then compare other children's understanding and responses.

Self-assessment is also helpful and formative. To do this, you could give children versions of the objectives which were child-friendly, ask them to use smiley faces, or mark themselves along a continuum (from 'I did not understand/achieve this' to 'I understood/achieved this very well') and ask for a brief statement explaining why they had assessed themselves this way and what they think they still need to work on. Group assessment is also possible, with a group coming to a decision about how well they managed a task, and giving an example to back their judgement. Self-assessment is particularly useful for metacognitive learning, or knowing about your own learning.

Another case study about developing skills of active citizenship

Classroom story

Charlene and Year 2: where shall we go for our summer outing?

Traditionally, Year 2 went to the Natural History Museum for their summer outing but I wanted to give the children the chance to choose for themselves. I took ideas on the white board, which included 'the seaside' (narrowed down to Littlehampton), 'Disneyland in Paris', Kew Gardens and the Chislehurst Caves. With the children on the carpet, I asked them to say how they could decide. This meant discussing not just majority and minority and voting, but identifying criteria by which some choices would have to get eliminated, and helping the children decide how they might vote one way or another.

I prepared a list of criteria, which I used to guide the children's thinking, for example:

- **How much will it cost and can we afford it?**
- **How long will it take to get there, and does that leave us enough time to enjoy ourselves?**
- **What will we do when we get there?**
- **Will it be a new and different experience for us, or something we've done before, and which we already know will be good?**

The latter provoked an interesting discussion in which children explored their feelings about doing something they knew about, *versus* trying something new. I felt this helped them appreciate different points of view based on feelings, as well as understand their own feelings.

Then I organised groups to find out about different places, using the net. I needed to help them of course, not just with finding the most useful sites but also in extracting the information they needed. We used our ICT time and had some support. My 'star' group quickly found out the cost of getting to Paris and to Disneyland on Eurostar and how long it would take, and reported ruefully that this option had to go!

Finally, each group presented their findings with posters they had made which answered the main questions. Then the class voted. The first vote showed Kew Gardens trailing in popularity, so I introduced a new idea – the transferable vote. We eliminated Kew and everyone could use their vote again, and now Chislehurst Caves came out top of the poll.

Reflective activity

Following Reza's example on page 59 try to identify CE learning objectives for Charlene. How successful do you think she was?

Classroom story

Learning to develop a persuasive argument: Connor and Year 1: the alternative Three Little Pigs

Connor liked to read alternative versions of fairy tales to his class, to get them thinking and laughing! He read them the alternative Red Riding Hood, in which the wolf is a badly-done-by good guy, who was only trying to help[5] and 'The True Story of the Three Little Pigs',[6] in which it also transpires that the wolf has been framed! Then he asked his class to think about a version of the Three Little Pigs in which nobody's house got blown down, the third little pig did not triumph and the wolf was persuaded to come in quietly and share supper. Working in friendship pairs, the children had to come up with a persuasive argument for their little pig, about why the wolf should not hurt them, but come in and be friends. Each pair would put together what they would say, and role-play their alternative drama to the others.

Citizenship learning objectives

- **Recognise what is fair and unfair and what is right and wrong.**
- **Share opinions and explain their views; take part in discussions.**
- **Consider dilemmas (e.g. aggressive behaviour, questions of fairness).**
- **Recognise how behaviour affects others.**
- **Listen to others and work cooperatively.**
- **Share responsibility for their behaviour.**

These learning objectives all come from the guidelines, but you may well think, as I do, that the children were in fact developing important skills of advocacy, recognising alternative points of view, and conflict resolution and persuasion, not actually mentioned in the guidelines.

Political literacy – participation in decision-making and learning about representation

There are more ideas about handling discussion and debate in the next chapter about tackling controversial issues in the classroom. But now we will move on, to a very different but important aspect of education for democracy – helping children learn about political systems and how to be active participants.

Let's just review some of the skills and attitudes that lie behind democracy, to remind ourselves what children need to be learning:

- **How to participate in decision-making that affects them.**
- **How to elect representatives who are accountable to 'the electorate', taking account of convincing arguments, and seeing through bias, manipulation or special pleading.**
- **How to debate and change laws, or make new ones for new situations.**
- **How to recognise and expect free and open debate.**
- *Anything else you'd like to add.*

There is more than one tried-and-tested way to develop the skills, attitudes and understanding which children need to develop for participative democracy, and they build on one another.

I. Class councils: formal class discussion about issues relevant to their life in school

Natalie's classroom story earlier in this chapter was an example of children participating democratically in decisions about their life in school. Many teachers try to build in some democracy into classroom life, for instance asking children to vote on which of their favourite songs they will sing at the end of the day, which game they might play at the end of PE or which story will be read from the book box. Classroom rules are also usually negotiated through whole-class discussion. Children will get experience of developing and presenting their research or work as a group through different curriculum areas, all part of their developing skills in political literacy.

Classroom story

Year 4: Kate's class council

In the early spring term, when I had got to know my Year 4 class pretty well, I decided to go more formal and set up a class council which would be 'in session' on the last Friday afternoon of each month, during the period allocated to Circle Time. The whole class was actually the council, in that everyone was involved in the discussions, and where appropriate voted. It was modelled on real local councils, with a mayor (me, though I hoped to train up a mayor to take over) and children taking responsibility for specific areas. The children had decided – with my help – on a 'Behaviour Issues Committee', a 'Classroom Organisation Committee' which dealt with the classroom as a physical space, and a 'Learning Committee' which dealt with the ways they were organised for learning. The children had elected three children to each committee. There were three boxes in which anyone could post a suggestion or issue that they wanted to have debated at the council meeting. The week before the council meeting, the committee members looked at the contents of the boxes. I helped them draw up an agenda, which was 'published' on the Monday so that anyone who wanted to talk to an issue had time to prepare, if necessary with a friend. I was available to the committee members and to other children for help in preparing for the meeting. The sort of thing which came up was 'Please can we do something about keeping the story books in our fiction shelf in decent order' (Classroom Organisation Committee); 'Can we sort out how we use the computers, and for how long, because not all of us are getting a proper turn' (Learning Committee); 'There is trouble on the stairs when we go out or come back from play. Some kids are pushing.' (Behaviour Issues Committee). Some council meetings were very short, as nobody had put in a note, and twice I put in a note myself, to stimulate discussion about things I was concerned about (expensive toys coming to school and getting damaged; some insidious bullying and exclusion of girls in the reorganisation of cliques). Even if there wasn't much, I felt it was important not to let the council die, so that there should always be this system in place, to deal with issues that came up.'

Reflective activity

What do you think the children in Kate's class were learning about democracy and particularly political literacy? You might find it helpful to look back at the first few pages of Chapter 1, and Figure 1.2, 'Some important concepts in being a citizen' on page 9. In Chapter 5, under 'Paula's story', you will find more about a class council.

2. School councils

School councils are increasingly common in primary schools. To be honest, their effectiveness either in implementing democratic procedures in the school, or in dealing with real issues at decision-making level, varies! In some schools, the younger children are not considered ready or capable of participating, while others have representatives from the nursery, who not only join in, but report back to their nursery classes. In one school, the council decided that they wanted to abandon stickers and stars as the reward system. The children themselves had started to feel that this was leading to bad feeling in their classrooms. Some of the teachers were less happy about abandoning behaviour management systems with which they felt secure, but the headteacher backed the children and so everyone agreed to give the new system a try. Instead, the teachers organised two big boards in the entry area, one for excellent work during that week and the other to commend children who had made progress on their personal targets, which included behaviour issues.[7]

Some school councils remain tokenistic because the children don't have sufficient back-up information and understanding about how decisions are made, in terms of budgetary constraints, or accountability to higher authorities such as the governors or the LEA. Without this it is easy for children to become cynical and frustrated, because they don't have a realistic notion of what they have the power to affect. We'll come back to this in the next chapter, in Paula's 'classroom story' where we talk about 'joined-up thinking', and we'll learn more about how a school council was initiated.

You will find quite a lot of material about how to prepare for, set up and run a schools councils or class council on the website **www.schoolcouncils.org/**. There is also good advice and information from the DfES about class and school councils on the QCA/DfES Standards site, under Citizenship.

Here is an extract from this site:

> **Participating in the life of the class and the organisation of the school**
> Children contribute to decision-making in, and the running of, the class and the school. A range of responsibilities can be developed for younger and older children alike, allowing them to progress in the development of their skills and accept more responsibility as they do so. Children need less support in this participation as they get older.

3. School parliaments

School parliaments are probably less common than school councils. Where school councils typically find themselves dealing with behaviour-management issues, 'Parliaments' in Britain are more concerned to help children learn about the actual processes through which our own government works, for example, ministers, and debates for and against issues, followed by voting. The next chapter describes how a teacher introduced a 'parliamentary debate' to help her class understand about the historical issue of women's suffrage. The Bibliography section has information about school parliaments and school councils.

An inspiring example about the possibilities of school parliaments comes from Rajasthan in India, where a Children's Parliament has been set up based on the Night Schools attended by children who have to work during the day.[8] The 'voters' are aged 6–14, but members of the parliament have to be 11 or older; 38% of the seats have been reserved for girls to counter traditions which limited girls' participation. The children debate problems that arise in their schools, for instance resource issues or difficulties with teachers. Though adults attend the parliament, apparently the children decide what happens. Interestingly, the parliament seems to have fostered a sense of community identity as well as responsibility, and its example has now been followed in nine other Indian states.

Summary

In this chapter you have encountered all the following concepts and read about activities and classroom practice where children participated in different ways to develop their citizenship skills and understanding.

- **Active citizenship.**
- **The importance of a democratic classroom environment.**
- **How self-esteem and trust relate to participative citizenship.**
- **Empowering children and negotiating the curriculum.**
- **Setting ground rules for democracy in the classroom.**
- **Developing thinking skills.**
- **Philosophy for Children and communities of enquiry.**
- **Persuasion, advocacy and debate.**
- **Political literacy, learning about voting and representation.**
- **School councils and school parliaments.**

You also thought about identifying learning objectives for your citizenship planning, and considered assessment, albeit at an introductory level.

Notes

1   American researchers Michelle Borba, Robert Reasoner and John Vasconcellos are all enthusiastic proponents of the importance of raising self-esteem (see **www.kidshealth.org**; **www.self-esteem.nase.org**). British research is more sceptical about self-esteem, though it endorses the notion that self-esteem is

correlated with the opinions of significant others: see **www.jrf.org.uk/ knowledge/findings/social policies**. **www.escalate.ci.uk** is another useful website.

2 See the resource section for references for emotional literacy.

3 Murris, Karin and Haynes, Joanna, 2000, *Storywise: thinking through stories: Teachers' Guidance*, DialogueWorks.

4 See Clough and Holden, 2002, pp.91–95.

5 There are a variety of alternative versions, including one on pp.275–7 of *Reclaiming our Pasts* (Claire, 1996).

6 Scieszka, J. 1991, *The True Story of the Three Little Pigs*, Puffin.

7 Thanks to Angela Piddock, headteacher of Wilberforce Primary in London for telling me about this initiative in her school.

8 Reported in Osler, 2003, 'The Children's Parliament in Rajasthan: a model for learning about democracy', by Mary John.

What will you learn about in this chapter?

- *controversies that can arise in the classroom because of different values*
- *the teacher's role in dealing with controversial issues*
- *the links between economics and political action: how values and politics link in active citizenship*
- *using drama and role-play for dealing with issues in the classroom*
- *formal debates and 'trials'*
- *theatre in education*

Dealing with controversy as part of CE

In earlier chapters we considered the impossibility of avoiding controversy when we teach CE. In a plural society there is bound to be a variety of values and interests. These are recognised and legitimised in democratic societies through freedom of the press and of speech, and through having opposition parties in parliament and local government. The skills to deal with controversy and conflict in a democracy, without resorting to insult or violence, are absolutely essential. They don't come naturally, and much as you need to learn how to do division or measure space, children need to learn a number of strategies for dealing with controversy.

What issues can be controversial in the classroom?

In Activity 4 towards the end of Chapter 2 you were invited to consider your own values with respect to certain controversies which could come up in the classroom. Broadly speaking, anything that is controversial in the wider society can enter the classroom, since few children are totally insulated from issues discussed by their parents/carers or other adults in their community, or the media. Controversy can arise because of different positions and values, and different customs. In our plural society, you can find that children are personally connected to some of the more contentious issues in the wider world – as teachers whose classroom stories figure below have found. Your children may well have conflicting views about the status and rights of refugees, about racism and sexism, about the politics of battery or GM farming, gay and lesbian issues, what to do about homeless people or people claiming social security. As I found when I was doing research with primary children a few years ago,[1] even young children are likely to know about, and may have strong views about, events in the wider world, like the train bombings in Madrid or escalating violence in Iraq (in 2004), as well as controversies on their doorsteps.

Political controversies about, for example, the Middle East, can lead to worrying confrontations and abuse in school, but subsuming everything under 'bullying' or 'fighting', which of course are not allowed, doesn't get to the heart of the matter. The religious divide which characterises many current international and national conflicts and which easily becomes linked with stereotyping and racism, can poison children's attitudes. For example, post 9/11, a Reception teacher found that her class were taunting a five-year-old called Osama; in another school children were calling Muslim girls who were wearing hijab (scarves) 'Al Qaida'. One Year 2 teacher became aware that a group of Muslim boys were whispering 'evil people, people of the menorah' and blocking their ears, when she introduced the Jewish festival Chanukkah as part of her RE lesson. Also in Year 2, I became aware that a small group of girls was isolating and taunting a girl of a different faith because she didn't believe in 'their God'.[2]

In addition, there is considerable evidence that children can be extremely anxious about damage to the environment in the world that they will inherit, and the dangers and possible implications of violence in the wider society.[3] It is part of PSHE and Citizenship Education to acknowledge such fears, and help children, rather than airbrush their anxieties out of existence through the 'cosy curriculum'.[4]

Conflict resolution

Conflict between children affects the smooth running of our classrooms and the well-being of our pupils. However, since CE is intended to help children prepare for being part of wider democratic society, not just for their contemporary lives, it is our responsibility to help them develop understanding of a variety of perspectives and be able to deal with difference and diversity. This implies more than simply putting a stop to the unwanted behaviours, and does not mean forcing everyone into the same mould. Within the limits of democratic behaviour defined in the first chapter, we need to deal with intolerance where it exists, helping children manage difference without feeling threatened by it or suppressing diversity. When you are trying to manage controversy, all the advice and suggestions in the previous chapter come into play about the necessity for a safe democratic classroom, where issues can be discussed.

The importance of whole-school policies on bullying and equality issues

Currently, much controversy which spreads from the wider community into the playground and affects relationships between pupils and parents on school premises, comes from reactions and anxieties related to the heightened international situation. Advice from LEAs, the DfES and bodies such as the Runnymede Trust concerned with racism, is to keep firmly in focus whole-school policies about dealing immediately with racism, promoting understanding and dealing with issues through a variety of curriculum areas. A considerable amount of personal abuse results from stereotyping, failure to emphasise common values as opposed to difference, and failure to recognise that though fundamentalism and terrorism occur, this is an extreme end of a political/religious continuum. By far the majority of children and parents do not subscribe to extreme views and thus are victims of a situation, not the perpetrators. The message is to be proactive, not reactive, and not to wait till there is a nasty episode. Policies which encompass the overt curriculum as well as the hidden curriculum, relating to equal opportunities, community and parental liaison, democratic values within the school and so on, must be actively enforced before trouble starts.

The teacher's role

You can no more launch into tackling controversial issues in the classroom without setting up an appropriate ethos and ground rules, than you can have a football game without establishing the rules. Just as children need to know the rules of the game, they also need considerable practice in specific skills, which over time will improve. Because practising skills can transfer to 'the real thing', there are some examples in this chapter which use other curriculum areas as the vehicle for learning to deal with controversy.

It is helpful to acknowledge that controversy in the classroom can be extremely uncomfortable for everyone, teachers included. Controversies are always around value-laden and emotive subjects, where people can easily feel threatened and upset. It is also very important to remember that it is not part of a teacher's job – and in fact very wrong – to try to indoctrinate children. The point about tackling controversy in the classroom is not to make children think your way, but to help them think about issues clearly and rationally, and develop their own values within a framework of rights and respect. Here, just as in the wider democracy, the limits to what you may say or do come from understanding the underpinning values of democracy, i.e. freedom of speech is encouraged, but actions or behaviour which infringe other people's rights to be respected and valued are not allowed, including abusive behaviour, humiliation, racism or sexism.

In an earlier chapter we considered our power as teachers, and how being liked and respected as a person who was fair and trustworthy contributed to a democratic ethos. With respect to controversy, the more pupils like and respect us, the more our opinions and values will be adopted by them. So we have a very special responsibility to look inwards and make sure that we are really trying to be unbiased and open to different points of view, within the law.

The QCA/DfES *Citizenship: Teachers' Guide for Key Stage 3* has a useful section on sensitive and controversial issues (Appendix 9, pp.46–8) which you can access through the DfES Standards Site (Citizenship – teachers' guide). Unfortunately it hasn't been replicated in the KS1 and 2 Guidance. The Crick Report is also on the web and has helpful and up-to-date advice on teaching controversial issues (pp.56–61). Otherwise, it's worth putting 'teaching' or 'dealing with controversial issues' into Google, since topical material comes and goes. At the time of writing (early 2004), I put 'dealing with Islamophobia' into Google and located a wide variety of sites from LEAs in the UK to academic and religious groups here and abroad, offering extremely helpful advice and suggestions about ways forward.

Establishing ground rules

This first section will remind you of the importance of classroom ethos generally, and ground rules within which children can safely voice their opinions, even if they disagree strongly with one another. 'Straight' discussion or debate is not the only, or necessarily the best, way to deal with controversy. However, there will certainly be occasions when you do want to have a straightforward discussion, and the following guidelines will be essential to prevent things deteriorating into a nasty free for all, which can be counterproductive. It is also worth remembering that some teachers have learned to their cost that controversy may be suppressed in the classroom but can erupt in the playground, where it is much more difficult to oversee or manage.

Guidelines and ground rules

- Show mutual respect and avoid put-downs.
- Give people space to say what they want to safely.
- Be rational, listen to evidence – but also expect evidence to back up statements.
- Respect truth and honesty – that is, don't manipulate or abuse evidence to try to prove a case.
- Be open-minded and prepared to change your mind.
- Be able to consider your own and other people's values, and come to decisions based on values and possible compromise.

Activity 1

What teachers can do

Ground rules need to be developed collaboratively with the children. Some American research[5] looked at the relationship between pupils' ability to handle difficult issues, a democratic classroom environment (which we discussed earlier) and the teacher's role. The following grid sets out the positive features of democratic classrooms where difficult issues are successfully addressed. Mark yourself on the scale 1–5 (1 = lowest, 5 = highest score) on each criterion. If you get between 40 and 50 in total, you are well on the way to managing controversy effectively. If you get below 25, you might want to work on some of your current strategies and practices.

Positive features	1	2	3	4	5
Give frequent opportunities for pupils to express their opinions.					
Respect pupil opinions and make this explicit.					
Encourage perspective-taking through modelling and making it part of a variety of curriculum activities.					
Use praise for behaviour management, smile and be warm and open with pupils.					
Establish a norm of openly discussing controversial issues as opposed to avoiding or ignoring them.					
Offer a range of viewpoints about issues under discussion.					
Use divergent questioning techniques (i.e. encouraging children to think in wide-ranging ways and avoid narrow approaches).					
Use a variety of sources and activities, e.g. role-plays, debates, working with texts or pictures, adverts.					
Interest in issues; make regular time for such discussion, perhaps through weekly 'what's in the news?' sessions, with children contributing subjects.					

Teachers' roles in debate and discussion

There are a number of possibilities, which are not mutually exclusive. We'll come to other strategies, particularly role-plays and drama, later in this chapter. The Crick Report[6] mentions the 'neutral chair' who facilitates discussion; the 'balanced approach', in which the teacher expresses her/his view about a number of alternatives to ensure that all sides of an argument are presented; and the 'committed approach', in which the teacher states her/his view quite clearly, and pupils are encouraged to agree or disagree.

A development of these roles might be:

I. THE JUDGE
- **Dispassionate, concerned that children stick to the point, back up their case, listen to one another, keep to the ground rules.**
- **Clarify where the discussion has got to, if necessary on a white board or flip chart.**
- **Sum up and manage the 'ending'.**

S/he can set the class up as a 'courtroom' so that children take advocacy or defence of a position very seriously in role.

2. THE DEVIL'S ADVOCATE
- **Make sure that children consider different sides to a story, if they are not offering these themselves.**
- **Challenge children's thinking and perspective, using words like 'what would you say to someone who said ...' or 'so-and-so ...' (a well-known figure) believes ...'.**

3. FACILITATOR
- **Make sure that everyone who wants to speak gets their chance.**
- **Watch for dominating people and keep them in check, or change the format.**
- **Ease the tension with a joke or some other strategy if necessary.**

4. SOCRATES
- **Push children to justify their position.**
- **Ask questions which get them to see for themselves the consequences of a statement or to think through the next steps in an argument.**
- **Question their assumptions.**
- **Help them make connections and understand the logic (or lack of it!).**

The notes below about the teacher's role and establishing ground rules for tackling controversial issues are adapted from an Australian site at Flinders University.[7]

I. YOU MAY NOT BE ABUSIVE, DEROGATORY OR PUT PEOPLE DOWN. THIS INCLUDES THE TEACHER

Encourage children to think carefully, and not to say anything that they would not be prepared to say directly to someone for whom the issue was important. Encourage positive responses and politeness, even in disagreements. Model this for children with words like 'I hear/understand what you're saying, but I disagree, and maybe you haven't thought about ...'.

2. YOU MUST BE ABLE TO BACK UP STATEMENTS WITH EVIDENCE AND EVIDENCE CAN BE EVALUATED

Children will need help in distinguishing between opinion and evidence. 'My Dad says so...' is not evidence, and one example may not be sufficient to back up an argument. You can help children decide on criteria for evaluating evidence and do this in a 'neutral space' so that you have already established what's acceptable and can call on earlier agreements. A variety of curriculum subjects could be the way in. In history, children can consider the idea of 'propaganda' and how history is often presented from a particular point of view (normally the victor's); they can consider how evidence is manipulated by people who have a specific agenda, whether through the media or advertising.

3. HELP CHILDREN TO THINK TENTATIVELY AND PROBABILISTICALLY

Help them reserve judgement, and be prepared to wait to hear a variety of points of view before they articulate a definite position. They can learn to use words like 'it may be that, but I'm not sure till I've found out more', 'I need to think about this, or see what happens if …'.

4. HELP CHILDREN BREAK FREE FROM 'CLOSED' OR 'BLACK-AND-WHITE' THINKING'

Model different perspectives; invite them to think of and represent someone else's position who might feel differently. Acknowledge that you have changed your mind about something and encourage them to see changing your mind and open-mindedness as a strength, not a weakness. Games like 'The Great Divide' (see below) can help here.

5. STEREOTYPES ARE NOT ACCEPTABLE EVIDENCE TO BACK UP YOUR ARGUMENT

Children will need help understanding what a stereotype is and how it can operate to wrongly include everyone in another attribute, just because they do share some characteristic. A good way to help them understand this is to use Venn diagrams with subsets and intersections.

Subsets work like this: first make a set of furry animals – cats, rabbits, etc. Then within your original set make a set of furry creatures that burrow underground. This shows that there are lots of furry creatures, but only some furry creatures burrow. (Analogy: all girls have certain biological characteristics, but only some girls like dolls.)

Intersecting sets work slightly differently: Make a set of 'people with brown hair' and a separate set of 'people who like Britney Spears' then 'pull them together' to show the intersection of brown-haired people who like Britney Spears. This shows that not all brown-haired people like Britney Spears, and that liking Britney is not a predictor of hair colour.

If you find children using stereotypes, use their experience with Venn diagrams to help them see the faulty thinking.

Classroom story

Saira and Year 5: playground troubles

Saira was on playground duty when two girls in her class came up to her. Chrissie had her arm round a sobbing Baljit. It transpired that following a conversation about a treat at MacDonalds, a group of girls had been mocking Baljit about being a strict vegetarian. Saira comforted Baljit, thanked Chrissie and said she would deal with this, but if they agreed, later in the day rather than immediately. She knew she could have done some moralising about respecting people's cultural or religious food preferences, but thought the children would all dutifully nod and agree and not alter their opinions one jot. Saira suspected there was an element of racism which she'd have to consider, but she could not do everything simultaneously. So, first, she decided to try an activity she'd encountered in an INSET session, called 'The Great Divide'.[8] Children had to literally 'take sides' about certain issues, justify themselves and then had an opportunity to alter their original position based on the variety of perspectives on offer.

She arranged a hall time, and got a soft ball and a couple of long skipping ropes, which she knotted together and laid across the floor. One side of the rope was the 'I agree' side and the other 'I disagree'. You positioned yourself near or far from the rope to represent physically your feelings about a statement. If you were neutral, you stood right by the rope. Saira called out a statement, and when the children had moved into position, she threw the soft ball to someone who had to explain their views as persuasively as they could. She kept control of the ball so that she could decide who would be invited to speak.

She started with statements that children probably disagreed about, but which were unlikely to be upsetting ... dogs are better than cats ... Weetabix is nicer than Rice Crispies ... but gradually introduced more controversial issues. Children soon got the hang of positioning themselves and having to explain their point of view. After she'd thrown the ball to a few people, she'd ask if anyone wanted to change their mind. There were no takers until the statement was 'We should all wear school uniform', when several children who'd been strongly against, changed sides on the basis of a very persuasive argument from Jasmine about people not being shown up if they didn't have the latest gear. Saira's last statement that day was 'we shouldn't kill live creatures'. Put like this there was a small minority on the 'disagree' side. No one initially seemed to be think-ing of killing animals for food; the first 'agree' child talked about fox hunting, and the 'disagree' person talked about killing dangerous snakes and rats. Then someone mentioned killing cattle with BSE, and someone else said that her cat had been put down because it was very old and very sick. Saira asked if anyone wanted to shift their position now and several children changed sides or moved closer to the line. Saira threw the ball a few more times. Baljit was on the 'agree' side near the rope, with two of the girls who'd taunted her quite nearby, when Saira passed her the ball. She carefully explained that she thought there were times when you would have to kill animals, for example if they were dangerous to people, but that she and her family didn't agree with killing animals for people to eat and there were plenty of other healthy things they could eat instead. People listened respectfully. It was as if the game had put vegetarian beliefs into a different perspective for them.

Saira left it there, but was really pleased when the next day the children asked if they could play the game again. In her own mind she hoped the day would soon come when she would feel confi-dent enough to let the children contribute the statements.[9]

Where next for Saira? Using drama

Though the children had listened respectfully to different opinions in 'The Great Divide', Saira had been rather disappointed at their ability to explain themselves articulately. She needed to build in more opportunities to debate and consider alternative positions to one's own. She decided not to plunge straight into a debate about a controversial issue in the contemporary world (and there were certainly plenty of them!) but to use a story by Anne Fine[10] called 'The chicken gave it to me'. This is a satire about little green space creatures who liberate some battery chickens and replace them with humans whom they are fattening up to eat. One of the chickens smuggles herself aboard the spaceship and becomes a television celebrity on 'Green Planet' with a message about allowing the imprisoned humans space to grow and eat normally. The children loved the witty story which touches on the conditions of factory farming as well as comparative land use for rearing meat and crops. Saira decided to use drama techniques to explore the issues of battery farming and organic food, and leave vegetarianism and meat-eating to a later date. First the children drew up lists of pros and cons for battery and organic farming, thinking about and researching websites to get information about the product's taste, cost to the producer and the customer, cruelty to animals.

For homework, she encouraged some children to get the prices for battery and free-range chickens from their supermarket, and compare the prices for battery eggs and free-range. Saira overheard an animated discussion about whether it was worth it, with two children arguing that poor people needed food, and it was just too bad if the animals had to suffer, because people were more important, and two others adamant that in this country we were all well off enough to afford to pay a bit more. Groups developed a series of freeze-frames to represent green people-eaters, 'battery humans' imprisoned in their cages, their advocates the chickens, and the space audience, responding to the chicken's television appearance with jokes, recipes for tasty humans and poems (using the story as inspiration). Finally, Saira animated each group, so that they spoke their lines.

Reflective activity

Learning objectives and evaluation, including self-evaluation of Saira's activities

In line with examples in the previous chapter, we need to evaluate our work in the classroom using CE learning objectives. We can start by evaluating Saira's initiatives.

First, draw up a short list of CE learning objectives that you think Saira needed, or indeed had for the first activity, playing 'The Great Divide'. Then draw up a second list for the 'green people/battery humans' freeze-frame work.

It's difficult to use the limited information you have here to do a genuine evaluation, but perhaps you could try something like this yourself, and evaluate your learning objectives. Don't forget advice in the previous chapter about formative, diagnostic and self-assessment, and don't get bogged down in summative assessment. Try to share your objectives with the children, and get them involved in self-evaluation, which research has shown is one of the best ways for children to learn.

Commentary on Saira's approach

Saira has not got started on her second objective, of exploring the possibility of insidious racism in her classroom. But her imaginative and oblique approach to issues would seem very helpful in diffusing personal animosity, and at the same time exploring genuinely controversial issues.

The economic concepts underlying some controversies

Saira deserves credit for building in work on resource allocation, which is in itself controversial. Some policies that we might advocate for humanitarian reasons, or because they seem just, may cost more than alternatives. This is a very important issue to introduce into CE planning, since many of the human-rights controversies or environmental issues the world now faces are the result of programmes which try to produce goods as cheaply as possible for consumers, or to produce maximum profit for producers. This can result in exploitation of some groups, or pollution to our environment. For children to have a genuine sense of what change would entail, they need a handle on the economic arguments.

1. MORE HUMANITARIAN PRODUCTION MAY BE MORE EXPENSIVE

To deal with this idea in more than a tokenistic way means children must face up to the value they place on alternatives. If they value treating live animals well, or eating organic food, or not exploiting people abroad who are part of the production cycle for their clothes, then they may need to pay more. According to the age of the children, you might help them understand the following ideas, possibly with mapping exercises which show how different ideas like 'price', 'producer's profit' or 'workers' pay and conditions' link up.

2. PRICES ARE DETERMINED BY COSTS TO PRODUCERS, THE PROFIT THEY EXPECT TO MAKE, AND CONSUMERS' WILLINGNESS AND ABILITY TO PAY

This is 'supply and demand' in action, and also reflects the fact that within private enterprise, no producers operate at a loss or without any profit. This is in itself a possible issue for debate with children. For example, some nationalised industries are prepared to operate some facilities at a loss for egalitarian reasons (normally making up the loss elsewhere), such as running a bus route to a small village.

3. COSTS RELATE TO PRODUCTION COSTS AND DELIVERY COSTS

Production costs are often held down by mechanisation, e.g. housing and feeding battery chickens with easily dispensed food, in tiny cages, as opposed to using land space where they can run around freely, and require more workers. Pesticides reduce losses from pests more efficiently and cheaply than labour and thus reduce production costs; in contrast, organic foods cost more. As well as paying the primary producers poorly, global monopolies which market, e.g. bananas or coffee, keep their prices

low by very large-scale production and sales (economies of scale). Independent producers can't do this. A good local analogy is the constraints on the corner shop when
compared to a supermarket.

In the case of cheap goods made abroad, the production costs are low relative to costs
in the West because, typically, people are paid much less. There is often less concern
with human rights, and work conditions are often poor; children and young women
may be employed at very low wages for long hours. Merely boycotting or closing
down their factories would deprive them of the jobs which keep them alive. If they
were to get better pay and better conditions of work, the production costs would be
transferred to the buyer. This does not prevent people in the West protesting about
human rights in the places where goods are made and putting pressure on large
corporations to reduce their profit margins, but higher prices are also likely.

Delivery costs are lower for mass-produced goods because of economies of scale in
distribution, and also because in the case of food, it may not be considered important
to deliver things fresh. Smaller-scale producers either have to use middle people for
delivery (who take a cut) or have the option of banding together for marketing and
delivery. This is why goods sold through Fairtrade can have similar prices to goods
sold through large monopolies. As more organic goods are bought, then larger production and delivery runs for the producers and distributors will work in their favour,
bringing the costs, and thus the prices, down.

4. YOU HAVE TO CHOOSE HOW YOU'LL SPEND YOUR MONEY –
OPPORTUNITY COST

This is the familiar idea that if you only have 10p to spend you can't have both the apple
and the pear. For CE, this is an important idea, which goes beyond personal choices.
Political parties offer us all kinds of economic inducements to vote for them, for
instance better education, better healthcare, better transport, and so on. However,
if you've only got £x in the kitty, you can't improve anything without giving up some
other 'opportunity'. Economists say the true cost of something is not its money cost
but its 'opportunity cost', which is what you must forgo in order to pay for something
else. The only way you can improve public services in total is to get more money in
the coffers, and this will mean taxing people more, or taking out loans. And loans
have to be repaid with interest!

A variety of resources from NGOs (Oxfam, Save the Children, UNICEF) address the
problems of exploitation through globalisation, but they don't always make the
economic choices and values clear to children (or teachers). It may help you teach
with more clarity if you can help children understand some of the introductory ideas
above.

Using drama to develop debate and understanding of controversial issues

Saira's story above and examples in Chapter 3 and in later chapters employ drama
techniques. Drama is a powerful vehicle for children to develop critical thinking and
articulate their engagement with issues. It is very valuable for addressing controversy

indirectly, allowing children to consider perspectives 'at one remove'. It is also fun. Some children who find more conventional textbook work boring or difficult can excel. Through taking different roles, children can consider and evaluate different dilemmas, possibilities, ideas and values imaginatively and without personal threat. However, good drama work requires research and preparation through exploration of meanings and emotional responses and planned objectives which you, the teacher, can evaluate. If you are using drama for CE, you need to set up explicit CE objectives which you can evaluate in their own right. In this case, Saira's CE objectives included children researching issues, and understanding and being able to present a variety of viewpoints convincingly.

'Conscience alley' – another drama opportunity to explore controversy

Classroom story

Sam and Year 3: children at work in Victorian Britain

Sam's class began their new project on children's work in Victorian Britain with a discussion about the kind of work they did themselves, and whether they were paid for it. Most of the children did jobs round the house and got some pocket money, and some of their older siblings helped their parents in shops or at the market. Some siblings in secondary school had proper paid jobs, but Sam soon established that they were all legally old enough to work in the British system. She asked them to think about why we now have laws to stop young children working. She intended to use material from UNICEF[11] about child workers, relating to the Convention on the Rights of the Child, to back this up. The class were quick to say that young kids should be able to play and go to school and not be working for long hours, but that their parents should support them. Then Sam was confounded by Zeinab, who put up her hand and said 'My sister Hala works for money. She works all day making shoes in a factory in Morocco. She doesn't go to school any more. She's twelve.' The class went silent. Everyone stared at Zeinab. Sam realised she had to do something about this, and like Saira, decided she would go about things in a round-about way.

The class moved on to talking about children at work in Victorian Britain, and learned about children going down mines, becoming chimney sweeps or domestic workers, or working in textile factories. As well as learning about the harsh conditions, the long hours and the cruelty that many suffered, they learned that there were few opportunities for working-class children to go to school, and that their earnings were an essential part of the family economy. Then, through asking them to take a slip out of a box with 'no' or 'yes' on it, she divided the class into two lines with a narrow space between them. The 'yes' side represented arguments 'to go to work', the 'no' side, 'don't go'. One child walked very slowly down 'conscience alley'. As he or she passed between the lines, each child had to express a point either for or against going to work in a factory, depending on which side they had been allocated. Sam was impressed. Even those children who had looked most shocked about Zeinab's sister understood about the economic imperatives driving a Victorian child to work. She decided to leave this for the time being, and to find an opportunity to discuss global issues concerning exploitation of child workers on another occasion.

Reflective activity

What do you think of Sam's solution to this controversial issue that arose unexpectedly in her class? She effectively deflected the issue away from Zeinab but could she be confident that the children would transfer their thinking from one context, which was historical, to the contemporary one? Secondly, even if they did understand that Hala might be obliged to work for economic reasons, they were left without any sense of what they could do about this.

Figure 4.1 Ridouan prepares to walk down 'conscience alley'

What could Sam do next?

Sam had already decided to use UNICEF material about child labour in her classroom. She might also have followed some of the ideas in Chapter 7 of this book explaining how a student called Patrick, also teaching the Victorian history unit, developed children's understanding of constitutional methods leading to change.

Other drama techniques

Along with a number of other drama strategies, conscience alley is described in the Primary National Strategy: 'Speaking, Listening, Learning; Drama – making it work in the classroom'.[12] All provide excellent vehicles for CE work, as our example of using 'meetings' and 'freeze-frame' has already indicated. Role-plays and simulations can all be part of developing empathy and understanding of other points of view. It's a good idea to start with moments in history or from stories which don't personally engage children's emotions. We've had some examples in previous chapters (for example, the Wolf and the Three Little Pigs). Francesca, a Year 4 teacher, had her class consider alternative endings to *Romeo and Juliet*, in which the Montagues and the Capulets sorted out their problems before Romeo and Juliet died. Pippa, a Year 5 class teacher, had her class role-playing the Pied Piper of Hamelin. The Hamelin Council met to represent the parents and the City Elders, and decide what to do when the Piper lured all their children away. This distancing technique is what Saira and Sam both used.

Hot-seating

This is a favourite activity in both literacy and history, in which either the teacher or a child takes the hot seat, presents her story, and answers questions from the class which can be prepared in advance. Whoever takes the hot seat needs to do their research in advance. It is an excellent way to personalise a subject, contextualise information and deepen children's understanding of quite difficult issues, which can be dry and abstract coming from a textbook. When hot-seating is done well, it has all the emotional power of good theatre or living history, with the added advantages of interaction. (See Chapters 7 and 8 for more examples.)

Forum theatre

Children act as 'directors' as a group acts out a scene, suggesting changes, interpretations, questioning the characters about what is happening or what they are feeling. They can also 'advise' a character in a dilemma what s/he should do, especially if the drama is being improvised, rather than a previously set story.

Flash backs and flash forwards

Children have to consider what has just happened and what will happen next, given a specific scene. They create all three moments in mime or freeze-frame and then animate them when they are 'brought to life'. This encourages reflective discussion, and can help children think about consequences and causes for what they or others say or do. For example, a child stands by the school gates looking nervously to left and right. What does s/he 'see' in the past (a gang of bullies waiting round the corner? a fierce dog?) What does s/he 'see' in the future (facing the bullies? getting a group of friends to accompany him home? going back into the school building and trying to explain to an adult?).

Paired improvisation

Given a subject and deciding themselves on their roles, children improvise a conversation in role which they then perform to the rest of the class. Examples will come from your own situation and issues you want to deal with, where there are different points of view. Some suggestions are 'child who doesn't want to go to school, talking to her mother'; 'elderly person talking to a child about the 'horrible music' which assaults his ears through other passengers' portable CD players'; 'conversation between two people who respectively love and loathe the countryside'; 'two children who disagree about beggars on the street'. Such work is not just about exploring different perspectives, but also to give children practice in expressing and articulating opinions. You would want to do preliminary work to move them on from 'I did/you didn't' arguments, if you find this happening.

Thought tracking

One child takes a role and another is her/his 'private thoughts'. The first child says and acts out something, e.g. 'overhearing someone cussing someone else's mum'.[13] The other speaks what she is actually thinking, as opposed to saying. A version of this is 'icebergs'. The tip of the iceberg is what you see and hear. Several other children play the submerged part and tell us what is really going on. These drama strategies can help children explore perspectives and undercurrents and be more open to feelings and alternative interpretations of events.

In Chapter 3 Joe used 'dear Aunty Aggie' work to give his class a forum to articulate some of the problems happening in their lives. These could be the subject matter for the drama work above, particularly if you have some idea who is the victim rather than the perpetrator of some injustice, and organise the groups so that children are actually having to play a different role.

Using Theatre in Education (TiE) to raise and develop awareness about controversial issues

Saira's classroom story implied racism lurking beneath some aggressive behaviour. At the time, Saira decided to take on the immediate issue first, namely intolerance about vegetarianism. Sometimes, especially if you lack confidence in your ability to manage issues like racism, you can deal with difficult and sensitive issues by inviting in professional outsiders who have the experience to handle difficulties that may arise. They will support you and the children in a structured context which both allows feelings to be expressed, but contains them. The examples below briefly outline the sorts of possibilities which may be available.

Challenging and combating racism through Theatre in Education

Most local authorities have a list of TiE groups, and your school may well have contacts which you can follow up. Mostly the group comes into the school itself, and works with the children, though sometimes you can take your pupils to an interactive performance. The best work is done where the group has identified a particular issue, and has developed cross-curricular strategies as well as specific drama techniques which you can follow up. An example is work of the Bournemouth TiE group, who during 2003 took a play called 'My Name is Savitri' by Tony Horitz into 24 Year 4 classrooms and reached over 1,500 children. The play and the surrounding work were designed to address the requirements of the Macpherson Report about the responsibility of schools to tackle racism.[14] As we pointed out in Chapter 2, the most worrying incidence of racism can be in largely white areas, rather than in parts of Britain with large communities from minority ethnic groups. In the play, 'Savitri', a child of mixed heritage, was being called racist names and bullied by Camelia. Through the drama, which uses flash backs and hot-seating, children hear an Indian traditional story about a princess also called Savitri, another story about slavery, and consider Savitri's feelings about being racially abused. As well as identifying with Savitri, the children hot-seat Camelia, trying to get her to explain herself.

Improving knowledge and understanding of diversity and introducing global citizenship

Another example of Bournemouth TiE's work on diversity is 'Surya's Story'.[15] Surya is a child from a village in Rajasthan who is employed hand-stitching footballs to sell in the West. She decides to join the 'Children's March', a peaceful walk like those under-taken by Gandhi many years before. The march was organised by Christian Aid to publicise the situation of exploited children. A resource book provides copious background information and suggestions for work in literacy, geography, RE, history, art and citizenship. All the suggestions have relevance to CE concepts. Directly or indir-ectly, they develop understanding about people from other societies, and with different religious traditions and customs, and challenge Eurocentric notions about rights and responsibilities. Material in the Teachers' Resource Book from Traidcraft about child labour in making footballs[16] and from Save the Children about child soldiers[17] is of direct relevance in developing a sense of rights and responsibilities, and possibilities for useful intervention. Information is given, but children are moved on from a simplistic 'boycott or send aid' approach to controversies about the relationship of the North and South. There are more examples of how to make links with global citizenship through material from NGOs in Chapter 6, on geography and global citizenship, by Julia Tanner.

Formal debates and 'trials'

We have already thought about the importance of having controlled, reasoned discussion about controversial issues and the need to give the children a structure. Not only does this help you and them manage the discussion, but it also allows you to intervene if children start to become personal or infringe the ground rules. In Chapter 3, you read about Reza's class who debated the Narmada Dam project. Saira and Sam could also have held debates about the issues that they explored through drama.

There are lots of opportunities for trials from fiction. Instead of the drama about the Three Little Pigs and the Wolf in Chapter 3, Connor's class might have put the Wolf on trial, or the Hunter who killed the Wolf in the original version of Red Riding Hood. Jackie, a Year 2 teacher, got her class to hold a trial of Goldilocks, accused of 'breaking and entering and destroying property'. As you will see in the example below, a real historical trial can be the vehicle, with children learning skills to deal with controversy, and also about real issues relevant to political literacy. In Chapter 7, you will find out how some students planned to use a project with KS1 about the suffrage campaigners, the Pankhursts, to develop CE concepts. Here now is an example with KS2 children, also using the theme of women's suffrage for a debate and a trial.

Classroom story

Caroline and Year 5: parliament meets in Crossgate School[18]

For Women's History Month, Caroline's Year 5 class had been learning about the Women's Suffrage Movement in the first decade of the twentieth century. As part of the school's celebrations, they were to do an assembly about the Pankhursts and women's struggle for the vote. Caroline got hold of a pack which gave quite a lot of information about the campaign, and also found a resource with some of the Pankhursts' and others' speeches and writing[19]. Her class wanted to do two short cameos for the assembly. In one they would recreate the famous trial of Emmeline, Christabel and their supporters in 1912, using the speeches they had actually given. The children were sentenced for conspiracy to incite violence and imprisoned in Holloway Gaol. The children would also recreate a session in Asquith's 1910 Parliament, when a draft women's suffrage bill was debated – and failed, though a significant number of MPs were in favour. Imprisonment, hunger strikes and force-feeding of suffragettes had started, as had Emmeline and Christabel Pankhurst's militant campaign of arson, window-smashing and fire-bombing. This gave the children plenty to incorporate in their speeches, both for and against the bill. Caroline decided that each child's position in the debate would be decided randomly. Each took a slip out of a box which said if they were pro-suffrage, against, unsure, or a suffragette unable to participate, but watching and commenting from the galleries. Caroline prepared resources which represented the range of opinions, and gave them time to develop their arguments in groups. Caroline herself took the part of the Speaker of the House. After everyone had considered their role and what they would say, they rehearsed the debate – conducted with all the drama and passion that Parliament is famous for! When they voted they were not allowed to falsify history and let the bill through. The assembly was memorable. The final touch was to tell the audience how the vote had eventually come to women, in 1918 and 1928. At the end, 'Emmeline', 'Christabel', 'Sylvia' and other key figures in the drama stepped forward in role, urging the children to make sure to exercise their right to vote.

Commentary

The work brought home to the children something they had taken for granted – the worth of the vote. The class had no idea that women had been unable to vote at one time. They also didn't know that in some countries women had been, till recently, or were still deprived of the vote (Kuwait, Bahrain: women enfranchised 2001; Switzerland 1971; South Africa: black men and women enfranchised 1994); or that voting was manipulated by the government (for example, Burma, Zimbabwe). The parliamentary debate increased their knowledge about the vote and about the workings of the House of Commons. Through an issue which was genuinely controversial at the time, they developed the necessary skills of advocacy and participation.

Strategies for debates

- **You can start with class or group brainstorms about the aspects of an issue. From this, children can refine their particular position.**

- Teach them that in a good debate you need to consider what your opponents might say, and have an argument ready to refute them.

- Remind them that people are persuaded to change their mind by the excellence of the evidence and the argument.

- Encourage pupils to argue from a viewpoint opposed to their own, by taking names out of a hat. This needn't preclude whole-class work on the pros and cons of a position, shared by everyone, so that they gain insights into the variety of arguments and perspectives.

- Remember to debrief, so that the children think about what persuaded them or made them change their mind, or what failed to. This can be as necessary and useful in the longer run than the debate itself, in helping them understand about strong, evidence-based argument, and how manipulative techniques or false analogies work.

- As part of the debriefing, ask children about thoughts and feelings before, during and after the debate on a controversial issue. You might want to record this, since being open about such things is more productive than pretending there is nothing emotionally laden.

- Follow this up with some discussion about how we can recognise and deal with negative emotions in other people and ourselves, such as anger or sadness. Ideas from emotional literacy (see resources at the back) will help here.

Summary

We have explored a variety of ways in which you could address controversial issues in your classroom.

- We acknowledged some of the controversies and conflicts that can arise.

- We acknowledged the importance of whole-school policies on bullying and equality.

- We thought about the teacher's role and looked at some specific strategies for managing discussion.

- We considered a variety of games through which children could learn to explore different perspectives, articulate their own thoughts, and take advantage of a 'games' context to change their minds.

- We followed through with some examples of teaching children to consider controversies and different points of view through drama and role-play strategies.

- We learned about two examples where external agencies are the catalyst for work with children about controversial issues.

- We looked at the potential of debates and the simulation of 'parliaments', councils and trials to explore different positions in a controlled environment, where the rules and structures for managing difference are quite explicit.

You have now come to the end of Part I of this book which has set out concepts, issues and approaches. In Part 2, we will look first at 'stand-alone' and cross-curricular work, and then at approaches to CE through geography, history and religious education.

Notes

1 See Claire, H., 2001, *Not Aliens*, Trentham.

2 See Claire, H. 2002, 'Why didn't you fight Ruby?' Education 3–13, June.

3 See Hicks, D. and Holden, C., 1995, *Visions of the Future: Why we need to Teach for Tomorrow*, Trentham. This is currently (2004) being updated to compare the original research findings with contemporary data.

4 Cathie Holden's powerful phrase for an unrealistic curriculum, divorced from the real world.

5 See **www.nwrel.org/scpd/sirs/10/c019.html** 'Attributes of a prepared citizen. What the researchers say', especially Harwood 1992, and Harwood and Hahn 1990.

6 Crick Report, 1998, p.59.

7 **www.flinders.edu/au/teach/teach/inclusive/controversial.htm**

8 Clough and Holden, 2001, pp.66–7.

9 Save the Children: 'Partners in Rights' has a variation of this game, with more challenging statements, such as 'Teachers should be obeyed at all times', 'Everyone should be able to say or write what they really think', 'Pupils should not have to go to lessons they don't enjoy', 'Pupils should have a say in what they learn'. With my own students, I have had a fascinating debate emanating from the statement which they proposed: 'Unmarried couples should have the same rights as married couples'.

10 Anne Fine, 2000, 'The chicken gave it to me', The Book People, Mammoth.

11 UNICEF: 'India – Children's Needs, Children's Rights', based on Article 28, rights to education and Article 32, protection from economic exploitation. With thanks to Charlotte Hunt from the UNICEF Education Department.

12 Primary National Strategy, 2003, DfES and QCA, Speaking, Listening, Learning: working with children in Key Stages I and 2; Drama – making it work in the classroom.

13 Research with Primary children has shown that 'cussing someone's mum' is one of the most hurtful ways to verbally abuse another child. See Claire, H., 2001, *Not Aliens*, pp.36–8.

14 Bournemouth TiE works across southern England. **tie@bournemouth.gov.uk**. They have now produced a short video of the play which is available from Tony Horitz at the above email address.

15 Surya's story comes from a larger project called 'Child of the World' by Sharon Muiruri. See **www.swgfl.org.uk/child**; for Bournemouth TiE use the email above. The play 'Child of the World' and Teachers' Resource Pack will be available later this year from Bournemouth Borough Council, Inclusion and Achievement (Publications), Dorset House, 20–22 Christchurch Road, Bournemouth, BHI 3NL.

16 **www.traidcraft.co.uk**

17 **www.savethechildren.org.uk**

18 With thanks to Theo Boyce, PGCE student at London Metropolitan University in 2004.

19 *The Pankhursts: Significant Figures*, 2004, Pictorial Charts Educational Trust.

PART 2

5 STAND-ALONE AND CROSS-CURRICULAR WORK IN CITIZENSHIP

What will you learn about in this chapter?

- *how 'challenging behaviour' led to children becoming involved in setting up a schools council and the cross-curricular work entailed*
- *whole-school issues and equal-opportunities practice which make democratic pupil involvement possible*
- *how underlying racism towards refugees and human rights education were tackled by a student through a cross-curricular CE project*

Introduction

Part I introduced you to the main principles of CE. You started to consider some practical ways to implement concepts and teach skills. Through two classroom stories, this chapter will develop your understanding about designing classroom work. You will see how an NQT and a student teacher seized the opportunity offered by children's own concerns, or worrying attitudes, to address citizenship issues. In the first story, with support from adults, children took responsibility for trying to intervene in an unsatisfactory situation and effect changes. The second classroom story shows how citizenship work can grow from a teacher's sensitive response to a situation he encountered in the school. The case studies are intended as examples of what is possible in a school which is responsive to children, and where committed and enthusiastic teachers are ready to support and promote the ideas of active citizenship.

We will explore the following ideas and processes which we introduced in Part I. The italicised items relate directly to the way the Crick Report set out citizenship concepts:

From 'Paula's story'

- *Political literacy:* working through school councils, class councils and school parliaments.
- The importance of whole-school ethos.
- The importance of effective equal-opportunities/anti-bullying and parental-liaison policies.

From 'Sohal's story'

- *Community action and global citizenship:* initiating work on an issue which goes wider than the school itself.

- Tackling a controversial issue in the wider community through school action.
- *Social and moral responsibility.*
- Working equal opportunities, anti-bullying policies and good parental liaison in a school.

Classroom story

Year 6 and the disgusting loos[1]

Paula was at the beginning of her NQT year. A mature student, she had worked in a variety of jobs and brought up two teenage children on her own, before she finally entered university to train as a primary teacher. All her school experience blocks had been successful, so she was dismayed to find herself in a very challenging Year 6 class who simply didn't respond to her strategies for establishing discipline. Paula was committed to running a democratic classroom, to respecting children and giving them a voice, but many of the children were openly dismissive of her efforts to reason and seemed to be pushing boundaries and forcing confrontations. Early in the autumn term, straight after lunch, things came to a head. One after another children asked to go to the loo, even though the school rule was that they must go at playtime or lunchtime. When she tried to enforce the school rules, children said they were 'busting'. She gave way, but her NQT mentor told her in no uncertain terms that she must learn how to discipline the class, and show them who was boss. I had been Paula's tutor at university, and she had remained in touch. Now I received a rather desperate email asking for help. Paula felt that she was being asked to compromise her deeply felt convictions about how to treat children and that bullying them into submission was not the way she wanted to behave.

I suggested that Paula was likely to be faced with the same problem the following day if she didn't get to the bottom of things. So despite her failure so far to reason with the children about the necessity for school rules, I suggested asking why they didn't go to the loo in the lunch break ... The next morning Paula's plans for literacy hour went on hold while she conducted a general discussion. It was difficult to keep to the ground rules of not interrupting each other but she kept going. With unconcealed anger and passion, the children told her that the outside loos were totally disgusting. They were filthy, there was no loo paper (they were supposed to bring their own), there was pee on the floors, the doors didn't lock, so you had to try to keep them closed with one foot, the flushes didn't work, the walls were so low that Year 6 children could easily peer over. The dinner ladies would not allow them into the school during dinner hour, so they 'held on'. By the time they actually came in, they were desperate to get to the inside loos which were kept in a reasonable state.

Paula was shocked about this unjust situation. Literacy hour resumed: but with a new agenda. First Paula scribed on the white board what the complaints were. Then briefly, she discussed with the children what they would like to be done. She sent the children back to their tables and asked them to draft letters to the Head, explaining the problem and offering their solutions. Meanwhile, until things could be sorted out, she said she would allow people to go to the loo in class time, provided they didn't take advantage.

That evening she read through the letters they'd drafted to the Head. Many of the ideas for change were sensible, but the children had a lot to learn about putting their case in a reasonable, responsible and persuasive manner. They needed help with the appropriate language to complain assertively, but without being rude or vulgar. They lacked informed ideas of what was or wasn't realistic. The discussion had only confirmed what she knew about their inability to listen to each other politely, and wait their turn in debate. Her new plans involved working on establishing ground rules for discussions. She got the children to role-play in pairs, asking assertively but politely for something. They also considered how they felt when things were demanded rudely, rather than requested in a reasonable fashion. She talked about the necessity to back up requests with reasons and evidence. Eventually, they collected a variety of statements in polite, persuasive language – 'we understand that there might be problems, but we would appreciate if...', 'we think it would help this problem if...' – which she scribed on to the white board.

In a couple of days the redrafted letters were ready to give to the Head. Paula emailed me reporting on progress, and mentioned how surprised and pleased she was that some of the behaviour problems (though not all!) seemed to be diminishing. There was a new buzz in the class, and she had stopped feeling such a failure herself. She realised that an important principle, both of democracy and behaviour management – to be fair – was becoming explicit in her classroom.

Soon after, the Head appeared unannounced in the Year 6 classroom. The class fell silent, expecting a ticking off. Paula was anxious. She didn't need to be. The Head beamed. 'I have come to congratulate you, Year 6,' he said. 'I have received your letters. They are well written, the complaints are justified and many of your suggestions are spot on. It will take a bit of time to get things sorted, but I give you my undertaking that I will find a way to deal with the issues you raise. Well done Year 6, you have shown yourselves to be responsible about sorting out a genuine problem.'

Later, the Head asked Paula to come and see him. 'I am impressed with how you managed that,' he said. 'I have been thinking for some time of setting up a school council. It's been on the back burner. But that business with the toilets could well have been dealt with that way.' Casually Paula dropped into the conversation that Jeanette (the other Year 6 teacher) was also interested in a school council and that perhaps they could work together on this. The Head was delighted that someone was enthusiastic and prepared to take an initiative.

Now, working collaboratively, she and Jeanette drafted a plan of action, using Paula's university notes, and material which they downloaded from the school council website. They explained the developments to their classes, what a school council did and that they would be the ones to launch the new initiative.

Paula and Jeanette planned that the children themselves would research how school councils worked, and then take the message round the school, giving them a sense of ownership and getting them started in their new roles of responsibility. This included considering advantages and difficulties which they worked on in class time. Paula, Jeanette and the Head formed a 'Panel' which would try to answer Year 6 children's questions. In art they would design posters to go up round the school advertising the new idea. Then they introduced the school council idea to their colleagues. By half term, the Year 6 classes had made considerable progress. The posters were up. They'd nominated a small committee from both classes to visit all the classes in pairs, including KS1, to explain about the school council and take questions. Finally, the 'committee' from Year 6 went to a Governors' meeting and presented their proposal for a school council.

Memorably for Paula, the behaviour difficulties she'd initially experienced seemed to have just faded away. Possibly the children had been testing her and they had come to accept her, but Paula felt the class had grown in maturity through being given responsibility, having their ideas taken seriously and their voices heard.

I got an email from Paula:

'... I have finally understood what Citizenship Education can mean in practice when children learn to make systems work for themselves. What I hadn't realised is that Citizenship in action could make such a difference to the ethos and enthusiasm of the children. It was only when they got really involved in this way with something they cared about that the potential they had in all sorts of different areas really started to show.'

Postscript ... one year on

I got another email from Paula the other day. In her new Year 6 class she has established a class council with representatives and secretary, and *ad hoc* meetings when necessary.

> The children set their own agenda, limiting themselves to six items maximum, which experience has shown is realistic. The Chair ensures that no one rambles, summarises items and clarifies what we are voting on before moving on ... My class will be going into other classes after Easter to explain the practicalities, processes and aims of class meetings.

Activity 1

In the grid below, try to match the children's activities to the concepts, skills, knowledge and understanding from the National Curriculum Citizenship Guidelines in your National Curriculum Handbook. Then see if you can categorise these under the three Crick strands (Political literacy and democratic action; Community action; Social and moral responsibility) using three different-coloured felt tips. To help you, I have filled in the first two. You can also 'fast forward' to Activity 6, page 101, where the grid has been completed for the second case study. This activity would be good to do in groups.

Children's activities	Concepts and skills	Knowledge and understanding
Putting their point of view with evidence.	Talk and write about opinions, explain views.	Healthy lifestyle.
Discussing how to write a persuasive letter about their concerns.	Explain views, recognise their worth as individuals, try to resolve difficulties.	Recognise range of jobs, responsibilities and duties in school
Developing and putting questions to the 'Panel'.		
Making posters about the workings of a school council.		
ICT and other research about how school councils work.		
Going round other classes to explain the school council.		
Putting a case to the Governors.		

Commentary

Decision-making and democratic action is not limited to schools councils, class councils or to Year 6. Elsewhere in this book you will find examples which develop other possibilities, across the age range. The QCA Standards site has helpful and relevant advice on how to involve children in decision-making, for example, 'Citizenship at Key Stages 1 and 2' (Year 1–6), **Unit 01:** *Taking part – developing skills of communication and participation;* **Unit 06:** *Developing our school grounds* **Section 4:** *Making changes* (**www.qca.org.uk/citizenship**). Note too, that the DfES/QCA are encouraging teachers to look for cross-curricular links to develop citizenship (**www.standards.dfes.gov.uk/schemes.3/combined**).

The case study shows you how an NQT used ideas from Citizenship Education to respond to a situation which initially seemed to be about behaviour management and even pupil insubordination. Paula's initial action about the disgusting loos involved her in setting up a school council in her school. In secondary schools, where Citizenship is a compulsory subject, there is normally a designated coordinator, but this can fall by the wayside in primary schools. On the other hand, if someone shows willing and is interested, they can find themselves as the Citizenship Coordinator. Whatever your subject specialism, you could make your mark! Paula was a maths specialist but that didn't stop her from taking an initiative.

Paula took responsibility for developing citizenship concepts and skills by:

- **being responsive to the pupils' concerns and being prepared to listen;**
- **harnessing the children's existing concerns and giving them a structured way to deal with them;**
- **taking things further than discussion through other areas of the curriculum, such as literacy time and art;**
- **going wider than her own class through involving a senior member of staff and other colleagues.**

School issues – some things to think about from this case study

- **Finding colleagues to work with – avoiding isolation when initiating change.**
- **The school ethos.**
- **Equal opportunities in democratic practice.**
- **Setting up a school council – 'political literacy' in action.**

It is significant that Paula found someone else on the staff who was also interested. Jeanette and Paula collaborated on the nitty-gritty, and gave each other psychological support in the initial stages. Not all the staff were convinced. There were doubters and cynics who tried to pour cold water on their enthusiasm, with put-downs like 'We've been there and it doesn't work', or 'Maybe it works in the green and leafy suburbs, but not with these kids'. Working together, they could identify staff who were interested, and build a little team. The support of a member of the senior management team made all the difference to their efforts (in this case the Head, and in due course the Deputy was convinced and came on board). Without this, they might have been able to set up some democratic processes in their own classrooms, but this would never have gone any further.

The ethos and culture of the school and how they relate to developing Citizenship Education

Here is an extract from one of the emails that Paula sent me when she was first trying to implement positive management strategies with her class.

> What makes life more difficult here is a divide about teaching approaches. The business of 'reasoning' alarms some teachers. They feel sort of threatened by reasoning pupils, and are perhaps apprehensive that it will open a Pandora's box of grief. There is a modicum of truth ... where does reasoning end ... but is it duping children to think they can exercise rights in what are essentially state institutions? Honesty is paramount. I believe it isn't duping, and it is building a better future. I've decided that when my mentor told me that I was 'too idealistic' he actually meant he wasn't idealistic enough!

Let's unpick some of the important considerations about power, democracy, discipline, children's rights and responsibilities in this thought-provoking reflection.

1. WORKING WITH THE TIDE AND AGAINST THE TIDE

It's a basic precept of managing change that powerless people can't initiate or effect change on their own. You can't suddenly implement a democratic, rational ethos, even in the context of your own classroom, if you are trying to go against the tide of the mainstream. That is why I emphasised finding collaborative, supportive colleagues.

Paula was up against a rather punitive attitude among some staff about discipline when she started her new job. In retrospect, she realised that her own difficulties with her new class had to be understood in relation to the children's experience and expectations about discipline. A visitor to the school would probably have noticed the very things that an earlier OFSTED inspection report had criticised – namely that children were not helpful to visitors, were often rough and rude with each other, dinner helpers and classroom assistants, and that those teachers who kept good discipline mostly did so through punishment and shouting.

Even if this is your experience too, do not despair about setting a new agenda with your own class, which is more responsive to children, gives them a voice, and values their opinions. Remember that they will have to unlearn old expectations and attitudes, and learn new ones, and this takes time. Make this new challenge explicit to the children, and give them positive feedback as they do start learning new ways of behaving and taking responsibility.

Paula had a gut response about the children breaking the 'loo rule', and it was only by asking them what was going on that she discovered that there were genuine grievances and opportunities to remedy the problem which could involve the children themselves. It took much longer to change things in the school, and with other teachers, but in her own class there were almost immediate signs of improvement.

2. ANXIETY ABOUT GIVING CHILDREN POWER

The subtext of Paula's email is that the teachers felt beleaguered by children whom at some level they feared, and whom they could only control through exercising quite repressive power. Some teachers were aware that once they started allowing children to reason with them, they would have to give ground, and some of their own power and control would be diminished. It is true that there is considerable tension between the limits of democracy and who is in control in schools. They are large institutions, and not only are adults older and more experienced, but they are also responsible and accountable in ways that the children are not. This puts a lot of pressure not to 'open floodgates', often exemplified by phrases like 'give them a finger and they'll take an arm'.

3. 'OWNERSHIP' OF EQUAL OPPORTUNITIES AND OTHER SCHOOL POLICIES

Equal opportunities, parent liaison and anti-bullying policies existed but, written some years before, they seemed dry, irrelevant documents, for which almost no one felt any ownership. They had to be dusted off and re-energised, identifying how they applied to specific situations, adults and children. Paula was able to contribute here too, because she had always taken a special interest in equal opportunities, and had written an assignment in her third year about this. In one staff meeting, she talked about equal opportunities with respect to gender, while her colleague (and increasingly her friend) Jeanette, who had a special interest in children of minority ethnic origin and bilingual children, gave a short presentation about some of the ways to support minority children, and involve their parents in the life of the school.

A democratic society, including the microcosm of a classroom or school, depends on thought-through, shared policies about equal opportunities, which are seen to be working. Fairness is at the heart of democracy, and also at the heart of equal opportunities. Not all schools make the links between equal opportunities and a democratic 'fair' school environment.

4. SCHOOL COUNCILS – DEMOCRACY IN ACTION

In Part I, Chapter 3, we discussed the implementation of political literacy through school councils, parliaments or class councils, at some length.

Reflective activity 2

Consider your own views about sharing some power with children, what the limits should be and why you do or don't feel comfortable with the idea. If you are at university, this could be small group discussion, shared later with the whole class. In a staffroom considering the initiation of a school council, this could form the basis for preliminary discussion. (See also Activity 3 in Chapter 6.)

Commentary

For school councils to be more than token gestures towards democracy, there has to be congruence between their overt aims, which are to give children a voice, to provide them with the means to discuss their own agenda, and to make decisions which affect themselves and the general ethos of the school. You can't run an effective school council which depends on respecting children and giving them some rights, in a context in which they are bullied by staff or each other, and endlessly subject to discipline and control which may seem to be operating merely for its own sake. Children, as we all know, are good at spotting such contradictions, and they are likely to recognise when staff are paying no more than lip service to the underpinning ideas of a school council.

5. WHAT ARE THE LIMITS – ARE WE 'DUPING' CHILDREN BY PRETENDING TO OFFER THEM A SAY WHEN WE CAN'T DELIVER ON THEIR EXPECTATIONS?

Paula put her finger on a critical concern about the ethos of the school, and honest approaches to democratic principles. Children will certainly be 'duped' if they are led to believe that their school will be run as a true democracy, where everyone has an equal say and an equal vote, and unless rights are being infringed, the majority will overrule minorities.

They will need to understand something about hierarchies and constraints on the school and its staff. For a start, not even the Head is autonomous. S/he is answerable to Governors, the LEA, the government, parents. Secondly, many important decisions involve money, and the people in control of the money normally have very stringent criteria before they will fork out. In Chapter 4 we looked at some of the economic principles which guide political decisions. Decision-making in school/class councils could be an opportunity for children to consider such constraints.

Along the same lines, some suggestions and requests that children might propose will be unrealistic, or go against rules and regulations which take precedence, e.g. to close the school earlier every day, or abandon KS1 and KS2 SATs.

This implies

a. that one needs to be honest and open with children about the limits on their power to implement changes, even if strongly supported by many of them;

b. that it is worth exploring some of their issues in depth, because even if their original request is unrealistic, there may still be something that can and needs to be addressed. (For example, though you can't abandon the SATs, you may be able to lessen the anxiety and stress round them.)

6. WHOLE-SCHOOL APPROACHES TO CHANGE – THE IMPORTANCE OF VALUES

Neither an individual teacher, nor the Senior Management Team, can change things on their own. Each depends on the staff understanding how the general ethos of a school seeps into and affects the workings of every interaction, between staff, between children and staff, and finally between children, whether negatively or positively.

In Part 1 we discussed how *values* threaded through Citizenship Education (without assuming that there was one monolithic value system which could be imposed on all pupils or schools). We noted that both the Statements in the National Curriculum itself and the new Professional Values statements in the Standards for QTS emphasised the teacher's and the pupils' values, the importance of an 'open school' with an open-door policy to parents and carers, and of considering pupils' self-esteem along with issues of achievement. One of the children quoted in a case study from the Scottish Schools Ethos Network research said tellingly, 'Teachers at Allan's don't humiliate you or embarrass you. If there is something wrong they talk to you privately.'

The Head of Paula's school saw the school council initiative as something which could be part and parcel of a wider change in attitudes and behaviour – itself something that was on the agenda in the aftermath of the OFSTED criticisms. He had a vision of 'a listening, caring school' which fostered emotional literacy (see Chapter 3).

Activity 3

Values for our class or school

Look back at Fig. 2.2 on page 30 of Chapter 3, and consider its message and concepts in the light of our case study, and your own school experience. As students or as practitioners already in post, can you articulate a values system that you are happy with for your school or classroom? When you have collected some initial ideas, and decided which are the most appropriate and meaningful to your setting and value system, you might try to express their 'heart' in a mission statement.

Commentary

It would be foolish to pretend that the initiatives to create 'a listening, caring school' effected a sudden, swift turnaround in attitudes and behaviour, either in staff or in pupils. Change of the kind that the Head envisaged goes very deep, and takes time. But gradually small successes start to persuade the pessimists and the fence-sitters, and confirm the views of the optimists that a school does not have to be run like a boot camp. For children to start putting the concepts of Citizenship Education into practice, the whole-school ethos has to be supportive. Piecemeal tokenism will never replace cynicism and apathy.

For further material, put 'Whole School Ethos' into Google, to find a range of reports and statements. Also, look at the Primary case studies from the Scottish Schools' Ethos Project.

Activity 4

Figure 5.1 summarises the citizenship concepts and skills that started in Paula's class and eventually permeated the whole school. It shows some of the wider issues about school ethos which are essential to success. Photocopy this, and use it as a model to develop your own concept map of opportunities to develop specific citizenship skills and concepts. Use the KS1/2 citizenship guidelines and the discussion in Part 1 to help you.

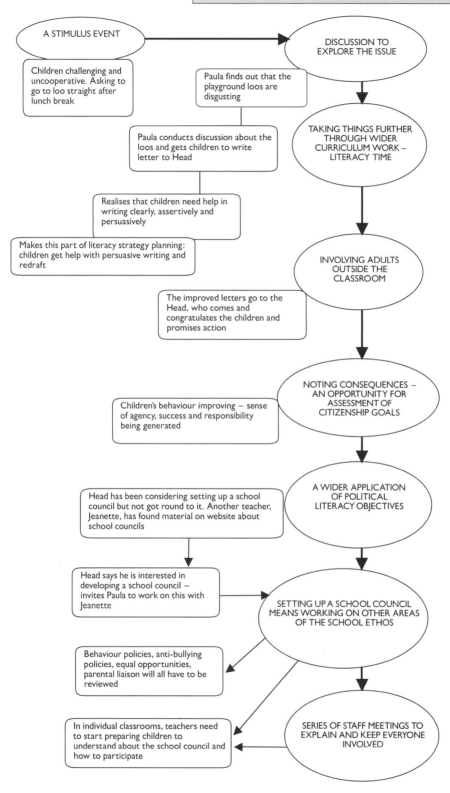

Figure 5.1 Flow chart of citizenship concepts and skills for Paula's initiative

Classroom story

Year 4 and the children from Eritrea[2]

Sohal was a PGCE primary student in his final Teaching Practice in a Year 4 class. He had been born and brought up in England, but his family came from Uganda and had been part of the large exodus of East African Asians in the early 1970s in the wake of oppression by Idi Amin. Sohal had grown up with stories about life in Uganda, and the awful events when the family were 'chucked out', lost everything and found themselves living in barracks in Aldershot, humiliated by having to accept charity and even choose coats for the bitter winter from the rails furnished by Save the Children. He and his family had encountered quite a lot of racism in their lives and he was sensitive to implicit assumptions about white superiority and explicit rejection of many minority ethnic people as truly 'belonging' in Britain. His placement school was in a largely white, working-class neighbourhood of London, and he had been rather nervous about this, as the borough had a reputation for having pockets of racism. But for some African-Caribbean dinner ladies, he found himself the only minority ethnic person on the staff.

During his pre-practice placement days he became uncomfortable about the dismissive way that some white support staff talked about a small group of African children who had recently come into the school. Several of the teaching staff were supply teachers, feeling their way in the system themselves, and as a 'mere student' Sohal didn't feel he could broach the matter with the Head or Deputy. It appeared that the African children were refugees from Eritrea. They had been granted asylum and settled by the local authority in a nearby estate but no one seemed to know much about them and they were regarded as 'a problem'. Their fathers and sometimes their mothers – veiled and in long robes covering their bodies – brought them to school, spoke quietly to each other before kissing their children goodbye, but barely interacted with other parents or the staff. None of these children was actually in Sohal's class.

During one of his practice days, Sohal did playground duty alongside his class teacher. He was concerned to notice that the small group of African children were all sticking together. The boys seemed excluded from the large football game that was going on, and the girls just stood near them on the sidelines, the younger ones holding hands. Watching when the bell rang, he saw some boys in his class deliberately pushing two of the black children out of the way, quite roughly. The victims did not complain to the teacher on duty. Over the following visits to the school, Sohal found out more. The children were refugees from the war in the Horn of Africa. He listened carefully to how children and adults spoke about the newcomers, and when he could, watched them in places like assemblies, going into the dinner hall and round the school. His impression grew of children who were being isolated and victimised, both subtly and openly.

His mentor was sympathetic to issues of racism and equal opportunities, so during planning week he asked what she thought of him raising concerns about tolerance and difference in Circle Time as part of the Citizenship Education curriculum. Circle Time had been chiefly devoted to quite safe issues of PSE and the mentor thought that Sohal should proceed gently, and not bull-doze straight into the issues of racism and hostility to refugees that possibly lay behind the behaviours he was witnessing. She also thought he should plan to use RE sessions to discuss toler-ance towards people of different faiths.

The first Circle Time session went well. Children contributed without rancour to a discussion in which they started statements with 'I feel comfortable when ...'. Sohal had planned that they would establish the positives before moving to 'I feel *un*comfortable when …'. He hoped that through this someone might introduce the idea 'I feel uncomfortable when … I see someone being treated badly'. But they didn't – the children seemed reluctant to move beyond superficial descriptions of physical comfort. His mentor suggested that he could go back to the original 'I feel comfortable when …' statement and introduce psychological and social issues himself. So he prepared a set of cards with ready-made statements which had to be completed. Here are some of them:

- **I feel comfortable when I am with my friends because …**
- **I feel comfortable when I am in the playground if …**
- **I feel comfortable in class when other children …**
- **I feel comfortable with the work I have to do as long as …**

The children were asked to discuss these in self-chosen groups of four, and to contribute another two statements themselves.

This scaffolding strategy worked, and Sohal completed Circle Time by discussing physical, psychological, social and educational 'comfort zones', scribing the conditions the children had come up with. It was important, in his view, to include the physical ones because he suspected that most of the refugee children were actually living in dire circumstances, well below the standards that other children in the class had come to expect, and that the circumstances of leaving Eritrea and first arrival in Britain would have been distinctly 'uncomfortable'. He wanted to include 'educational' comfort zones because he wanted the children to think about how their own learning depended on a safe, secure and welcoming environment in school, tolerant of difficulties and differences. His mentor also pointed out that he would be working in the spirit of QTS Standard 2.4: 'understand how pupils' learning can be affected by their physical, intellectual, linguistic, social, cultural and emotional development'. He hoped that he would be able to move from this to empathy with the children who were being marginalised. At the heart of his plan was that children should come to see that the idea of 'comfort zones' could be translated into human rights. Working from their own needs and feelings, he intended to coax from them their own versions of the Golden Rule: ' I will behave to other people, or be prepared to grant other people, the same things I want for myself.'

Now he moved into the negative areas. Next Circle Time was spent with children considering what it was like for them if the various criteria for 'feeling comfortable' were not met. As expected, children tended to translate ideas into practical examples, such as 'I would feel uncomfortable if one of my friends turned against me, like the time when Sam wouldn't let me join in the football game.' Sohal pressed on, getting children in pairs to try to articulate just what it was that made these situations uncomfortable, and eventually creating a list of synonyms, like miserable, upset, lonely, rejected, let down, embarrassed, to match 'feeling uncomfortable'.

Now that the emotionally charged connotations of the rather bland adjective 'uncomfortable' had been explored, Sohal asked the children directly how they felt about seeing other people 'made uncomfortable'. They had to work in friendship pairs and report each other's opinions. Immediately, things took an unexpected turn. Emma said: 'Rosie says she feels uncomfortable when she sees a beggar woman with a baby coming round on the tube and asking for money. And I would feel angry if I saw Rosie made uncomfortable like this.'

In response, Jamie put up his hand: 'Sir', he said, 'it's true – you get accosted all the time by these people – they're refugees and they've just come to our country to get what they can take from us, and they don't work, they just beg.' 'Yes', said Angie, 'they just have their babies with them to make us feel guilty and give. My Dad says they shouldn't be allowed in.' 'There's too many. They take our jobs and the Council puts them in expensive flats,' said Rachel. Just one small lone voice sounded out. Peter said, 'It's us who are not being fair. What we're saying is prejudiced.' Thank goodness for Peter, Sohal thought, and wrote his remark up.

Sohal now had to think fast on his feet. He decided not to challenge any of this on the spot, but to receive the different views without comment, and give himself time to work out a plan of action, and to consult his mentor. He told the class that their ideas were extremely interesting and that they would be coming back to them.

The mentor suggested that he work from human stories from the Refugee Council's pack 'Refugees: a primary school resource' to help children move from their 'us and them' position towards recognising that refugees were people very like them, whose situation they might identify with if they knew more. She recommended that as far as possible, Sohal come obliquely at the issue of the refugees in their own school, allowing the children to make connections themselves. Otherwise, things could backfire on those vulnerable children. Sohal decided that he would use some of literacy time as well as Circle Time to develop his ideas. He learned that a Year 4 class in a North London school which had a number of refugee children coming in and then moving on, had worked with a refugee support teacher to make the school more understanding and welcoming for the newcomers. This class had talked about feelings when you start a new school, the things that helped them feel better, and what other people could do to welcome newcomers.

Then, without focusing on the circumstances which had led children and their families to become refugees, the children had produced little booklets to help new children settle in, designing covers, contents pages, welcome text and so on. (See Rutter, 2003, Chapter 10.)

Sohal decided he would follow this pattern too, using literacy and D & T time, but he was anxious to go further and give his class some insight into the political background of becoming a refugee. He wondered about talking about his own family, but didn't feel confident enough. He knew Benjamin Zephaniah's novel *Refugee Boy*, which was about the conflict in the Horn, and the traumas that Alem Kelo faced both before he left Eritrea, but also as news from 'back home' reached him. It had helped his own understanding, but he thought the circumstances in the novel might be a bit too sensitive for him to read out loud to his class and they wouldn't identify with Alem, who was much older than them. Instead, he decided that Beverley Naidoo's prize-winning children's novel *The Other Side of Truth* would be the way to introduce the children to the conditions that led people to flee their countries, and the difficulties they could face. Coincidentally, the Literacy Strategy for Year 4, Term 3 recommended using fiction that raised issues of bullying and injustice, and he followed this up with the recommended activities for text-level work from the strategy (NLS, pp42–3).

In Circle Time he now felt able to move the work on from 'I feel uncomfortable when …', in which children were increasingly identifying bullying and ostracism, to looking at specific instances which were based on 'being different'. As before, so that they could concentrate on issues, and not personalise things by focusing on the actual children in the school, he started with ready-made statements written as if to an 'agony aunt'. These were deliberately framed in the first person so that children should identify directly with the problems. They had to develop a response and bring the dilemma to a satisfactory conclusion.

Here are some examples of the starter statements:

My name is Ahmed. I feel I am an outsider and not really accepted in my school because I am Muslim and most of the children here are Christian.

I am Felicia. I am sometimes embarrassed in my class because my Mum is Spanish and doesn't speak very good English. Sometimes she comes to school to pick me up, and I hear other people giggle about her accent and the mistakes she makes in English.

My name is Mustafa and me and my sister Salima have come from Bosnia to England because of the war. We still remember some of the horrible things that happened to us, and sometimes we still have nightmares. It is very noisy and crowded where we live and often we don't sleep well, so I am very tired the next day. Salima likes to stay with me in playtime because she is young and hasn't made any friends. I am trying to make friends but the boys laugh because I let my little sister hang around with me.

Sohal had decided to wait patiently and see if anyone mentioned the Eritrean refugee children and finally, of course, they did. It was Angie and Rachel, working on the Salima–Mustafa statement who said, 'This is actually just like Jemal and his sister isn't it? She always runs up and holds his hand in playtime, and the others laugh at a Year 6 boy holding hands with a little girl.' 'Yes, I hadn't thought that maybe she was doing that because she felt scared.'

Sohal let the conversation run while the class meditated on how the things they'd identified as making them feel 'uncomfortable' probably applied to Jemal and some of the other refugee children. So far, of course, the children did not know they were refugees anyway. But you could trust Peter to be one step ahead of the game and to know intuitively why 'Sir' had introduced this example.

'Sir, are Jemal and his sister refugees like Mustafa and Salima?' asked Peter. 'Mustafa and Salima were probably white if they were from Bosnia. I know about Bosnia, I've seen about that on the telly, but until you read us that book about Sade and Femi from Nigeria, I didn't actually know there were refugees from Africa. Where is Jemal from sir, and why did they leave their country?'

'Well,' said Sohal, 'we could try to find out if you like. How will you start?' 'I suppose I could go up to Jemal and ask him what his country was? I mean that wouldn't be insensitive would it?' 'I don't think so, if you do it in a friendly way, and then ask him to join your game or something like that,' said Sohal, 'but I don't think you should ask him too many direct questions. He could find them very difficult. He might be able to tell you after a while, but meanwhile, when you know where they came from, why not get into the Refugee Council website and see if they have some information about their country.'

That was only the beginning of the project. Peter and a couple of friends pursued their research on Eritrea, partly in their own time. Peter was given a copy of Zephaniah's novel to read on his own and to report on to his class. Sohal's mentor said that actually this work would meet some of the criteria for supporting very able children and developing creative approaches to the curriculum, in line with the initiatives from DfES and QCA (**www.ncaction.org.uk/creativity/index.htm**). Sohal himself moved on to some work on human rights during Circle Time – which is what he'd been planning all along – using ideas in 'Our World, Our Rights', the Save the

Children and the UNICEF websites. The mentor negotiated on his behalf with the Head and the class teacher, and gave permission to change the existing RE medium-term plan to teach about Islam, which he also felt would improve understanding and tolerance of the refugee children, who were part of a small minority of practising Muslims in the school.

The senior school staff had realised that they were not responding proactively to the refugee children, but probably needed the evidence from the hostile remarks that had been made in Circle Time to appreciate that attitudes might be worse than they'd imagined. The Head came to look at the work on human rights, and also at Peter's developing project about Eritrea, which eventually was shown in a special work assembly. She went out of her way to invite the parents of the Eritrean children. She found that there was an Eritrean Advice and Support Group nearby and invited their workers to the assembly too, who were thrilled to make contact with the school.

On the grapevine, after he left, Sohal heard that the school had taken more refugee children in the following autumn, and had contacted the refugee support worker for the local authority to do some staff INSET and set up whole-school work. He never did get to tell the class about his own family history but knew he had gained confidence which he would draw on when he had a class of his own. Reflecting on his block practice, Sohal remembered his father's favourite phrase: 'From a small acorn a mighty oak can grow.'

Activity 5

Let's try to track the concepts, skills, knowledge and understanding which have been covered during this work, using the National Curriculum Guidelines. I have kept concepts and skills together in the grid as the NC does, as the overlaps are often stronger than the distinctions. You may disagree with my categorisations, and as well as discussing them, you may feel like changing them. Doing this retrospectively is clearly odd, since your planning will always be done 'forwards'. However, it is worth thinking about this grid, even though it has been produced by 'thinking backwards', because it shows how specific work could be expressed as learning objectives with outcomes that you would hope to achieve (and evaluate). One of OFSTED's criticisms of Citizenship Education work in primary classrooms has been the unfocused approach to citizenship goals (see p 46 Chapter 3), so you must plan CE, just as you do other curriculum areas, using clear learning objectives.

Photocopy the grid below. Look back at page 30 in Chapter 3, at the summary of the Aims, Values and Purposes Statement, and try to complete the empty column of the grid. Lastly, make some notes of things you would like to follow up yourself, perhaps through discussion with others, thinking about them on your own, trying something out in your practice classroom (or your own classroom if you are already a teacher), and by reading.

Children's activity	Concepts and skills	Knowledge and understanding	Aims, values and purposes
Talking about what makes one feel comfortable or uncomfortable and what might make others feel comfortable or uncomfortable.	*Social and moral responsibility/values.* Reflecting on feelings underpinning overt behaviour. Developing self-knowledge and raising self-esteem. *Political literacy.* Discuss and debate problems, including controversial issues.	Understanding consequences of bullying and racism.	
Learning about refugees using the Refugee Council's Primary Pack, and reading aloud from *The Other Side of Truth.*	*Social and moral responsibility/values.* Extending and developing existing concepts about 'who belongs', rights and responsibilities, justice and human rights.	Learning something of the contexts and situations leading some children to become asylum seekers. *Political literacy.* Learning about rules and; laws and how they are enforced. Recognising the role of voluntary, community and pressure groups.	
Making 'welcome' booklets for newcomers.	*Political literacy/community action.* Researching and making booklets, considering audience and purpose: a case of 'active citizenship'.	Researching what newcomers might need to know about, e.g. playtimes, school meals, local community – library, swimming pool, mosque/church/temple.	
The 'Agony Aunt' work.	*Social/moral responsibility/values.* Considering peer pressure, taking responsibility for racism/bullying.	Recognising and challenging stereotypes and differences between people.	
Small-group work on Eritrea (mainly web-based). Reading and reporting on *Refugee Boy.*	*Political literacy.* Understanding the framework within which support is available. Summarising and communicating findings and opinions.	Where people can get help and support; knowledge about a specific situation. *Community action.* Becoming aware of the range of different communities	

Commentary

The grid makes clear how PSE and citizenship are often woven together in practice, in the primary setting. This case study was obviously stronger on social and moral responsibility and values education, than on political literacy and community action. It would be important for this class to experience more work in those two areas, to meet OFSTED's criteria.

This case study also shows how a sensitive teacher can pick up on and develop work with his class which is directly relevant to children's attitudes about difference and diversity.

These are some issues you might reflect on:

- **Dealing with controversial issues.**
- **Refugees and asylum seekers in our schools; human-rights education.**
- **Going beyond CircleTime:** [3] **starting with PSE, but going wider, both to cover Citizenship Education and to draw on other subjects.**

1. CONTROVERSIAL ISSUES

As we emphasised in Chapter 4 of Part I, controversy is inevitable in CE, and you will need not only excellent classroom management skills, but some quite specific ground rules to avoid your class locking horns or getting mired down in pointless argument. Look back now to page 71 in Chapter 4, which discussed the teacher's role in managing controversial issues in the classroom. Which of the roles would seem most appropriate here, faced with some of the children's prejudice and lack of knowledge – neutral chair, devil's advocate, facilitator, etc.?

2. REFUGEES AND ASYLUM SEEKERS, AND HUMAN RIGHTS

Human rights and responsibility within a wider community are fundamental concepts in Citizenship Education, as we explored in Chapter I. Chapters 6 and 7 include more examples of how to develop this particular aspect of CE. Like adults, children can be more comfortable with according human rights to people far away (the NIMBY syndrome!). Still, the issue of refugees and asylum seekers is about human rights on our doorsteps, though the water is often muddied by sensationalist reports from the less responsible press, about abuses of the system by 'bogus' refugees (see the Refugee Council's site, which deals with some myths and falsehoods). The whole question is extremely contentious: the main political parties have different stances and each uses its own to try to attract support, which means that children who are aware of their parents' attitudes may bring very strong views to school. We also know that areas where refugees are housed can produce the most virulent hostility (see Rutter, 2003, Chapter 10).

It is very important to remember that CE is not about silencing some points of view, or indoctrinating children. In a democracy, we recognise differences and try to find ways to resolve them, 'by looking at alternatives, making decisions and explaining choices' (NC Guidelines, p.139, 2f). We try to educate children towards tolerance, understanding of difference, and if necessary, to think in new ways which do not always coincide with their parents. If this worries you as an idea, consider whether you would be prepared to allow a child to say or do racist or sexist things in your class, on the grounds that they were just copying their parents.

Work on refugees and asylum seekers can be the vehicle for children to research factual background and present arguments. This is a strong part of political literacy, but also may help to shift some children's attitudes towards greater tolerance (another strand of Citizenship Education). Sohal might have developed the work towards considering resource allocation. One could ask children to decide how to spend a pot of money, if they were 'the government', giving them a range of possible recipients of funding, including education, health, transport, defence, and so on, and including support for refugees (2j – Preparing to play an active role, in the NC Guidelines).

Again, this can be controversial, and would only be sensible with a class who had learned to debate contentious issues in a rational manner.

3. BEYOND CIRCLE TIME
Sohal started with the fairly conventional procedures of PSE and Circle Time, but had the courage and the conviction to go into deeper waters. In doing so, he unleashed overt prejudice among his pupils that he could not ignore. With support and advice from his mentor, he then reconsidered his planning in a cross-curricular fashion, both to allow him to address the issues in more depth, but also to use time differently, using literacy time. Making books, reading a novel and research on the web were all part of the way the work developed.

He might have gone further, and considered the possibilities from art and music, for example:

- **Making posters to welcome newcomers or protest against perceived injustice.**
- **Expressing one's feelings about an uncomfortable or comforting situation through art.**
- **Finding out about the artwork of the country of origin of refugees they are learning about, trying to paint/model etc., in these styles.**
- **Making music to express feelings.**
- **Listening to music from the Horn of Africa (or Nigeria, where *The Other Side of Truth* originates).**

Remember that QCA/DfES is encouraging teachers to work in creative cross-curricular ways, as their website testifies (**www.ncaction.org.uk**). Citizenship Education, as both Paula and Sohal's case studies indicate, may be the launching point for a wonderfully creative curriculum project in your class or school.

Summary

In this chapter we have:

- **considered how valuable, worthwhile Citizenship Education can start with an issue in the school itself;**
- **looked at the actual implementation of the three 'Crick strands of Citizenship Education' introduced in Part I.**

How the three Crick strands were exemplified

POLITICAL LITERACY
- **Participation and active citizenship through developing a school council and campaigning around an issue.**
- **Instituting democratic frameworks to address problems in a school.**
- **Researching about an issue of current concern, and developing a knowledge base to consider the situation of asylum seekers.**
- **Learning about rules and laws in the wider national context.**
- **Learning something about the political situation in countries that some refugees are fleeing.**

SOCIAL AND MORAL RESPONSIBILITY AND VALUES

- Considering and starting to empathise with the situation of people who are different and may be bullied or victimised.
- Developing tolerance and tackling prejudice and problems in an evidence-based, rational way.

COMMUNITY ACTION

- Learning about a new community and their problems and support systems.
- Considering how the more long-standing community can give support.

In addition, we have considered the following concepts and processes which were discussed in Part 1:

- The work of school councils.
- Whole-school ethos as the context for creating a democratic school community in which Citizenship Education can flourish.
- Equal opportunities and parental liaison.
- Tackling a controversial issue.
- Taking a cross-curricular approach to Citizenship Education.

Appendix 1: Supporting refugees and asylum seekers

In 1989 the staff and children at William Patten Primary School in Hackney mounted a campaign to try to stop the deportation of one of their pupils, Zeynep Hasbudak, with her Turkish family. They were not successful, but the moving story of the campaign to try to change the mind of the Minister in the Home Office, and the photos and detail of the campaign, are recorded in a book which All London Teachers Against Racism (ALTARF) published in 1989. It is no longer in print, but it is available in some libraries and is recommended for its practical example of how a whole school became involved in trying to prevent a deportation. You will also find examples in Chapter 7 which suggest how to introduce refugee status and experience through history.

Since the case of Zeynep Hasbudak, another school has become involved in campaigning to prevent the deportation of one of their pupils, Natasha Matambele, an Angolan refugee. Like William Patten Primary School in Hackney, Natasha's friends and teachers made sure that their campaign was reported in the press, TV and radio. Finally, Natasha and her family were allowed to stay. As a result of the pupils' campaign, the school thought about other things they could do to support refugees. They started an early-morning homework club for children living in hostels or over-crowded housing, which helped many children, not just refugees. Another primary school raised money for the Refugee Council and for the Medical Foundation for the Victims of Torture, which works directly with refugee adults and children in England. This project involved secondary pupils working with the younger children, helping them design and make Christmas cards which were sold in a local shop. Go to www.refugeecouncil.org.uk/diary/ to find out about events in your area related to Refugee Week (normally in June). This could be an opportunity for schools to focus on the plight of refugee children, even if there are none in the school itself.

Notes

1 With thanks to the 'real Paula' who has chosen to remain anonymous.
2 With thanks to my colleague Suresh Jethwa, who gave me information about Ugandan refugees in the early 1970s.
3 Cathie Holden emphasises the importance in Citizenship Education of going beyond the 'cosy curriculum' in Circle Time.

What will you learn about in this chapter?

This chapter has two main sections: citizenship and geography, and the global dimension of citizenship. It focuses on:

- *some ideas for developing all three aspects of CE: political literacy, social and moral education, and community involvement*
- *the relationship between geography and citizenship, including a local environmental issue*
- *global citizenship, focusing especially on the study of distant places*
- *controversial issues of social and economic justice, such as child workers or fair trade*

Introduction

Geography, like history, is a natural ally of Citizenship Education in the primary curriculum. Both geography and CE are concerned with helping children to understand the world and their place in it. Both are concerned with vital local, national and international issues, such as environmental protection, sustainable development and social justice for all. Both help children to develop the knowledge, understanding and skills to make a personal contribution towards creating a better future for themselves, other people, and the planet. Preparation for active citizenship is at the heart of primary geography.

PART 1: GEOGRAPHY AND CITIZENSHIP EDUCATION

Linking geography and citizenship: an initial example

The study of places and contemporary environmental issues, as required by the National Curriculum, provides an excellent context for the development of CE. The emphasis on using an enquiry approach in geography provides many powerful learning opportunities for children to develop some of the skills and attributes of active and concerned citizens. The focus on places, both local and further afield, lays the foundation for understanding how places work and are interconnected with one another. The attention given to environmental matters highlights the particular contribution of geography to education for sustainable development, which itself is an important part of CE.

One of the great strengths of the primary geography curriculum is that it offers many opportunities for *authentic learning activities*. Authentic learning activities are those which have real purposes, real audiences and real outcomes. As the Crick Report (QCA, 1998) makes clear, authenticity is a crucial element in effective CE. A good example is given in the illustrative case study below.

As you read the case study activity, think about how this approach provided authentic learning opportunities in both geography and CE.

Case study

Kings Norton School becomes involved in a local traffic issue

Kings Norton Primary School in Birmingham has not only managed to fit Safe Routes to Schools into its curriculum, but its pupils are also influencing the decisions of local politicians. Transport is a huge issue for the school, which is situated on the busy Pershore Road, a main arterial route through south Birmingham, with traffic jams, heavy lorries thundering past, and frequent accidents. Children were asked to complete online surveys on how they came to school, and the information was used as part of the school's travel plan. The survey highlighted real issues for those walking to school. A main pathway was blocked with overgrown ivy, and drivers were parking on double yellow lines opposite the school, causing a hazard for children crossing the road. Kings Norton school council was invited to put its case to Birmingham City councillors. The pathway has now been cleared, and some of the children's suggestions have been incorporated into transport consultation for the area.

'I think it's brilliant,' said the senior teacher responsible for citizenship. 'They've developed confidence in talking in an adult environment and in expressing their opinions in a way that understands that people have to make priorities.' (TES Teacher 23/1/04, p.28)

Activity 1

Whether you are working by yourself or as a group, try to identify the following:

How does this case study provide for authentic learning opportunities?

How does dealing with a real-life local issue relate to the PoS for geography, and the guidelines for CE?

For geography, how does this project enable children to develop enquiry and other geographical skills, knowledge and understanding of the local area, and knowledge to enable the understanding of environment issues?

For citizenship, how can it provide opportunities for developing the key concepts of CE: rights, responsibilities, political literacy, social and moral responsibility, identity and multiple identities, self-esteem, values and active citizenship (all discussed in Chapters 1 and 2).

Refer to the programmes of study for geography in Key Stages 1 and 2, and the guidelines for PSHE/Citizenship in the **National Curriculum Handbook.**

Commentary

A group of primary PGCE students who looked at this case study structured their thinking around the following three questions in Activity 1:

- **Is this an authentic learning activity and why/why not?**
- **What opportunities does it offer for geographical learning?**
- **What opportunities does it offer for Citizenship Education?**

Here are their responses, which you may like to compare to your own.

- **This *is* an authentic learning activity, in that the real purpose was to improve an aspect of the immediate environment, making it safer for children to walk to school. There were several real audiences, including other children in the school, local councillors and the local authority planners. There were real outcomes in that the overgrown path has been cleared and the children's ideas have been used in a public consultation exercise.**
- **There were many opportunities for geographical learning. An enquiry approach was adopted through the use of a survey and the results of this were analysed and communicated to the school council, local politicians and LA officers. The place studied was the local area, and the project focused on a real-life environmental issue – children's journeys to school. In completing this work, the children used a range of geographical skills (e.g. geographical vocabulary, mapwork, decision-making).**
- **It provided powerful practical learning of important aspects of Citizenship Education. *Political literacy* was developed in two ways. First, through the school council, and second, in making representations to local politicians and planners, children were able to engage directly in the political process.**
- **The topic of travel and transport raises many *social and moral issues* connected with the impact of car use on other road users and the environment.**
- **Finally, this project involves *community involvement*, in that the outcome has been a direct impact on a local footpath, and the local Transport Plan.**

Geography and citizenship within the National Curriculum framework: exploring the links

In this section we will explore the natural links between geography and citizenship, and investigate the particular role of geography in preparing children in primary schools to become informed, concerned and active citizens.

The whole curriculum framework

One very welcome benefit of the revision of the National Curriculum (2000) is that it provided an opportunity to reconsider the structure of the primary curriculum. Following widespread consultation there is now a new emphasis on the *whole curriculum*, and the interrelationships between subjects and cross-curricular elements.

There is also an explicit statement about how the curriculum serves the wider purposes of education in society now and for the future, especially in relation to values, personal, social and health education, and citizenship (see Chapter 2: AVPS).

Careful reading of the details of the guidelines for PSHE/CE reveals that geography has much to contribute to education for informed and active citizenship. At Key Stage 1, for example, children should be taught about what improves and harms their local natural and built environments, and about some of the ways people can look after these. At Key Stage 2 they should research, discuss and debate topical issues, problems and events; recognise that resources can be allocated in different ways; and that these economic choices affect individuals, communities and the sustainability of the environment. In both key stages, children should have the opportunity to develop, express and share their opinions, take responsibility, make real choices and consider social and moral dilemmas such as environmental issues they come across in everyday life.[1]

Geography in the Foundation stage

Very young children are avid learners, naturally curious about the world around them. Indeed, young children are sometimes described as natural geographers. The Foundation stage curriculum advocates a holistic approach to teaching and learning in the early years, and this is endorsed by the Geographical Association position statement, *Making Connections: geography in the early years*, which makes a direct link between early geographical learning and citizenship.

> The Geographical Association has developed a strategy for the Foundation stage. The strategy is embedded in the Foundation stage curriculum, and its overriding intention is to develop in young children a keen interest in, and desire to learn about, the world in which we live. Directly or indirectly, young children experience the world every day. The early years are an ideal time to build on children's images of places, near and far, and to lay the foundations for their understanding of the world. In turn, this will contribute to their development as a global citizens.(Geographical Association, nd)

Geography in KSI and KS2

Geography is a practical subject. It involves children in learning about real places through active enquiry and investigation. In learning about places and what they are like, children use enquiry and geographical skills, and develop understanding of the patterns and processes which give particular places their character. They also learn aspects of the three themes of physical, human and environmental geography through their investigations. At Key Stage 2, there are specific thematic studies in physical geography (rivers or coastlines), human geography (settlements), and environmental geography (a specific environmental issue). As the programmes of study make clear, geography is also concerned with learning about more distant environments, and the impact of our actions on the environment now and in the future. Geography helps children to understand how decisions are made about the world, how the local and global are interconnected, and that we have individual and collective responsibilities towards others and Planet Earth.

The QCA provides excellent advice on promoting citizenship through geography at KS3 (QCA, 2001). Much of this is equally relevant to KSI and 2, as examples in Table 6.I show. The QCA suggests that geography contributes to CE by enabling pupils to understand and reflect on

- **how decisions are made about places and environments across a range of scales (local to global) and appreciate opportunities for their own involvement;**
- **discuss topical social, environmental, economic and political issues;**
- **the diversity of cultures and identities in the UK and the wider world;**
- **the issues and challenges of global interdependence;**
- **the consequence of their own actions in situations concerning places and environments;**
- **their rights and responsibilities to other people and the environment.**

Understand how decisions are made about places and environments and appreciate opportunities for their own involvement.	Involvement of school council in school decision-making. Participation in school grounds improvement project. Write to or meet local politicians/planners to suggest how local area could be improved (e.g. road safety, play facilities).
Reflect on and discuss topical, social, environmental, economic and political issues.	Observe and discuss changes in the local environment. Discuss issues in the national/international news (e.g. famine, habitat protection, climate change).
Understand the diversity of cultures and identities in the UK and wider world.	Twin with a UK locality with a contrasting ethnic mix to own area. Read stories, sing songs, play games, handle artefacts, listen to music, look at pictures/photos, etc., which reflect diversity in the UK and wider world. Study an overseas locality.
Understand issues and challenges of global interdependence.	Investigate how we are linked to the wider world through everyday items, e.g. food, clothing, media. Investigate a controversial issue such as fair trade, child labour or global warming.
Reflect on consequences of their own actions concerning places and environment.	Identify opportunities for environmentally friendly action (e.g. not dropping/ picking up litter; recycling paper, glass, etc; saving energy; looking after school grounds). Explore their own environmental footprint.
Understand their rights and responsibilities to other people and the environment.	Explore concepts of rights and responsibilities in everyday situations (e.g. playtime). Participate in environmental campaign (eg, to reduce energy use in school).

Table 6.I Opportunities for citizenship through geography (summary of QCA advice)

In the rest of this section, we look at the relationship between CE and the three key elements of primary geography – skills, places and themes.

Geographical enquiry and skills

The programmes of study emphasise the importance of an enquiry approach to learning about places, geographical patterns and processes, and environmental issues and sustainable development. The process of enquiry at KSI, described in PoS Ia–d, suggests that children should be taught to ask questions, observe and record, express their own views, and communicate in different ways. The same essential process is described in paragraph la—e of the KS2 PoS, with the additional expectation that children will learn how to analyse evidence and conclusions, and recognise that other people may have different views from themselves.

In many ways the enquiry process embedded in the geography PoS reflects the key responsibilities of citizens in democratic societies. Active citizens need to be willing to ask questions; seek answers; make judgments based on sound evidence; formulate their own opinions, while still respecting those of others, and communicate these in appropriate ways, such as writing to newspapers, joining campaigning groups or voting in local and national elections.

There is also a correspondence between some of the geographical skills listed in paragraph 2 and those required for active citizenship. Of these, perhaps the most important are using secondary sources to acquire information, and decision-making. Informed citizens need to understand that all information, whether in oral, written or visual form, is created with a particular audience and purpose in mind, and that it may be partial, incomplete, biased, or even deliberately misleading. As suggested later in this chapter, learning about distant places from a variety of resources, such as books, photographs, the internet, artefacts and teaching packs, can help children to understand the limited nature of most sources of information. An understanding of decision-making processes, that there are consequences of individual and collective decisions, and that there is a power dimension to decision-making, are all crucial elements of effective Citizenship Education.

Places and environments

This emphasis on enquiry means that geographical work is often formulated through a series of questions. For example, at KSI, children need to learn about their own area and a contrasting locality either in the United Kingdom or overseas. For each place, children need to investigate the following questions: What is this place like? Where is it? Why is it like this? How is it similar to and different from other places? How is it linked to other places in the world?

At KS2, children are required to study a wider range of places and environments in different parts of the world, including a locality in the United Kingdom and another in a country that is less economically developed. They also need to answer similar questions to those in KSI, but in a more sophisticated way. There are also additional, more demanding questions which require more analysis and explanation: How may it change in the future? How are decisions made about this place? How is it interdependent with other places?

The primary focus on place in the geography curriculum provides a natural context for CE. People care about places, particularly their local area, and much of local politicians' work is concerned with very local issues such as road safety, the provision of amenities, planning applications and environmental enhancement projects. As a student teacher, you will have noticed that primary children may have strongly held views about their school and local area. Local area work can be enhanced by building on their ideas about how it can be managed and improved. As they grow and mature, children are more able to understand the complexity of decision-making about places, and that people have different points of view. Role-play or simulations can be very helpful in supporting children's learning in this area, as illustrated by the local quarry case study described later in this chapter.

Place studies offer particularly good opportunities for CE in relation to understanding decision-making and the interdependence of people and places. Well-informed citizens understand that open and fair decision-making processes are an essential element of a healthy democracy, that decisions have consequences for the present and the future, and that we all have individual and collective responsibilities towards other people and Planet Earth. Geography provides an immediate and meaningful context within which primary children can begin to make sense of democratic decision-making, as the case study in the next section illustrates. Equally, the study of distant places and environments can provide a vivid illustration of how places are interdependent, and linked through the movement of people, goods and products, and by the communication of information and ideas. In particular, it helps children to see and understand the link between the local and the global.

Thematic studies

At KS2, children undertake three thematic studies:

- **Water and its effects on landscapes and people, including the physical features of rivers or coasts and the processes of erosion and deposition that affect them.**
- **How settlements differ and change, including why they differ in size and character, and an issue arising from changes in land use.**
- **An environmental issue, caused by a change in the environment, and attempts to manage the environment sustainably.**
  (DfES/QCA, 2000)

All of these offer considerable opportunities for CE work. When you are planning a theme, you may find it helpful to create a spider diagram with the key elements of CE from Chapter 1 and consider activities which develop each element (namely self-esteem, identity, rights and responsibilities, political literacy, social and moral development and active citizenship). Now that you have read this far, you should be able to identify for yourself some of the ways in which the key concepts of CE could be embedded in the study of rivers/coasts, settlements or environmental issues.

Case study

A simulated local issue

This case study describes some work undertaken by third-year student teachers on a BEd degree course. It is part of a school-based module, in which students are given the opportunity to work intensively with small groups of pupils. Certain Year 6 children had been identified as gifted and talented, and the focus of the work was speaking and listening. The challenge for the students was to create and develop teaching and learning activities which would stimulate and stretch this group of pupils. They were able to work with the children intensively over three successive full afternoon sessions.

They chose to work with a simulation of a local issue, using as their primary resource a detailed A2 picture of a protest outside a quarry and a newspaper account of the protest. The picture shows a quarry in a rural setting. In the background can be seen a small town, hills and trees and a house near the quarry edge. Part of the quarry is being worked and the picture shows machinery extracting the limestone rock. The extracted rock is shown being removed from the quarry by a lorry heading towards a cement works seen in the distance. Another part of the quarry has been worked out, and is now being used as a tip for local refuse. One lorry can be seen dumping its load, and another is approaching. In the foreground you can see a number of people. On the left, protesters can be seen holding banners, protesting about the tipping. They are accompanied by young children, and a reporter is with them. On the right, four quarry workers, dressed for work in dungarees and overalls, are standing uncertainly, watching the protestors warily.

The newspaper article accompanying the picture provides further information about the situation.

Protest at Greenfield quarry

The families living near the Greenfield quarry are very worried about the dangers to themselves and their environment. Every day, big lorries carry household rubbish past their doors. The lorries are on their way to the quarry to dump the rubbish. Flies and other insects are attracted to this and cause a nuisance to the people living nearby. Mrs Lloyd's house backs on to the quarry. She has seen rats in her own garden and also in her neighbours' gardens. 'When will the Council do something?' asked Mrs Lloyd, who has three children, yesterday. 'Do we have to wait until the rats invade our homes?' Yesterday, mothers with babies in pushchairs marched to the quarry, and demanded that the tipping of rubbish should stop. Mrs Lloyd and some of the mothers handed in a petition asking the Council to stop the tipping. Greenfield quarry is owned by Cement Makers Ltd. They have been extracting limestone there for nearly 50 years. Part of the quarry is now worked out. This means that the limestone found in that part is not very good quality and so is not suitable for making cement. On this part of the site, Cement Makers Ltd let the Council dispose of household waste. A spokesman for the Council said today, 'We are pleased with the quarry as a site for rubbish disposal. It is close to the town, and there is room for a great deal of rubbish. After the infilling of the gravel pit in Green Lane was completed in June last year, much of our rubbish had to be transported to the next town for disposal. This solution is much less expensive. When parts of the quarry are full, we will landscape them and plant them with trees, shrubs and grass.'

Activity 2

Before you read on, identify the opportunities that this scenario offers for Citizenship Education. Make some notes of your ideas under the headings Political Literacy, Social and Moral Responsibility and Community Involvement, so that you can compare them to the ideas of my students. Now consider how you would use these materials as the starting point for creating a stimulating learning experience for Year 6 children. Again, you can compare your ideas to those of my students.

Commentary

My students came up with these ideas in small group brainstorms. Some of the ideas appear to belong in more than one column, or it is debatable where something belongs (see Table 6.2). What do you think? You could also represent the grid as a series of Venn circles which would clearly show the overlap.

Political literacy	Social and moral responsibility	Community involvement
Understanding how decisions about local issues are made. Knowing one's rights as a citizen. Possible impact of 'official' decisions on individuals. Understanding the role of the local council, councillors, and officers. The mechanics of protest and campaigning, e.g. organising a petition, contacting the media. The role of the media in publicising local issues.	'Not in my backyard' responses to local authority decisions. Balancing individual rights and collective responsibilities. Understanding different points of view. Conflicting priorities, e.g. jobs v development. Caring for others and the environment. Sustainable development. The impact of protest on others, for example the quarry workers.	Getting involved to make things better. Problems of rubbish disposal. Our collective responsibility for creating waste and finding acceptable solutions for disposal. Alternatives to waste dumping – re-use, recycling, composting.

Table 6.2 Citizenship Education from the Greenfield quarry simulation

Case study (continued)

The student teachers decided to create a role-play scenario, culminating in a simulated television broadcast. This was to take the form of a studio discussion, involving all the major players in the quarry protest, and would be videoed.

The first afternoon was devoted to helping the children understand the scenario. They were divided into small groups, each supported by a student, and given a copy of the picture and a newspaper article to study. Each group was asked to look at the picture carefully, and think and talk about what they could see. Some prompt questions had been prepared to support their discussion of the picture: What sort of place is shown in the picture? What is happening in the picture? What sort of people can you see? What are they doing? However, these proved unnecessary. The children were interested in the picture, and eager to read the accompanying newspaper article.

The second part of the afternoon was used to set up the role-play scenario. The children were told that each group would take the part of one of the protagonists in a televised studio debate about the issue of waste dumping at Greenfield quarry, which would be recorded the afternoon after next. Their challenge was to prepare for the debate. Each group was then issued with a briefing sheet, and given a card naming their protagonist. These included Mrs Lloyd, her neighbour, the Managing Director of Cement Makers Ltd, the council Waste Disposal Officer, the local ward councillor, an unemployed lorry driver, the owner of a small landscaping business, a protester, a quarry worker, and Year 6 children who attend the primary school next to the quarry.

During the second afternoon, the children worked in their small groups, discussing what their character would feel/think/want to happen. They also identified key points they would wish to make when invited by the presenter to contribute to the studio discussion. Each group chose one child to play their assigned role, while the others would be part of a studio audience, which would also be invited to contribute. Some groups prepared themselves prompt sheets, while others produced banners. Several used the internet to research relevant information.

On the third afternoon, the television discussion was videoed live and unrehearsed. One of the students took the role of the anchor person, ensuring that all points of view were heard. Both the main contributors and the studio audience made well-considered and effective contributions.

Commentary

This sort of approach in geography and CE can have drawbacks as well as advantages. Simulations can be very powerful learning experiences if they really engage and motivate the children, but any underdeveloped or insufficiently resourced role-play situation can seem irrelevant or pointless.

PART 2: THE GLOBAL DIMENSION: WHAT IS IT AND WHY DOES IT MATTER?

Traditionally, geography has had very strong links with the international dimension in the curriculum. It helps children interpret their environment and understand the world around them, and unlike some other subjects, its content explicitly deals with the world beyond the UK. It has always helped children to understand the links between their own lives and the wider world. Today, this is more important than ever. The following quotation shows the importance of the global dimension:

Young people are growing up in an increasingly global context. Many of us have family origins or family members in other countries. Many of us live, work and study alongside people from all over the world. More and more people are travelling for work or for leisure. All forms of culture are shaped by global influences. Each decision we make as consumers or electors has an impact on global society. To understand the nature of citizenship, young people need to learn about their position and role in relation to the world in which they live. They also need to develop the skills that will enable them to participate fully in society at a local, national and international level.

The global dimension to citizenship is more than learning about 'global issues' such as sustainable development or international trade – as important as these are. It is also about understanding the global factors to local issues which are present in all our lives, localities and communities.

Presenting the global dimension to citizenship helps young people to understand the issues that are around them, such as racism, the plight of refugees, the impact of international legislation, and effects of environmental change.

It provides young people with the knowledge and understanding to make use of the opportunities available to them and to react responsibly to these issues so that they can live, work and participate fully in society at every level.
(DfID/DfEE/QCA/DEA/The Central Bureau, 2000)

As the statement above suggests, children in school today must be prepared to live in an increasingly interdependent world. They need to understand that in addition to being members of their local community and nation state, they are also citizens of a wider, global society. In the past, many individual teachers, supported by organisations such as Oxfam, Save the Children, the World Studies Trust and local Development Education Centres, have tried to ensure that children learn about the wider world. Now, the global dimension of the school curriculum is also high on the agenda of government agencies such as the DfID, the DfES and QCA.

In this section, I first invite you to reflect on your own views about the global dimension. Then we will compare two attempts at conceptualising the key components of a curriculum which incorporates a global dimension. Finally, we will consider the particular contribution of geography in promoting global citizenship.

The global dimension: where do you stand?

Activity 3

Consider each statement in Table 6.3 in turn. Then decide where you stand, and record this by choosing the number which best matches your view: 1 equals strongly disagree, and 5 means strongly agree. If you are working as part of a group, compare your response with others, and discuss your reasons for adopting your particular viewpoint.

The world we live in is unfair and unequal, and education should challenge and change this.	1 2 3 4 5
We live in a diverse society, and education should give children the tools to counter ignorance and intolerance within it.	1 2 3 4 5
Learning about the wider world, and their place in it, is exciting and relevant to children, and education should extend children's horizons.	1 2 3 4 5
We live in an interdependent world, and education should encourage us to recognise our responsibilities towards each other.	1 2 3 4 5
We live in a rapidly changing world and education should prepare children to be flexible and adaptable to prepare them for the future.	1 2 3 4 5
We all have power as individuals, and education should help children to recognise that we can change things, and that each of us has choices about how we behave.	1 2 3 4 5
We can all learn from the experience of others, both in our own society, and beyond it, and education should recognise this explicitly.	1 2 3 4 5

Statements adapted from Oxfam Cool Planet website

Table 6.3 Where do I stand?

Commentary

If you found that you agreed or strongly agreed with most of these statements, you are committed to the principles of global citizenship. You will want to ensure that the children you teach have opportunities to develop the knowledge and understanding, skills, values and attitudes associated with this aspect of the curriculum. You could give this questionnaire, or a version of it, to children in your own class. When they have filled it in individually, they could compare their responses in small groups. This in itself would be a valuable experience in CE.

Comparing two models of global citizenship

The first model we will look at, Figure 6.1, was developed by the education team at Oxfam, who consulted widely to produce a curriculum framework for global citizenship (Oxfam, 1997). The second, Figure 6.2, was produced by the Development Education Association for DfID and the DfEE (2000). Both these frameworks have been widely distributed and publicised. Photocopy them and lay them next to each other.

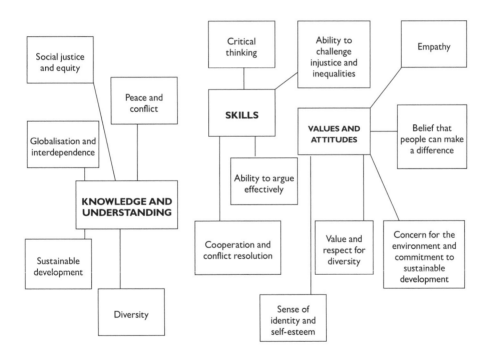

Figure 6.1. Curriculum framework for global citizenship
(Source: Oxfam Education, 1997)

Underlying the notion of a global dimension to the curriculum are eight key concepts. These underpin subject areas and help us clarify what the global dimension means.

1. Interdependence
Understanding how people, places and environments are all inextricably interrelated and that events have repercussions on a global scale.

2. Citizenship
Gaining the knowledge, skills and understanding necessary to become informed, active, responsible global citizens.

3. Sustainable development
Understanding the need to maintain and improve the quality of life now without damaging the planet for future generations.

4. Values and perceptions
Developing a critical evaluation of images of the developing work and an appreciation of the effect these have on people's attitudes and values.

5. Conflict resolution
Understanding how conflicts are a barrier to development and why there is a need for their resolution and the promotion of harmony.

6. Social justice
Understanding the importance of social justice as an element in both sustainable development and the improved welfare of all people.

7. Diversity
Understanding and respecting differences and relating these to our common humanity.

8. Human rights
Knowing about human rights and understanding their breadth and universality.

Source: DfID/DfEE/DEA/Central Bureau, 2000

Figure 6.2 Key concepts for a global dimension in the curriculum

Activity 4

Ask yourself the following questions as you compare the two models:

- **To what extent are there areas of compatibility or overlap between the two?**
- **Are there any major differences in approach or emphasis?**
- **What core values seem to underpin the two models?**
- **What implicit model of the citizen is embodied in each model?**
- **How might they be used in planning for classroom work?**

Commentary

You probably noticed that although there are considerable areas of compatibility, these two models do differ in significant ways. The DfID/DfEE model is based on eight key concepts, whereas the Oxfam approach identifies the key elements for developing responsible global citizenship in the three areas of knowledge and understanding, skills, and values and attitudes. The Oxfam model is more complex, and gives more emphasis to the personal development of children as global citizens. It suggests a great commitment to challenging injustice and inequalities. The DfID/DfEE model, in contrast, emphasises knowledge and understanding. These two models illustrate the continuum that exists about interpretations of global citizenship. Some advocate a strong interventionist stance, whereas others prefer a less radical approach.

Geography, global citizenship and sustainable development

As we noted earlier, geography has always made a significant contribution to education for international understanding, but the notion of global citizenship goes beyond this. It involves more than learning about the lives of people in places beyond our own locality. It also involves learning about the economic, political and cultural relationships between ourselves and others. Crucially, it is also concerned with issues of sustainable development — how we exploit and care for the local and global environment.

The Earth Summit in Rio in 1992 focused attention on the vital role of education in securing more sustainable development at local, national and global scales. It is increasingly clear that children in primary schools today — the workers, consumers and voters of the future — need to be educated to be able to respond appropriately to the critical development and environmental challenges which face humankind. This means that they must

> *develop the knowledge, skills, understanding and values to participate in decisions about the way we do things individually and collectively, both locally and globally that would improve the quality of life now without damaging the planet for the future. (DfEE/QCA,1999, p.23)*

There are opportunities for schools to develop their pupils' understanding of sustainable development in many areas of the curriculum, particularly science and design and technology, but geography, PSHE and citizenship are noted as having a particular contribution to make to this vital aspect of Curriculum 2000.

Many schools already undertake studies of local environmental issues or are involved in projects to improve the local environment. Many have made links with Local Agenda 21 networks through their local authority. These were created following the Rio Earth Summit to promote local sustainable development awareness and activity. Work on issues such as rainforest destruction, global climate change, or the impact of tourism on local people, economies and environments, are common in Key Stage 2. These topics represent excellent contexts for citizenship education.

Studying distant places

The programmes of study for Key Stages 1 and 2 require primary children to study places beyond the local area. In Key Stage 1, this can be in either the UK or overseas, provided the place has 'physical and/or human features that contrast with those in the locality of the school'. In Key Stage 2, children learn about both a contrasting UK locality, and a locality in 'a country that is less economically developed'. However, there are other, more important reasons than National Curriculum requirements why primary children should learn about the wider world!

Reflective activity 5

Before you read on, consider how you feel about this issue. Make some notes of your thoughts, so that you can reflect on them as you read the section below.

Overseas localities

There is considerable research evidence that even very young children can express negative attitudes towards people living in other countries, and that their ideas about places are often partial, negative and stereotypical (Tanner, 1999). This is because children learn about the wider world not only in school but also from the rest of their lives. Each child develops a unique 'personal geography', which is shaped by their individual experiences. This personal geography is derived from their first-hand experiences, their interactions with people and events in their immediate environment, as well as from secondary sources such as television, music, newspapers and photographs.

When teaching about overseas localities, it is important to recognise that children will already have some ideas, images and attitudes related to that place; and also to acknowledge that these may be limited and inaccurate. Just as in science, in geography we need to recognise that children have misconceptions, which need to be challenged appropriately and constructively. An excellent model for the study of distant places can be found in 'Speaking for Ourselves, Listening to Others', a Leeds Development Education Centre publication (Leeds Development Education Centre, 1996). This proposes a three-stage process for learning about overseas localities.

Preview: Children consider what they already 'know' about the locality to be studied, and explore and record this through, e.g. drawing pictures, small-group/whole-class discussion, brainstorming, etc.

New view: Children extend their original ideas by learning about the locality from as many different sources of information and activities as possible, e.g. photographs, the internet, artefacts, videoed television programmes, newpapers, weather data, information books, picture/story books set in the locality, meeting someone who has been there, contact (via email, fax, post, etc.) with children from the area, etc.

Review: Children compare what they now know with their original perceptions, and consider both what they learned and how they learned it.

This three-stage process for learning about distant places reflects both the geographical enquiry approach and good CE approaches. It encourages children to reflect on what they think they know, and to recognise how their ideas can change through exposure to new information. It also fosters a critical approach to different sources of information, and the recognition that they may be limited, biased or partial in some ways. This is a crucial understanding for informed and thoughtful citizenship.

Dealing with controversial issues

In Chapter 4 we discussed the necessity to accept controversy as part of Citizenship Education, the shortsightedness of offering children a sanitised curriculum, and we considered some classroom strategies for addressing controversy. Because it is centrally concerned with social, economic and environmental issues, geography has always dealt with controversy. In primary schools, children frequently investigate real, locally contentious issues such as traffic-calming measures, land-development proposals or amenity-improvement plans. Older primary children may learn about global environmental issues such as global warming, international trade patterns, habitat destruction, or the problems of waste disposal. All these topics are potentially controversial, given that different people will have different views and opinions about them, and that they may challenge people's cherished beliefs and daily actions. For example, many people in the affluent West behave as if they have an inalienable right to use the world's energy resources, despite the contribution this makes to global warming. This raises issues of a conflict between our right to use energy and our responsibility to ourselves and to other less-advantaged people who bear the brunt of our irresponsible actions. The following extract from *The Guardian* could be a discussion point among yourselves, or with your pupils:

> Each long-haul flight burns thousands of gallons of jet fuel and emits global-warming carbon dioxide gas ... these flights damage the upper atmosphere with nitrogen oxide and disturb the sleep of thousands of people living near airports ... every flight leads to more road traffic, more political pressure to build 12-lane motorways to get people to airports, more urban sprawl and more social problems.
>
> But if the real price of air travel today is the inexorable deterioration of the environment, what can people do? Unless we stop flying altogether – which very few are prepared to do, especially when we can travel round the world now for little more than the average British weekly wage. For every 4,000 miles flown by each traveller, one tonne of carbon dioxide pollution is produced. [But you can] make your flight 'carbon neutral' by offsetting an equivalent amount of carbon by reducing emissions elsewhere. This may be by tree planting, distributing energy-saving lightbulbs to small communities in the developing world, or investing in renewable energy projects. And it couldn't be easier to do. By logging on to the Future Forests website (www.futureforests.com), for example, and clicking on the flight calculator, you can work out what the carbon dioxide emissions are for any flight from Albania to Zambia and how many trees or lightbulbs you need to buy to offset these

emissions ... A long-haul flight from London to Australia produces 3.55 tonnes of carbon dioxide per person and would need five trees to be planted at a cost of £42. With the average return ticket to Australia costing £700, that works out at less than 6%. (www.guardian.co.uk, 23 November 2003)

Research suggests that British children are highly conscious that their future adult life will be greatly affected by what is happening in the world today, and that they are concerned about a range of local and global issues. These include crime and violence, unemployment, environmental damage, war and peace, poverty and hunger, international tensions, and natural and human disasters (Hicks and Holden, 1995). If we avoid these potentially difficult topics in the classroom, we risk children finding their education irrelevant to the real world and their concerns about it. The implication for geography teaching is that we must provide opportunities for honest and truthful discussion, for children to express opinions, and debate and develop their ideas about disturbing issues.

Classroom story

Nicola and Year 6: fair trade

This case study reports the work undertaken by a young NQT called Nicola during her first term as a teacher. She was working with a challenging Year 6 class in an inner-city primary school in Leeds, who were studying the rainforest as their geography topic. The more experienced teacher in a parallel Year 6 class was interested in fair-trade issues, and so suggested that they focus on chocolate as a rainforest product. Together, the two teachers investigated the resources available on the internet, and found a Comic Relief resource which focused on fair-traded chocolate.[2] They then used this to plan a sequence of teaching and learning activities which are shown on the left-hand side of the grid in Table 6.4.

When I first spoke to Nicola, she was part-way through this unit of work. She said the topic had really captured the children's interest, and that she thought that this was because it deals with a product that they know and love themselves. She realised that they were acutely aware of mainstream chocolate products and brands, and speculated that this was because the brands are 'in their face' all the time, through advertising. She had noticed that the questionnaire devised by the children for KS2 did not include any fair-traded products, and was surprised by this. She knew one child came from a family that routinely bought fair-trade chocolate, as his mother was employed by a school as a LSA, but reported that 'he didn't speak up'. Nicola felt that the majority of the children in her class were very capable of understanding the issue of fair trade, and that the farmers who produce the cocoa beans should be paid a fair price for their crop. She felt that this work was making them 'think about where our products come from, and that for chocolate it's a complicated chain ... and that they are involved in it, as consumers.' They were now aware of where chocolate comes from, and of the Ghanaian farmer at the other end of the chain. 'The resource pack helped with that, and helped them to empathise with the farmers, because it had pictures of a village in Ghana where cocoa is produced.'

Activity 6

In Table 6.4, use the PSHE/Citizenship guidelines to record the relevant elements from the Programme of Study.

Teaching and learning activities	PSHE/Citizenship guidelines
What are our favourite chocolate bars? • Class discussion	
What are the favourite chocolate bars of KS2 children in our school? • Design a survey re: favourite chocolate bars • Conduct survey with eight KS2 classes • Analyse results and draw conclusions	
Where are cocoa beans produced? How are they turned into chocolate bars? • Study pack photographs • Chocolate journey – picture-sequencing and caption-sorting activity	
Can we tell the difference between different chocolate bars? • Chocolate-tasting activity – blind comparison of familiar brand and fair-traded chocolate	
What is fair trade? • Investigating the fair-trade concept • Debating the merits of fair trade • Considering different perspectives: growers, multinationals, consumers • Developing a personal position on fair trade	

Table 6.4 Fair trade and CE

Commentary

My view is that this represents some good geographical work. The theme of fair trade is explored in the context of a wider study of the rainforest, and is relevant to the children because it deals with an everyday product they frequently buy. The work is structured as an enquiry, through a series of questions, and the children used a variety of strategies for establishing the answers to these questions. There are opportunities to develop specific geographical skills, e.g. using geographical vocabulary; designing, administering and analysing a questionnaire; using maps; using photographs; using ICT. The focus on a particular product helps the children to see how places and people are interdependent, and to begin to understand the patterns and processes of international trade in a meaningful context.

In terms of Citizenship Education, Dubble, who produced the resource, suggest it offers opportunities for children

- **to understand that real-life choices and decisions on how to spend money can affect individuals and communities locally and globally;**
- **to reflect on spiritual, moral, social and cultural issues, using imagination to understand other people's experience;**
- **to learn about the interdependence of communities within the wider world;**
- **to explore how the media present information, and begin to appreciate the influence and power of the media and advertising on consumer choice.**

When I asked my student teachers how they thought this topic might raise controversial or uncomfortable issues, they came up with the ideas presented in Figure 6.3.

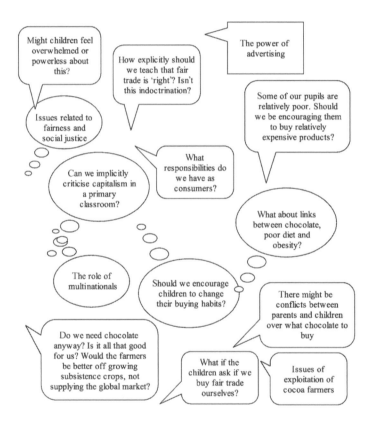

Figure 6.3 Controversial issues in a topic about fair trade

Where would you draw the line?

Controversial issues are always going to provoke uncomfortable feelings, and it is important for you to decide where you, personally, would draw the line. The next activity will help you do this. Although it will provoke more thought if done by a small group working together, you could do it by yourself.

Activity 7

Photocopy the statements in Table 6.5, and cut them up, so that you have nine separate statements. Then, on a table try to order the statements on a continuum from acceptable to unacceptable, carefully considering your reasons for placing each statement. Finally, when you have put all nine statements in place, decide where you personally would 'draw the line', i.e. what you consider to be unacceptable.

When you have completed this exercise, try to identify why you personally 'draw the line' where you do. If you have been working as a group, discuss these questions:

- *Which of these actions involve education for citizenship through geography?*
- *Which should we encourage?*
- *What are the implications for us as teachers?*

Statements for discussion
A group of children decide to bake and sell cakes to raise money to send to the people who live in a village in India they have been studying.
After learning about child labour, children want to boycott some local sports shops and encourage others to join in.
The local town council asks for a group of pupils to be released from school to attend a meeting on developing a piece of wasteland for leisure activities.
After some work on local transport problems, children want to write to their local MP on school-headed paper about the need to improve the local bus and train service.
The head teacher instructs children to collect rubbish from the playground during lunch breaks.
A teacher works with his class to discard school library books which misrepresent the lives of people in less economically developed countries.
As part of a local study, a teacher encourages children to learn more about why a new group of refugees has moved to the area and how they might be helped.
Through the school council, children complain that the playground is always dominated by older boys playing football and other children have no room to play, and suggest setting up a working party to look at how playtime could be improved for all.
Children discuss the pros and cons of fair trade in a literacy lesson on discussion texts, and ask the teacher for her views. She gives these, along with her reasons for holding them.

Adapted from Clough and Holden, 2002

Figure 6.5 Where do we draw the line?

Summary

In this chapter you have learned about the ways that geography provides a meaningful and powerful context for CE. As a subject, it deals with important social, political, economic and environmental issues which affect the lives of people now and in the future.

Through the use of case studies and activities, we have explored how good practice in teaching and learning provides a natural and powerful context for authentic CE.

In summary, I have argued that:

- **there are strong parallels between the geographical enquiry process and the skills required for responsible citizenship;**
- **the study of local and distant places and environments lays the foundation for informed environmental citizenship;**
- **geography makes a particular contribution to the promotion of international understanding and global citizenship;**
- **the investigation of decision-making processes in local and more distant places provides powerful opportunities for the development of political literacy;**
- **the inclusion of controversial issues in geographical work ensures relevance, and supports children's understanding of challenging issues and contributes to social and moral education;**
- **the emphasis on the local area in geography promotes meaningful community involvement;**
- **students and practising teachers have great opportunities through their geographical work to ensure that children acquire the knowledge and understanding, skills, and values and attitudes that will contribute to their development as active, informed and participatory local, national and global citizens.**

Notes

1 An excellent Geographical Association publication, *Geography and the New Agenda: Citizenship, PSHE and Sustainable Development in the Primary Curriculum* explores the links between these aspects of Curriculum 2000 in considerable detail (Grimwade, 2000).

2 **www.fairtrade.org.uk/downloads/pdf/fairtradeinyourschool.pdf**

7 HISTORY AND CITIZENSHIP EDUCATION

What will you learn about in this chapter?

- *how to develop all three of the 'Crick strands' – political literacy, social and moral responsibility and community involvement – through KS1 and KS2 history*
- *how history can be the vehicle for processes of CE*
- *history as the vehicle for some of the knowledge and understanding of CE*
- *history as an important context and reference for considering current issues*

Introduction

History and Citizenship Education are natural allies. In Key Stage 3 the QCA exemplary schemes have located excellent work for CE within the history curriculum, and in the primary years there are also powerful opportunities for working through the content and processes of history.

The actual content of history provides both direct and analogous material for CE, whether in the Early Years or beyond. One of your tasks, as you read this chapter, will be to think about the possibilities within a scheme that you are asked to teach. In this chapter, I only have space to offer a very few examples, but I do recommend that you extrapolate from these to other periods and issues, and that you make it a practice to think about CE whenever you plan and teach history.

The concepts of history are particularly relevant to citizenship. Let's start by reminding ourselves what these are, using the National Curriculum as our guidelines. In Figure 7.1a the main key elements (concepts) are in ovals, with 'using evidence' right in the middle, with virtually everything connected to it, and interpretations of what these mean in primary practice in the speech bubbles. Start with 'chronology' at the top and work out from there, to make sense of the diagram.

In Table 7.1, history concepts are set against equivalent citizenship concepts, and there are some examples and discussion points in the last column. You will be able to think of many other examples and probably want to develop the ideas in the middle column too.

Case study 1

The history tutor's story: planning a unit on significant people for a KS1/2 class

OFSTED reports, the 'Literacy Across the Curriculum' Project (LAC), the Creativity Initiatives and the QCA 'Respect for All' response to the Race Relations Amendment Act had all made me aware that my students needed to be better prepared to develop Citizenship Education through

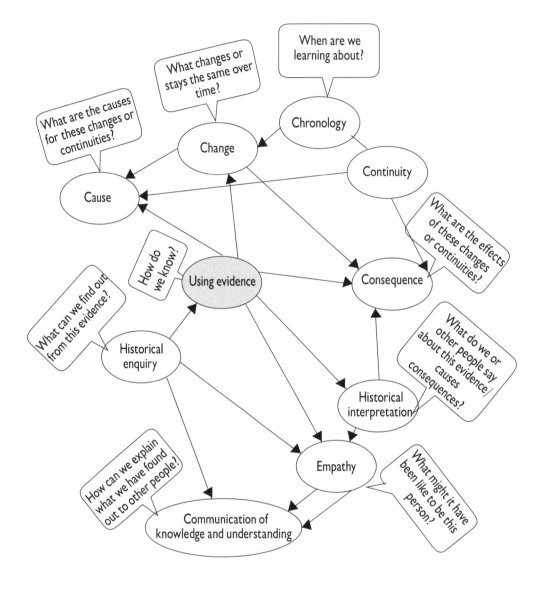

Figure 7.1 History concepts

History concepts and processes	Citizenship concepts and processes	Examples and discussion points
Changes and continuities over time and in comparison to different periods. How is our society similar to or different from a previous period?	Does change/continuity represent progress, 'being stuck' or moving backwards?	*Transport*: more convenient, cheaper, available to everyone BUT what about congestion, pollution, accidents? *Schooling*: an entitlement now for all British children – but what about other countries? Is disaffection of older pupils a problem of compulsory schooling? *Shopping*: there used to be an open market, now there is a shopping mall. What are the pros and cons of this change?
Explaining why change occurs	How could we make changes to try to improve our society?	In history, sometimes technology, sometimes a campaign (including in Parliament), sometimes a war has caused changes. What changes would we advocate for some contemporary issue? Could the campaigns to improve conditions for child workers in Victorian Britain help us think about child labour now? What combination of pressure and necessity leads to changes?
Consequences of change	Tracing the origins of our own society and getting a chronological perspective. How far are changes beneficial – weighing up the pros and cons of proposals. Who benefits and who doesn't?	We have a multicultural society both because of the Empire/colonial history and because of labour needs postwar. Have people who live in or use the countryside benefited or not from technological changes?
Using evidence to find out about other periods and people	Using evidence to counter prejudice, find out the facts or different perspectives on an issue, so that one can discuss rationally.	Evacuee children had very different experiences – not all happy. Their hosts also had different perspectives on the city children. How does this relate to the experiences of newcomers to our communities now?
Evaluating evidence in terms of validity, bias and relevance	Using these skills and concepts with contemporary material – what's the subtext or hidden agenda? What is being suppressed? What different points of view are there?	Can we believe what different people say about GM crops? Why do we only hear the 'bad news' about refugees or issues in the developing world? What do different people say about 'progress' and the death of traditions?
Empathising with and 'getting under the skin' of people from different periods and places	Developing understanding, respect and tolerance for diversity.	Does it help us think about choices available to us today, to think about the kinds of choices people had in the past? In what ways are people of different religious/cultural backgrounds similar or dissimilar to the majority in the wider British community? Can we start considering historical reasons for differences?
Communicating one's knowledge and understanding	Political literacy and advocacy, debating, presenting a case, representing your class or school on an issue.	Being a member of the children's parliament or school council, making a poster about a local issue, writing a letter to the papers about the local traffic problems.

Table 7.1 Links between history and citizenship concepts

history. So I gave the PGCE students the following task to research and present to each other for a seminar.

The QCA has provided exemplary material on significant people for KSI but without making explicit the opportunities for developing work in CE. In KS2 you are expected to include some significant individuals in different units. Working in small groups, choose one or two significant people who have *not* been covered in the QCA Schemes. You can also plan to introduce your significant person during Black History Month (October) or Women's History Month (March).

The brief

a. Develop a scheme to run over several weeks (not specified exactly, to give flexibility). Make sure it meets the requirements for the History Key Elements (check your NC document).

b. Ensure that work on this person/people will involve the children in considering social and moral issues of relevance to their current world.

c. Look for an opportunity to focus on an issue which helps children's developing political literacy (possibly only through process for younger children, but include content if possible for older children) and/or develops community identity and understanding.

After I had told my group about a term's project I had team-taught myself to a Year 2 class on Ruby Bridges, Bessie Coleman and Frederick Douglass,[1] several students decided to focus on more than one person.

In the Year 2 project the class teachers and I had developed children's understanding of resistance to racism and sexism, ideas of human rights, the importance of clear goals and moral courage. In the initial brainstorm the students had to justify why they would focus on their chosen person/people. There were two history graduates in the group, and their in-depth knowledge contributed to the range of names that came up in the initial brainstorm, as did the personal knowledge of several black students about people who had never appeared in their school syllabuses! I have turned some of their suggestions into a partly completed grid. The first thing you could do is extend the list. Your next task is to find out about people who are unfamiliar to you, and why and how teaching about them would contribute to CE.

Person or people	Year and history unit	Citizenship issues to be explored
Pericles, Socrates and Aristotle	KS2 Year 6 Ancient Greeks unit	The nature of democracy in Athens compared with Sparta in the 'Golden' Classical period – who had rights as citizens and who didn't – compared with the present; Socratic dialogue as a way of drawing out people's thinking; Plato's idealistic Republic compared with our views about representation; Aristotle's views about women; the fate of Socrates for challenging conventions – how do we treat iconoclasts and rebels now? Banishing dissidents by majority vote (the *ostrakos*).

Queen Hapshetsut	KS2, Year 4 Ancient Egypt Women's History Month	A powerful black Queen who sent her fleet to the Land of Punt (Eritrea); importance of trade for a viable civilisation; symbols of power – obelisks and temple at Thebes; comparisons with Elizabeth I; what are the current symbols of power of our leaders? What is their power? How important is trade now?
Boudicca	KS2, Year 3 Romans in Britain	*Your chance to consider the possibilities.*
Elizabeth I, Sir Walter Raleigh and Sir Francis Drake	KS2, Year 5 Tudor Britain and the Wider World	*Your chance to consider the possibilities.*
Richard Oastler, Michael Sadler and Robert Owen	KS2, Year 3 Children at work in Victorian Britain	*For you to find out more.* A clue: all were appalled by conditions for working children and were influential in different ways in improving these, through example and direct political action.
Elizabeth Fry	Victorian Britain; Women's History Month	*Your chance to consider the possibilities.*
Barbara Bodichon, Caroline Norton, Elizabeth Garrett Anderson	Women's History Month and Victorian Britain	*Your task to find out more.* All contributed to challenging Victorian sexism and expanding rights for women, including for women to become recognised doctors.
Harriet Tubman, Ellen Craft, Sojourner Truth	KSI significant people Women's History Month, Black History Month	*Your task to find out more.* 'Freedom Fighters' in the anti-slavery cause, brave inspiring women who put struggling for a better society above their own safety.
Sarah Parker Remond	KSI significant people Black History Month	*Your task to find out more.* An advocate of women's and black people's rights; one of the first black women to become a doctor in Europe.
Annie Besant	KSI significant people, KS2 Victorian Britain	The leader of the match-girls' strike in Bow, East London, in 1888.
Sylvia Pankhurst[2]	KSI significant people Women's History Month	Socialist, feminist and anti-racist.
Charles Edward Drew; Garrett Morgan, Benjamin Banneker; Dr Harold Moody	KSI significant people Black History Month	Scientists who made significant contributions to medicine or scientific knowledge.
Anne Frank[3]	KSI significant people KS2 Britain since the 1930s	An example of a courageous, sensitive young girl who tried to make the best of a horrendous situation; the story of the helpers who selflessly, and at great personal risk, helped keep the Jews alive till they were betrayed; for older children, an insight into the nightmare world that extreme racism can create for innocent people.

Case study 2

Learning about Sylvia Pankhurst in Year 2: a vehicle for Citizenship Education

Of the many exciting projects presented by the different groups, I have chosen one about Sylvia Pankhurst, developed for a Year 2 class by Rachael, Sylvana and Chantel. Their plans, which set out history concepts and learning as well as citizenship, were detailed and comprehensive; I have extracted the core relating to Citizenship Education.

Familiar with the names of Christabel and Emmeline, the group were intrigued to hear that there had been 'another Pankhurst', an artist who had designed the posters and much of the publicity material for the Suffragettes, but in 1914 had broken away from her mother and sister to work with poor London East End women. Sylvia had been a socialist and anti-racist, a friend of Haile Selassie, Emperor of Ethiopia, and was buried in Ethiopia where she had spent the last years of her life.

They designed their project on a simple chronological basis, taking the children through the period of activism in the suffrage movement alongside Sylvia's sister and mother – including imprisonment and the Cat and Mouse Act – and finally the achievement of partial suffrage for women in 1919. This gave plenty of scope for children to work through role-play and drama, taking roles as people who would or would not follow the Pankhursts. They planned hot-seating about rights for women (a student teacher in role as Sylvia); discussion about the importance of the vote; whether other people could really represent your needs if you didn't have the vote (which was the argument of some men hostile to women's suffrage); how far you would be prepared to go for 'the Cause'; and what the children thought about the deliberate law-breaking and ways to achieve publicity adopted by the militant Suffragettes.

However, going beyond the suffrage issue, the group was very interested in Sylvia's work as the organiser of the ELFS (the East London Federation of Suffragettes) and planned that children would learn not just about suffrage but about Sylvia's efforts to help East End women become self-sufficient and represent themselves. Sylvia had set up a toy factory to provide employment, a nursery/crèche called 'The Mothers' Arms' during World War I, a cost-price restaurant selling healthy food, and a newspaper for women – the 'Woman's Dreadnought'. They wanted the children to think about poor people's need for work, healthy food and the importance of having a say in how your life might improve. They planned for children to debate their needs and rights, and to make their own 'Children's Dreadnought' newspaper, emphasising community issues.

They planned that they would bring photos, clothes to dress up and convert the role-play corner into the offices of the 'Children's Dreadnought', with material for writing and reading set out ready. They would use freeze-frame techniques from the original photos with some children being hecklers and others supporters of 'the Cause'. They would learn that Sylvia had been committed to working collaboratively with others, including many men (unlike her sister and mother, who were very dictatorial and militaristic in their management of the WSPU[4] and would not work with men), and would practise 'discussing', taking turns to listen to one another. They learned through their own research that the ELFS had later become the Workers' Federation for Suffrage – that is, they wanted the vote for everyone who didn't yet have it, including the vast majority of men in the East End, not just women. They wanted to hold a mock election set in 1919, with debates and finally voting, but with women under 30 still unable to vote. They planned (sensibly) that they would not decide on the election issues themselves, but that it should come from something important to a class. As part of their project, children would design posters and publicity, as Sylvia had done, for 'the Cause'.

Lastly, they wanted to introduce Sylvia's membership and commitment to the peace movement in the postwar period, and her concern for the rights of black people. For example, they found out that she had been one of the first people to publish the writing of the black South African advocate of rights for Africans, Sol Plaatjie, and a Caribbean journalist, Claude McKay, who wrote about the racism against black sailors stranded in Britain after World War I.

School issues – some things to think about from this case study

- The value of focusing on a significant person in history to further CE.
- Being aware of the possibilities and knowing how to exploit them: the necessity for your own research and knowledge.
- Planning for imaginative, creative work which engages even the youngest children.
- Social and moral development from the life of a significant person/people.
- Rights and responsibilities.
- Anti-racist work.
- Political literacy.
- Community involvement.
- Self-esteem and identity issues.

1. Focusing on a significant person in history to further CE

I hope that the sketchy ideas in the grid and those in the case study about Sylvia Pankhurst will stimulate you to consider the immense possibilities of working from the life of a significant person. Significance itself is an important concept in history, closely related to the concepts of change and continuity but also important for CE because of its relationship to economic, political and social issues. You should encourage your class to think about significance – long-term and at the time – not just with respect to influential individuals who are leaders or who initiate change, but focusing on important social and political issues. Someone like Sylvia is significant not just because she was part of the suffrage movement, but also the peace movement and efforts to improve the conditions of working people, particularly women, and black people in the then colonies. All those issues are not just historically significant, but of considerable contemporary relevance. Children can be encouraged to take on the role of ordinary people who were inspired by individual leaders to help them understand that you don't have to be a famous name to have your part in making change happen. You could also ask your children to think about why some people who have made great contributions to human life are not so well known as others: this will help them think about the bias in selection of what we learn about.

2. Being aware of the possibilities and knowing how to exploit them: your own research and knowledge

Rachael, Sylvana and Chantel hadn't even heard of Sylvia Pankhurst before they came into my history class. This means that they had a lot of research to do to get up to speed. They had erroneously imagined that for KSI history they could rely on their general knowledge, till I pointed out that the limitations of their own education and of published children's material which might be Eurocentric or biased would just be recycled. One or two students in the group had heard of Sylvia, but didn't know she had broken away from her better-known sister and mother, because of political differences. The implications are clear: if you want to bring a cutting edge into your teaching, you may have to stray from the well-trodden paths of powerful white males (and some powerful white females, typically royal or upper class) which give elitist and racist messages to our children about who is important. Still, even if you choose someone who is very well known you will need to do some reading to round out your planning so that you genuinely do understand the possibilities to develop political literacy, social and moral and/or community issues.

3. Planning for imaginative, creative work which engages even the youngest children

Throughout this book we emphasise 'active citizenship'. In the context of a subject like history this means exploiting cross-curricular opportunities and creative approaches. Your pedagogy needs to be rooted in an understanding of how children learn. This means that you are always looking for ways to scaffold their learning, to differentiate and to support 'multiple intelligences' in your class. Rachael's group planned for a strong emphasis on speaking and listening as well as reading and writing (which OFSTED itself is encouraging[5]). The children would explore pictorial evidence and make their own art; they would use drama, role-play in the home corner, debates and hot-seating to take on the complex issues that faced women and working people in the early twentieth century.

4. Social and moral development from the life of a significant person/people

There are a number of strands to be explored here with respect to Sylvia's life and the comparison with her mother and sister. Your task, as someone thinking about citizenship and not just history, is to encourage children to consider issues which have contemporary as well as historical relevance. You may do this explicitly, or decide to sow the seeds by letting children ponder on issues, and make connections later.

Firstly, children could think about whether they would have joined the WSPU in the early years. This would have meant going against social conventions because of something you strongly believed in and going right outside the conventions of how females were supposed to behave. Many, but not all, suffrage women had support from their husbands or fathers – and they needed it. Sometimes it was frankly dangerous to go out and speak in public for women's right to the vote, let alone what happened if you got arrested! Within Sylvia's suffrage organisation there is a role for the boys too:

will they give support or will they be among those throwing rotten fruit and heckling? Children could consider what the limits might be for protest, and especially if you work with older children, they could make comparisons with contemporary protests – the most extreme being suicide bombers, and less contentious being large demonstrations which are peaceful, or broken up by police, abroad as well as here.

There are moral issues to do with how people are treated in prison. I wouldn't introduce children in KSI to force-feeding which the suffragettes endured, but what about the Cat and Mouse Act[6] – children can certainly debate the ethics of this! Through hot-seating and other drama techniques (such as 'mantle of the expert', where someone tries to persuade others to join them), children could reflect on the moral and physical courage it takes to protest against injustice.

Activity 1

There are other moral issues to be explored from this topic. Thinking about the age of children that you personally teach on school practice, or as a class teacher, what would you feel able to work on? Collaborate on developing some ideas with people teaching a similar age group. You might like to think about Sylvia's involvement with the peace movement after World War I, and that fact that she rejected pacifism in World War II.

5. Rights and responsibilities

The students planned to get into issues of rights and responsibilities through learning about the campaign for the vote and whether this should be a 'right', and how the suffrage women were treated, which many might consider as enfringement of their human rights. They could also learn about Sylvia's work in the East End, which would take them into how far people had a right to good healthcare, employment and enough money to live on. The student group found it harder to think about how to develop the concept of 'responsibilities' within this theme, till someone pointed out that the women who financed the ELFS welfare projects, and often worked in them, such as the crèches and cost-price restaurants, were themselves quite privileged, but took responsibility for the needs of others less fortunate, and like Sylvia, went and lived among them. Then they realised that the whole notion of working for peace was about taking responsibility for a wider world situation, not just for oneself. Once they'd started to approach things this way, they also suggested that Sylvia's sponsorship of black rights and the rights of colonial peoples was also a matter of taking responsibility and taking action for others.

What do you think? Start by debating these issues in your student or staff group, and then consider how far such discussion could go into your classroom.

6. Anti-racist work

In Chapter I we talked about how CE in the Primary phase might respond to the Race Relations Amendment Act (2000), and the government's concern about addressing diversity and inclusion. Your choice of 'significant person or people' is an excellent opportunity to address these issues through history. Some significant people, for example Martin Luther King, Rosa Parks, Harriet Tubman or Nelson Mandela, take you straight into anti-racist activism. The case of people like Gandhi[7] is more complex, because colonialism was also at issue. Sylvia is interesting because she was a white person who was anti-racist. It's important to include this dimension in order to offer positive models to white students and children, and a broad perspective to minority ethnic groups. Only the other day one of my black students said to me, 'Till I came to uni. I had this simplistic notion that all white people were either racist or indifferent. I really didn't know about white people who made a stand.'

7. Political literacy

As you learned earlier, political literacy is certainly not a boring recital of which prime minister or royal was in power, or how many people sit in the House of Commons. We pointed out in Part I, it's probably helpful to have a sense of what issues you might include. Voting is certainly one of them – not just how to do it, but why it's important. The struggle for suffrage is a powerful way for you or your pupils to debate the importance of the vote. With hindsight we know that having the vote hasn't proved the panacea that many of the suffrage women (and men in earlier decades) thought it would be. But even that would be a great debate or opportunity for role-play... Might 'Sylvia, Emmeline and Christabel' visit us in the early twenty-first century asking us to explain what we had done with the hard-won vote? A hundred years have passed since they formed the WSPU. How have things changed? Is this because of the vote? What else has affected change? The group could have extended their plans to address the civil rights campaign for the vote in the southern states of the USA, or the achievement of black suffrage in 1992 in South Africa, to bring home the contemporary significance of voting.[8]

Political literacy, as we explained, is also about process – learning how to speak for oneself and make a case, argue cogently, persuasively and rationally, keep an open mind, and recognise and respect differences in opinion. The WSPU's publicity campaign was extraordinary for its time. It is part of political literacy to recognise how publicity/propaganda works and deconstruct its methods and messages. You could use the posters, badges, leaflets and banners that came from the movement (many designed by Sylvia) to discuss the power of such publicity.

In my history class I set up a debate between those who would have supported the militant suffra*gettes* or the constitutional non-militant suffra*gists,* who always followed legal means to achieve their ends (led by Millicent Garrett Fawcett and actually a much larger organisation than the militant suffragettes, though less publicity-conscious and now much less well known).

8. Community involvement

There are two possible ways to develop this strand. One is to consider how the WSPU and the ELFS both strove to involve women in the local communities in the cause of suffrage. The national campaign was only as strong as its local branches. Both encouraged local activists; the WSPU went into every area of the country where local women joined up, went to meetings, and tried to persuade their colleagues, families and friends of the importance of the vote. This is an opportunity for you to think about how a small group of people can harness the energy in the community and build a national movement. The second strand is to think about the community work of the ELFS in East London. This was directly concerned with the needs of local people, involved them in running the ventures that were set up, empowered them and was not just about charity.

9. Self-esteem and identity issues

Rachael, Sylvana and Chantel wrote a rationale of their work on Sylvia Pankhurst. Here is part of it:

> One of the difficulties of much work on significant people is that by concentrating on elite groups we give 'ordinary' children little to identify with. Granted, the Pankhurst family were from the privileged middle class but Sylvia's flight from her family into the East End, her espousal of socialism and anti-racism gave us an opportunity to bring the lives of ordinary people, including from Britain's ex-colonies and the wider world, into our classrooms. We think this is good for the self-esteem of our pupils and good for their sense of being part of history.

Activity 2

Can you design a project on another significant person either for KS1 or for Black History Month/Women's History Month for KS2 and try to unravel the opportunities for citizenship work, using this example to get you started?

Summary

Case study 2 has addressed:

- **Political literacy – acting as an 'advocate' for a cause; why vote? how to exercise the vote.**
- **Social and moral responsibility– considering issues of justice and rights responsibilities beyond oneself; children considering personal goals.**
- **Community involvement – introducing material relevant to the identity of the local community, raising self-esteem and profile of members of the local community.**
- **Anti-racist approaches – the responsibilities and attitudes of white people.**

We explored how the life of a significant person could connect to CE if carefully chosen:

- **Introducing such personal qualities as courage, concern and a sense of responsibility for the welfare and rights of other people.**
- **Exploiting cross-curricular approaches, including drama, art and literacy.**
- **Important moral and ethical issues such as how to treat people in prison, the limits of legitimate protest, whether pacifism is justified and in what contexts.**
- **Challenging racism and offering white children a positive example.**

- Developing notions of community.
- Making children aware that ordinary people are also part of history and can effect change.

Going further with social and moral responsibility through history

The previous case study showed that social and political history provides valuable opportunities for children to learn about social and ethical issues, and the difficult choices that people have had to make. For CE, it is important for children to move beyond 'learning *about*' people in the past, which implies that the subject remains remote and unconnected to their own lives, towards 'learning *through*' history. This means that they actively engage with dilemmas and challenges that people have faced in the past. Imaginative teachers and students are increasingly realising what a rich resource such work can be, particularly through drama and role-play. Faced with uncertainty, and without relying on the hindsight which allows you to know what happened, children are invited to make difficult decisions about what to do, as a particular story unfolds. A few years ago I conducted some research with primary children exploring the nature of their developing ethical systems.[9] They put themselves in the shoes of such people as Nelson Mandela's wife and children in 1962; Allen Jay, the Quaker boy who helped the escaped slave Henry James in the 1840s; Miep Gees, who helped keep the Frank family alive; or Cissie Foley, a young trade unionist in the nineteenth century. You may like to try some of the ideas and processes in your own classroom.

Classroom story

Learning about Victorian Britain in Year 3

Siobhan was a final-year BEd student, with history as her subject specialism. The history topic for her school practice Year 3 class was 'Victorian Britain'. Her teacher was happy to let her design the work. She decided to divide the Victorian scheme in two, one half devoted to 'children at work' and the other to the famine in Ireland (see also 'Sam's classroom story' in Chapter 4).

In the first half-term, Siobhan planned a variety of opportunities to develop CE, partly through using the evidence that children had brought to the Royal Commissions on Child Labour in the mid-1800s. She set up role-play, taking the role of a reformer come to gather evidence to take to Parliament in order to try to change the law, and interviewed children working in different occupations, for instance in a mine, in a textile mill, and several decades later in an agricultural gang. She used a timeline and pictorial evidence to help the children with the chronology. The children had pictures and some of the evidence collected by the Royal Commissioners, downloaded from the web.[10] They used this to find out about working conditions for children and to develop their roles as working children in the mid-nineteenth century. They had to explain what work conditions were like, and what they would like to be changed. Memorably, Kyle in role as a child worker in a mine, pushed up his trousers and showed Siobhan (imaginary) bruises and cuts from his exploitative physical labour.

Finally, in a later session, the children talked about child labour today. Siobhan brought in some pictures and simple stories from a charity organisation about children working for very little pay, making carpets in India, and asked the children to think about why they might need to work, but also what we in the West might do to improve the situation. You'll remember that Sam (in Chapter 4) also made links with child work in the contemporary world.

Figure 7.2 Amina gives evidence to the Royal Commissioner, 'Mr Richard Oastler'

The Irish famine

In the second half of term, Siobhan planned to teach about the famine. Her own heritage was Irish and ever since she had been shown some materials produced by the 'Ireland in Schools' project[11] she'd wanted to teach about Ireland. Besides, many of the children in the school had Irish origins, so she felt it would be good to include an aspect of their history. She did not want to concentrate on the more horrific details of the famine but she did want the children to learn about charity and the limited government support, and sponsored emigration, all of which she felt had connections with contemporary CE issues. In Circle Time she extended the topic to talk about what they thought should be done about people in need, for example people they saw near cashpoints with notices saying 'homeless and hungry'.

She also thought they should know about the evictions. At the back of her mind were links with contemporary issues of people losing their livelihood through no fault of their own, and needing help. She used contemporary pictures of the soup kitchens provided by the Quakers, the government work which was supposed to help starving families earn enough to buy food (breaking stones, building roads, etc.) and of evictions. The children used these to develop a series of freeze-frames to express their understanding.

The last part of the project involved children thinking about the reasons why people have to leave their homes. They talked about famine as one reason; some children knew there had recently been famines – and also floods – in some parts of the world. They talked about other reasons, like wanting a better life or job, or needing to escape from a war. Siobhan completed the project by telling the class that many of her own family had left Ireland for America and England in Victorian times, and so, though she sounded completely English now, she had roots in another country. Sean and Maria's parents came to tell her how pleased they were with the work their children were doing, and brought some photos of their families in Cork. Kathy asked to sing the class an Irish song, and together with her friend Corinne, they taught it to the whole class.

Figure 7.3 Freeze-frame of the Irish famine: Natasha, Zehra and Hamza – evicted!

School issues – some things to think about from this classroom story

- Having support and taking the initiative to develop your own scheme of work within the NC for history.
- Planning a history scheme which incorporates elements of CE from the start.
- Taking a cross-curricular approach.
- Considering the history of Great Britain and not concentrating exclusively on England.
- Making connections to contemporary issues.
- Encouraging children and their parents to take ownership of the work.
- Children's reactions to difficult/sad history.

1. Having support and taking the initiative to develop your own scheme of work within the NC for history

It is becoming increasingly common for schools to develop their own schemes for history, even if they still use the QCA exemplary schemes as initial models. OFSTED and the QCA welcome this, as they never intended the QCA schemes to become the official curriculum. Even if, as a student, you find yourself constrained by the school's long- and medium-term planning, prepare yourself for more flexible approaches, and when you are in post, consider arguing for schemes which reflect the needs of CE and the community itself.

2. Planning a history scheme which incorporates elements of CE from the start

Siobhan's scheme was strengthened because concepts of CE were integral, and not bolt-on or tokenistic. She appreciated the need, and planned for discussion about contemporary issues as the children learned about analogous past situations. This approach supports CE, but also makes sense pedagogically, working from children's interests and existing knowledge.

3. Taking a cross-curricular approach

We have already pointed out that OFSTED and QCA are encouraging cross-curricularity and creativity in primary classrooms. Siobhan tended to use drama and literacy – particularly speaking and listening – and note-taking (for their roles as child workers to be interviewed). She included art, but might have done more music (particularly some of the poignant and beautiful Irish songs from the period like 'Athenrye'). She could have brought in maps to show both the areas of the famine, and where the majority of emigrants went, in England and abroad. She also might have used oral history, through inviting a parent or member of the community whose origins were Irish, to talk about their experience of living in England, and their continuing connections with Ireland.

4. Considering the history of Great Britain and not concentrating exclusively on England

The biggest minority group in England is in fact the Irish but their identity, culture and history are somewhat neglected in English classrooms. This is a CE issue, since as we pointed out in Chapter 1, to marginalise the contributions and history of groups in our society is to marginalise their identity as citizens. This work does something to redress the situation with young KS2 children. The 'Ireland in Schools' project provides many other opportunities, including for KS1, for example through learning about Grainne O'Malley, the pirate queen in Elizabeth I's time, Irish saints or the Vikings in Ireland.

5. Making connections to contemporary issues

Siobhan used the issues that arose naturally in this scheme to get the children thinking and discussing some contemporary issues, such as child labour in the developing world, and responses to disasters. In addition, being forced to leave your home and your country continues to be a relevant contemporary issue. Many children in our schools are economic or political refugees, victims of war, poverty and natural disasters in their parents' countries of origin. In Siobhan's school experience class in an inner-city school, virtually every child had connections to another country in one or two generations. In rural schools this might be less common, but it does not prevent discussion about the reasons why people emigrate.

6. Encouraging children and their parents to take ownership of the work

The Head came and told Siobhan that other parents of Irish heritage had been remarking how pleased they were to see work about Ireland going up in the corridor. Some children from other classes came and told Siobhan that their families were also originally from Ireland, and that they went back there on holidays. Siobhan was of course delighted when Kathy and Corinne wanted to teach their class an Irish song.

7. Children's reactions to difficult/sad history

Siobhan had been a bit worried that the miserable story of the famine (and also of Victorian children at work) might be upsetting for Year 3 children. On the contrary, they seemed to wallow in the misery! Their 'real teacher' said afterwards, 'Isn't it strange, the more miserable the more they like it!'

Summary

This classroom story has addressed:

- *Political literacy* – developing and presenting a case for your situation.
- *Social and moral responsibility* – considering the rights and wrongs of child labour from different perspectives; considering what to do in a national disaster like a famine.
- *Community involvement* – considering community support and solidarity.
- *Identity issues* – including the history of the biggest minority group in Britain.

Activity 3

How does this classroom story develop CE?

In the previous case study, we considered some concepts, knowledge and processes of CE that emerged from the work. This time, you will be drawing out these threads yourself. Starting points and the beginnings of a spider diagram are set out in Figure 7.4. When you have explored the citizenship threads, see if there is anything missing and consider how you might develop that marginalised aspect in a creative and imaginative way.

Summary

In this classroom story we looked at:

- Developing a NC history scheme so that it included aspects of CE.
- Considering the ethnicity and identity of children in the class and the school.
- Making links with contemporary issues such as child labour, emigration and disasters, and exploiting opportunities for developing children's social and moral thinking.
- Active engagement with citizenship concepts, especially political literacy, through the opportunity to be part of an historical campaign.

Case study 3

The history specialists' story: teaching CE through the World Study Units

Our history tutor gave us a challenge in our final year. We had to find a way to develop CE through one of the World Study Units for KS2. She reminded us that political literacy was the most neglected of the 'Crick strands' but said she would be happy with anything we researched and planned that contributed to CE. We worked in small groups and presented our findings and plans to the whole group. Here are some of our ideas.

Sandy, Fatima and Chris – Ancient Egypt

We were interested that Ancient Egypt was in fact an African civilisation, though it is often portrayed as European. We thought this could contribute to recognising, understanding and respecting the achievements of Africans, and self-esteem and identity for black minority groups in Britain. Our specific CE focus was 'rights and responsibilities' with respect to the Egyptian treasures now housed in the British Museum. We thought it would be interesting for children to debate whether these should be returned to Egypt, or whether they should remain in England. We would hold a 'trial' with a prosecutor and defence barristers, arguing whether or not the treasures should stay or go back to Egypt. We had found out that some of the treasures had come legitimately; some, particularly in private collections, had been stolen by travellers in the nineteenth century, but also that in Ancient Egyptian times there had been a run on the treasures in the tombs and a thoroughly fishy trial in which the main culprits – wealthy and powerful overseers – went free, while lower minions carried the can.

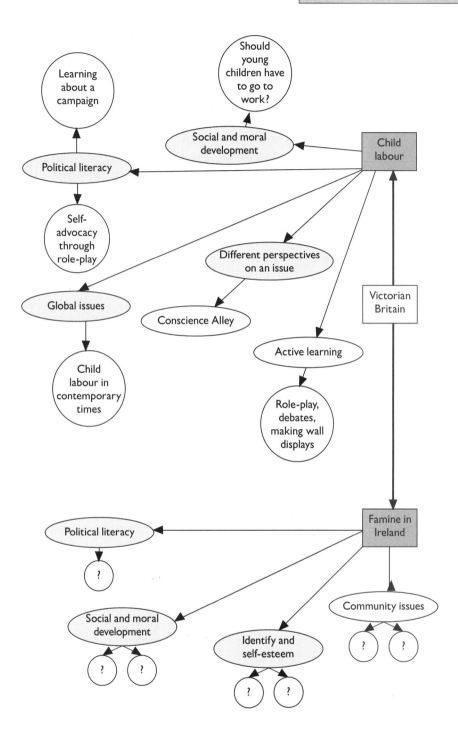

Figure 7.4 Citizenship concepts and processes in work on Victorian Britain

NB: the group thought the idea of 'trials' about whether treasures should be sent back or stay in Europe could be used for several of the World Study Units, such as Assyria, Benin and also Ancient Greece – the Elgin Marbles being the obvious one. The recent raids on the museum in Baghdad were another relevant contemporary issue.

Paul and Theo – Mesopotamia

We were interested in raising the profile of a Middle Eastern civilisation – the so-called cradle of civilisation and the site of modern Iraq – given the contemporary political problems in that area, and danger that the occupants could suffer from blanket stereotyping. We wanted to emphasise the extraordinary achievements of the people who lived between the Tigris and Euphrates. They were the first to use writing, had a knowledge of medicine, a sophisticated artistic and political culture and, in the Code of Hammurabi, ruler of Mesopotamia in the eighteenth century BCE, a written legal system which allowed us to discuss issues of justice, mercy and punishment with our pupils. The Code set out a whole variety of punishments. The death penalty was rather frequently invoked, so some transgressions were more appropriate for children to consider, e.g. stealing, cheating or failing to be socially responsible. For instance, '53: If any one be too lazy to keep his dam in proper condition, and does not so keep it; if then the dam break and all the fields be flooded, then shall he in whose dam the break occurred be sold for money, and the money shall replace the [grain] which he has caused to be ruined.' '54: If he be not able to replace the [grain], then he and his possessions shall be divided among the farmers whose corn he has flooded.' '108: If a [woman wine-seller] does not accept [grain] according to gross weight in payment of drink, but takes money, and the price of the drink is less than that of the corn, she shall be convicted and "thrown into the water".' '142: If a woman quarrel with her husband, and say: "You are not congenial to me," the reasons for her prejudice must be presented. If she is guiltless, and there is no fault on her part, but he leaves and neglects her, then no guilt attaches to this woman, she shall take her dowry and go back to her father's house.' '143: If she is not innocent, but leaves her husband, and ruins her house, neglecting her husband, this woman shall be cast into the water.' We discovered that this was a trial by water, a bit like Tudor trials of witches. If the person did not sink, then s/he was innocent!

Agriculture in one of the Mesopotamian cities, Mashkan-shapir, had probably failed when the land became poisoned with salt because the irrigation system had failed. This was apparently happening now in California in the San Joaquin Valley, so this ancient example would take us into a contemporary ecological problem. We thought that the importance of the Tigris/Euphrates would allow us to consider the importance of water, in the light of droughts which are currently causing famine.

Maggie and Vicki – Benin

We wanted to work on Benin because it was a powerful African civilisation, at its height at the same time as the Tudors, with magnificent artistic and craft traditions. We thought improving knowledge and understanding about Africa was good for intercultural-global understanding. We would use the Dutch and Portuguese descriptions and lithographs of Benin city from the seventeenth century, as well as the carvings and sculptures in the British Museum, to introduce pupils to the sophisticated culture (or if we couldn't go, use COMPASS, the BM website). For direct CE work we would like to 'fast forward' to the end of the nineteenth century and do a drama based on the Sack of Benin in 1897. Children would have to think about the rights and wrongs of the invasion, the massacre of the British who refused to wait till the holy ceremonies were over before trying to enter Benin, and the subsequent retaliatory destruction of Benin city. This was when most of the treasures brought to Europe were taken. We would use role-play to debate if the sack of the city and the Oba's banishment were fair and just. Some children would take the role of ordinary inhabitants of Benin, others of the families of the British soldiers who were killed.

Leila, Tracy and Tayo – Aztecs

We found it really difficult to find a CE focus for KS2, from a study of the Aztecs. We spent ages discussing this and eventually decided on a debate about why an Empire fails and what our judgement of the Spanish invaders might be. These questions are about the ethics of war and conquest, revenge and treatment of the defeated, really only suitable issues for the oldest KS2 children. We thought that they had relevance to twentieth and twenty-first century events and might help older pupils think seriously about power and its abuse.

We did a lot of research about the Aztecs. We wanted to keep some kind of balance, and not imply simplistically that the Spanish were superior to the Mexica, or vice versa. We did not want to dwell on blood sacrifice, though we could not exclude it, since Aztec religious beliefs and rituals seem to have been so central to their civilisation. Trying to make ethical judgements using contemporary beliefs about human rights was, we thought, anachronistic. But a focus on very different attitudes towards life and death could help children think about the value *they* placed on life. Though contentious in some circles, Mexica attitudes seemed matched by the Spaniards' assumptions that they could destroy a civilisation in the name of Christianity. We thought children could discuss Cortes' decision literally to 'burn his boats' as an answer to the men's reluctance to wage this war. We discovered that Cortes seemed unconcerned about the sophisticated art and culture of the Mexica, and was happy for his men to destroy the wonderful city of Tenochtitlan – 'the Venice of America'. We realised that the Aztec Empire fell not just because the Spaniards had superior weapons, but because they had treated their neighbours so harshly that 150,000 were easily recruited to join the tiny invading Spanish army. It appeared that Montezuma had made peaceful overtures to Cortes, which the Spaniards initially accepted, and then betrayed. Apparently too, though Montezuma begged his people to give up peacefully, the warlike Mexica regarded this as cowardly, and so colluded in their own destruction. We did wonder, however, whether everyone had a say, particularly women, or whether a powerful male elite imposed this decision, which was to prove so disastrous.

We planned to use a version of the game 'The Great Divide'[12] to encourage thoughtful responses and to allow for differentiation. This is a version of 'Conscience Alley'. After studying the Mexica civilisation and the Spanish conquest, children would be asked to consider quite a complex statement: 'There is little to choose between Cortes and Montezuma'. We would give them quite a bit of time to prepare their point of view, in groups, and the groups would take their place on either side of a line, which represented neutrality. In the second part of the game, the statement would be 'Mexica's enemies who joined the Spanish invaders were right to want to take revenge', with the same procedures. When each group had had their say, children could move physically to represent a change of opinion, including into the neutral zone.

Summary

This case study has addressed:

- *Political literacy* – learning about laws and comparing them with contemporary ones; a simulated trial – advocacy: prosecution and defence.

- *Social and moral responsibility* – considering whether treasures from world civilisations should be housed in European museums; how should conquered people be treated? the rights and wrongs of invasion and conquest.
- *Community involvement.*
- *Identity and self-esteem – potentially for some children in the class through addressing their heritage.*
- Developing understanding and respect for people in other parts of the world.

Activity 4

Use the grid below to identify the CE concepts and issues that the different World Study Units could develop. Add columns for Ancient Greece and any of the other units in Key Stage 2 to summarise your own ideas. One or two are filled in for you, to get you started.

	Ancient Egypt	Mesopotamia	Benin	Aztecs
Political literacy – content (e.g. laws, hierarchies, justice)		The justice system in the Code of Hammurabi and comparing with contemporary laws.		
Political literacy – processes (debate, advocacy, weighing up different perspectives, etc.)			Debating the pros and cons of the Sack of Benin, in retaliation for the murder of British soldiers, who had disrespected Benin religious rituals.	
Tolerance, respect and understanding				What does it mean to respect another culture? What do we feel about the Spanish actions? Were they justified?
Identity and self-esteem		Work on a Middle Eastern civilisation could counteract some of the current ignorance and negativity about this part of the world and its history.		
Social and moral responsibility – considering ethical issues	Should the Egyptian treasures in the British Museum be returned?			
Community involvement				
Any others?				

Commentary

Which concepts are more difficult to develop through the World Study Units? Why do you think this is? If you identified 'Community issues', you are not alone! The answer is probably to develop this strand of CE through local studies or through the British units, particularly Britain since the 1930s. If you are interested, a project I team-taught to Year 6 is written up on the QCA site *Respect for All*.[13] It describes work on the Commonwealth contribution to the war effort, and the experience of the Jewish children brought to England on the *Kindertransport* in 1938–9. This same class also studied the experience of Caribbean immigrants in the postwar years, which gave them wide opportunities to consider community issues, including support systems.

Summary

This chapter has explored some of the possibilities for CE developed through history, with a particular emphasis on active approaches to political literacy and social and moral responsibility. We have emphasised planning to incorporate concepts and issues from CE from the start, but also being open and flexible about children's responses to the content as you go along. It will be obvious that good subject knowledge is imperative not just for good history lessons, but to draw out the CE aspects in an informed way. You will need to be as critical of web material as about any other resources on offer, and read widely, to establish not just the so-called 'facts' but the interpretations, and make sure that children are aware that there is always more than one point of view about an issue. Once you develop your own awareness of the possibilities in history for CE, it becomes easier to make connections.

Notes

1 See Claire, 2002 and QCA *Respect for All* website.
2 PCET Educational Charts, 2004, Significant People, 'The Pankhursts'.
3 PCET Educational Charts, 2004, Significant People, 'Anne Frank'.
4 WSPU – Women's Social and Political Union, founded by the Pankhursts in 1903 with the slogan 'Deeds not Words'.
5 Personal communication: Scott Harrison, HMI responsible for history, November 2003 at the Historical Assocation Primary Meeting.
6 The Cat and Mouse Act meant that women who went on hunger strike were released and then re-arrested as soon as they had gained their health.
7 PCET Educational Charts, 2004, Significant People, 'Gandhi'.
8 A picture book, Sisulu, E. B., 1996, *The day Gogo went to vote*, Little Brown and Company, would be ideal to introduce and discuss how black South Africans finally got the vote.
9 See Claire, 2004, in Osler.
10 www.spartacus.schoolnet.co.uk/Rchild.main.htm
11 www.irelandinschools.org.uk
12 In Clough and Holden, 2001.
13 www.qca.org.uk/ca.inclusion/respect_for_all/index.asp

What will you learn about in this chapter?

- *the place of RE in the primary curriculum*
- *how the aims, skills and processes of RE and CE are related*
- *how RE and CE promote active learning*
- *opportunities for CE through RE*

Introduction

> *In RE, children reflect on spiritual, moral, social and cultural issues, using their imagination to understand other people's experiences. It provides a valuable context for children to learn about and appreciate the range of national, regional, religious and ethnic identities in the United Kingdom.*

> *RE contributes to citizenship by providing opportunities for children to explore what is fair and unfair, recognise what is right and wrong, and understand and exercise personal, social and moral responsibility.* (QCA Citizenship: Teachers' guide, 2002, p. 17)

Religious education and CE have a great deal in common:

- **They are both concerned with investigating and appreciating diverse religious and cultural experience in Britain today.**
- **They both have at their heart the spiritual, moral and cultural development of children.**
- **They both require very careful planning in the busy primary timetable to ensure time, fair coverage and quality teaching.**

A brief introduction to the place of RE in the basic curriculum

The 1944 Education Bill and the 1988 Education Reform Act required that all pupils in full-time education should be taught RE unless withdrawn by their parents (DFE Circular 1/94, para. 44). The general assumption in 1944 was that Christianity was the religion taught and that most of the children attending schools would share a common faith. The Act stated that an agreed syllabus 'must not be designed to convert pupils, or to urge a particular religion or religious belief on pupils' (Education Act 1944, Section 26 (2)). As the social fabric of Britain has become more complex, the delivery of RE has changed to reflect and support the wide range of religions represented in local communities. The 1988 Act recognised that an agreed syllabus should:

> *reflect the fact that the religious traditions in Great Britain are in the main Christian, while taking account of teachings and practices of the other principal religions represented in Great Britain* (ERA, 1988, Section 8(3)).

Although there has been much debate about this statement,[1] ERA confirmed that Agreed Syllabuses should develop their approaches to the teaching of *all* religions represented in Britain, and since 1988 RE has developed substantially in its understanding and delivery of education about a range of religions and life stances. In this, it reflects the diverse needs of pupils, British society and a growing engagement with a range of world views. Indeed, some believe that

> for the vast majority of British young people, religious education today offers the main way whereby the plurality of the modern world is recognised, and a dialogue between alternative world views is encouraged. (Hull, 1998, p. 27).

There is no National Curriculum for RE. It is taught through Local Agreed Syllabuses which are written and reviewed by local education authorities or by religious bodies who write syllabuses for their schools. LEAs establish SACREs (Standing Advisory Councils for Religious Education) who organise and revise their Local Syllabuses. These SACREs include members of local faith groups who can advise on the representation of their faith in the local community. Although RE is organised and taught through Agreed Syllabuses, advisory documents such as the QCA exemplar schemes of work help teachers plan RE, and a recommended eight-point scale can be used for assessment. During 2004 the QCA is consulting on a non-statutory national framework for RE. This would be designed to fit within the current legislation and would support the delivery of RE so that it can benefit from some of the advances made in National Curriculum subjects.

Model Syllabuses and non-statutory guidelines for RE

To assist LEAs in drawing up Locally Agreed Syllabuses, SCAA (now QCA) published two 'Model Syllabuses' in 1994. Because there is a wide range of Agreed Syllabuses across the United Kingdom, some of the work in this chapter will refer to the Model Syllabuses which are available on line (**www.qca.org.uk/ca/subjects/re**). Both are based on teaching religions as separate entities, through studying the major tenets of religions and through investigating their expression through local religious communities. More recently, some thematic models between religions have been developed, allowing children to engage with a range of religious answers to living issues. This approach has been reflected in the draft non-statutory framework. Actual Agreed Syllabuses should be used when planning specific work for pupils in class whichever approach is used.

The Attainment Targets

The Model Syllabuses have two Attainment Targets which are also used in a large number of Agreed Syllabuses.

Learning about religion – where pupils study information about the different religions (usually Buddhism, Christianity, Hinduism, Islam, Judaism and Sikhism) so that they understand their individual beliefs and practices.

Learning from religion – which develops the pupils' engagement with religion in the light of their own experiences. Children are encouraged to 'give an informed and considered response to religious and moral issues' and to 'reflect on what might be learned from religions in the light of one's own beliefs and experiences' (QCA Model Syllabus 2, p. 6). The delivery of this Attainment Target is discussed further in the QCA non-statutory guidelines (QCA, 2000, Section 3).

Summary

- Religious education is organised and taught through Local Agreed Syllabuses rather than through a national syllabus.
- RE should be provided for all pupils in all schools, although individual pupils may be withdrawn by their parents or carers.
- There are two widely used attainment targets: learning *about* religion and learning *from* religion.
- RE engages with both the concept of community and the expression of religion in communities.

RE aims and how they relate to CE

Each Local Agreed Syllabus sets out its aims for RE. The grid below sets out widely held RE aims based on those in the Model Syllabuses.

Activity 1

Using the aims for RE set out below, consider how the knowledge and understanding generated in RE can be related to CE. The first and third examples are completed for you so that you can see the different Attainment Target strands.

RE aims	Relationship to CE
1. Develop knowledge and understanding of the principal religions represented in Britain today.	Reflect on how religious communities are represented in Britain and how religious communities express themselves in society (e.g. places of worship, care in the community, food and dress, festivals and celebrations).
2. Develop an understanding of how beliefs, values and traditions can influence individuals, communities, societies and cultures.	
3. Develop the ability to make reasoned and informed judgements about religious and moral issues with reference to the teachings of the principal religions.	Consider the teachings of religions on care for others in the light of equal-opportunities, social-justice and human-rights work in CE (e.g. voluntary service, charity giving, respect for diversity, rights of the individual).
4. Enhance their own spiritual, moral, cultural and social development by awareness of the fundamental questions of life raised by human experiences and how religious teachings can relate to them.	
5. Reflect on and respond to these questions in the light of their own experience and with reference to the teachings and practices of religions.	
6. Reflect on their own beliefs and way of life.	
7. Develop a positive attitude towards others and respect their right to hold different beliefs in a society of diverse religions.	

Commentary

This activity shows how both the RE Attainment Targets are involved in CE. The first two aims involve knowing about religions. This is important for CE because pupils learn about the place and role of religions in society. They learn why and how religious believers practise their faiths and about the impact religions can have on social structure. The next five aims all relate to the pupils' own understandings which are developed in the light of religious teachings. RE helps pupils to develop a dialogue between their own ideas and those of major religions. CE benefits from these aims because they complement the active learning strategies which pupils need to engage with citizenship. Both areas are identified in the Teachers' Guide for Citizenship quoted at the beginning of this chapter.

Skills and processes

Activity 2

As well as developing similar areas in terms of knowledge and understanding, RE and CE both make use of a similar skills base. Figure 8.1 shows the similarity and relationship between the concepts, skills and processes developed in RE (as listed in the Model Syllabuses) and those for CE. Your task is to consider the links made on the diagram and add others to complete a grid of linked skills and processes.

Commentary

You should now have further links across the two subjects on your diagram, and you will have noticed how closely the skills and concepts developed in RE and CE relate. Both subjects engage pupils in higher-order thinking, requiring not only knowledge acquisition but also a range of different types of analysis and application, including skills of reflection and empathy. Although the two subjects share common skills and aims in terms of pupil development, it is important at this point to identify their differences and consider their relationship.

Using RE as a context for citizenship

As chapters in Part I illustrated, recognition of shared values and negotiation about different values are important aspects of CE. This is where RE can play a major role in CE. Clearly, as Figure 8.1 shows, RE and CE have much in common in terms of processes and attitudes, but we still need to be aware that the two subjects are not in complete agreement over aspects of purpose or delivery. Also, we must make sure to clarify the purposes of a lesson which involves both subjects and decide how different objectives are being addressed, as well as where objectives overlap.

Concepts from religion

RE aims to investigate and teach about the ways religions express their beliefs and values. There are many values which are shared across different faiths, such as the

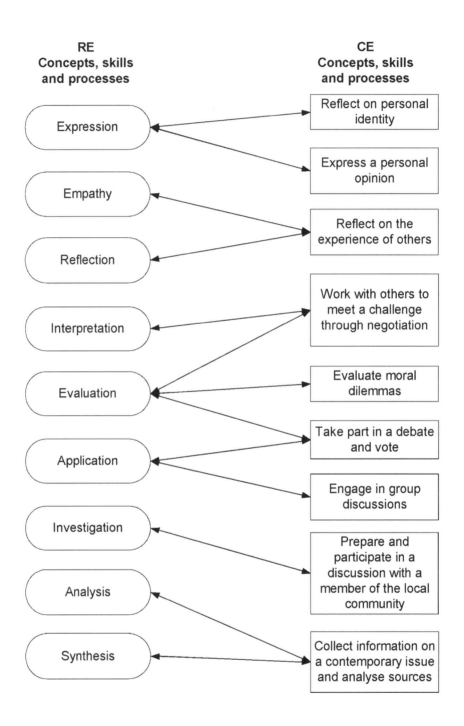

Figure 8.1 Similarities in concepts in RE and CE

sanctity of human life or care for the oppressed. However, there are some values promoted by specific faiths which are not held in common, for example about divorce or acceptable clothing. The faith communities themselves nurture their adherents in their beliefs, values and practices, and RE examines those values in the contexts of the faiths which hold them. It is not the role of RE teachers in non-denominational state schools to inculcate or nurture children in a specific set of values from one religion alone and RE has taken immense care over the years to distance itself from accusations of indoctrination. By learning *about* religion and learning *from* religions, values are discussed within the context of the religion or religions investigated.

Concepts from CE

CE has at its centre 'education for citizenship' which includes 'behaving and acting like a citizen' (QCA/DfEE, 1998, p.13). This could be interpreted as moving away from RE's base of developing knowledge and understanding of difference and moving towards a specific model of behaviour or 'common citizenship'.

Can RE and CE share the same definition of citizenship? The potential for tension between a believer's adherence to his/her faith and the expectations of the society in which he/she lives lies at the heart of much religious teaching. Understanding these tensions and the negotiation undertaken by adherents of faiths who find themselves exercising different values from the general society in which they live, is part of RE. It is essential that RE and CE undertake a dialogue between their approaches. Both teachers and children need to keep in mind the individual identities of the two subjects. RE and CE can sometimes be combined when they have common objectives, but neither should be assumed to have the same aims and purposes as the other in all circumstances. As previous chapters have suggested, citizenship is a secular concept in which the law and human-rights conventions form the overarching ethical framework. In contrast, the authority of religious teachings provides the framework for specific faiths.

The 'Crick strands'

RE is closely linked with two of the three strands from the Crick Report, namely social and moral responsibility and community involvement. Material taught in RE can be used not only to teach about attitudes in religions but also as a starting point for discussions in CE.

Social and moral responsibility

Religions have at their core teachings which affect the way their adherents behave. For example, Hindus speak of their *dharma* or 'religious duty' which includes social responsibility as part of the development of the self; Muslims have *Akhlaq,* the code of moral rules which cover responsibilities, conduct and attitudes based on the *Qur'an* and the *Sunnah*; and Christians use Jesus' life and teachings as examples of social and moral responsibility. Apart from individual action, religious organisations are involved in socially responsible action, drawing on religious precepts as their justification, since they regard social and moral responsibility as inherent to belief.

An example of a topic looking at social and moral development which includes both RE and CE is the local and global work of charities. Pupils could look at the development and work of large and small charities which have religious and non-religious affiliations. Here are some examples of charities which are inspired by their religious beliefs to aid others.

Name of charity	Religious affiliation	Type of charity and relief work
Islamic Relief **www.islamic-relief.org.uk**	Muslim	Providing emergency and long-term relief for the needy, regardless of colour, race, background or religion.
Christian Aid **www.christianaid.org.uk**	Christian	Agency of the churches in UK and Ireland. Works wherever need is greatest, irrespective of religion.
Khalsa Aid **www.khalsaaid.org**	Sikh	Established 1999 when British Sikhs delivered aid to Bosnia. Since then there have been further missions to Orissa, Gujarat and the Congo in response to natural disasters.
TZEDEK – Jewish Action for a Just World **www.tzedek.org.uk**	Jewish	Tzedek is a Jewish word meaning 'being fair' as well as 'charity'. Based in the UK. Administers small-scale sustainable projects regardless of race or religion.
Sewa International **www.sewainternational.com**	Hindu	Based in Leicester. Helps victims of man-made and natural disasters in developing countries through immediate relief aid and long-term community-based projects.
Karuna **www.karuna.org**	Buddhist	Karuna is a Tibetan word for 'help' or 'serve'. Founded 1980. Developed work among Dalit groups in India. Aims to promote dignity and self-confidence. Has branches in 18 countries and projects in Tibet, Nepal and Zimbabwe.

Children should also learn about charities and organisations which are secular and are guided by humanitarian or ecological aims so that they understand a range of motivations. Examples of secular charitable organisations are Amnesty International, Oxfam and the Worldwide Fund for Nature.

When children investigate different motivations for charitable giving they should also consider their own motivation to behave responsibly and charitably. Do they act responsibly towards others because they are fulfilling a religious duty; because they really want to; because they are motivated by a sense of common humanity; or is responsible, social action just a pragmatic way to stay out of trouble?

These questions lie at the heart of understanding how religious belief can influence individual actions. But we need to acknowledge that you do not have to be religious to be 'good' or to consider ethical behaviour as part of social responsibility. So while RE helps us understand how religions can lie at the heart of moral and social behaviour, CE is about understanding the need for behaviour which benefits society as a whole, and this may be secular or religious in origin. There is a wealth of debate about how one should behave and why; what one can do on behalf of humankind; and what is unacceptable in social and moral terms. The wellsprings of motivation for ethical action are relevant for both RE and CE, especially when children investigate religious teachings to develop their own ideas.

Community involvement

RE's connection with this strand of CE is through understanding how individuals, groups and communities show their beliefs, how they negotiate with others in relation to those beliefs and how they use their beliefs to be part of society in general. Religious and secular teaching and common values can be compared and discussed.

Classroom story

Teaching about the importance of community to Islam

Julie decided to invite her neighbour Mumtaz to visit her Year 4 class and talk about the importance of community in Islam. The children had already learned about the Five Pillars, especially *salah* (prayer), *sawm* (fasting) and *zakah* (almsgiving), each of which contributes not only to the values of the individual but to the expression of community.

When Mumtaz visited the class, the class first asked her about *zakah* and how her family organised their giving. (*Zakah* is a welfare contribution which is calculated on all wealth after paying for such necessities as food, clothing, housing, vehicles and machinery.) She explained some of the arithmetic needed to work out how much was given each year. The pupils wanted to know how she felt about the money not being spent within her family. She explained that in Islam all people are equal and that it is a duty for the rich to help the poor. Giving *zakah* is a recognition that wealth should not be hoarded when others are suffering. The money is sent to an Islamic organisation so that it can be sent to people who needed it. Mumtaz explained that there were other ways in Islam to give . She explained about *sadaqah*, which are voluntary gifts or charitable acts which can be at any time and in response to all sorts of needs in the community, such as a neighbour who is ill and unable to care for her family.

Julie invited her class to tell Mumtaz about their collection of tins of food at Harvest Festival and how they had made up parcels for a local old people's home. They also explained how they had organised a cake sale in school which was in aid of Oxfam. Julie and Mumtaz encouraged the children to make connections between *zakah* and *sadaqah* and how they had felt involved with both projects at school. The lesson ended with a discussion on how belonging to a community meant that people could pool their resources to help others.

Commentary

Inviting a member of a faith community into your classroom is an important and valuable way to help children understand issues, and means they are not always learning 'at second hand'. Julie prepared the class for the visit, but she also briefed Mumtaz in advance, so that she knew what sorts of questions to expect, and could prepare herself. Mumtaz felt it was very important to move the children on from thinking about the amounts of money involved in *zakah* to the reasons why it is part of the Five Pillars. She was able to weave in the references to the children's own activities to help them understand the concept of community which they were investigating.

There are opportunities within other religions to develop the idea of community:

Judaism: Leviticus 19, 15–18 teaching on social responsibility to your neighbour and how this can be carried through today.

Christianity: The Good Samaritan, Luke 10, 25–37 with particular reference to the question, 'And who is my neighbour?' – which prefaces the story.

Sikhism: The story of Bhai Khanayah which illustrates *sewa,* the Sikh and Hindu word for service to humanity regardless of colour, creed, caste or gender.

Buddhism: The way Buddhists involve themselves in the community, for example by supporting the monastic *sangha* (community).

RE also teaches pupils what the different practices of religions mean in terms of social, ethnic and cultural diversity. It teaches about understanding the needs and preferences of members of society whose beliefs are reflected in the way they live, e.g. food laws and dress codes. It teaches tolerance and respect, enquiry and self-understanding as part of the attitudes which are valued in religious, social and personal development. In this it is directly relevant to CE with respect to understanding diversity, tolerance, justice, individual rights and the nature of community.

Classroom story

Fatima's hijab

Fatima was on School Experience in a Year 5 class. Some non-Muslim pupils questioned her about her dress and, in particular, wearing *hijab* (a veil). Some of them thought it was a restriction which they could not personally envisage accepting. It was obvious that they had been influenced by recent media coverage about wearing *hijab* in French schools. Fatima carefully explained that for her it was a liberation, not a restriction, that she felt empowered to be herself when she wore *hijab*, and that it was part of her identity. 'I had to explain to the children that I do not wear *hijab* at home, but that I choose to wear it when I am outside in public. Then, when people look at me they are not judging whether I'm pretty or not, they are not just summing me up by my appearance. It means when I am talking, people listen to the words I say. It means I can be free to focus on how I behave. I try to live my life through the teachings of Islam. Wearing *hijab* means I can concentrate on my actions and whether they are just. We should not judge people by their appearance.'

Commentary

Both RE and CE were addressed in the ensuing wide-ranging discussion about dress codes. The children were keen to discuss their own views and explore Fatima's reasons. Children learned about Islamic teaching, considered the issues from a Muslim's point of view and their own, and developed their own understandings of cultural diversity. They also considered stereotyping and prejudice, and developed empathy and respect for the beliefs of others.

This was a very valuable experience for the non-Muslim children and also offered support to Muslims in the class. Fatima was confident about this discussion, both because she had thought through her own position and because she was knowledgeable. Those of us who want to encourage such debate but are not part of the specific faith ourselves need to find out about the faith perspective and develop confidence to handle such discussion, using the strategies outlined in earlier chapters about sensitive or controversial issues.

Table 8.1 suggests some opportunities to link RE and CE, developing the two attainment targets for RE, and social and moral responsibility and community involvement for CE. The last column is for you to look for links to the CE guidelines for KS1 or 2. The first example is filled in for you.

	Learning about religions	**Learning from religion**	**Activities**	**CE links from NC guidance**
KS1	Investigate what is most important to people from various religious backgrounds.	Talk about what is important to pupils. Investigate their behaviour and the things that influence it.	Talk to representatives of faith communities about what they value. Discuss what is valuable to individuals and to the class as a whole.	*Playing an active role as citizens by: taking part in discussions, recognising choices, beginning to know about different cultures and beliefs.*
KS2	Investigate what is involved in being a member of a specific religious community.	Consider what it is like to live your life in a community with shared values. Which shared communities do pupils belong to? Which shared values do they have?	Listen to people talking about their religious beliefs and values. Discuss class and school values and other expressions of value pupils encounter.	

Table 8.1 Linking RE and CE

How RE pedagogy can develop CE

Developing self-confidence and self-esteem

In Chapter 1 we looked at the importance of self-confidence and self-esteem for healthy attitudes. We noted that believing that you matter, and that your opinions count, were the bedrock to valuing other people's individuality and opinions. Self-confidence is central to RE as well as to CE. Some pupils struggle to express themselves and feel vulnerable about discussing personal issues. Many children find talking about their religious beliefs challenging, especially if they are in a minority, so creating an atmosphere of respect is very important. You shouldn't expect children to be able to articulate their religious beliefs clearly and act as teachers. You should welcome contributions from children who are happy to talk about their own beliefs or practices but remember that some children keep a very clear divide between home and school life and do not want to discuss their religious practices. As we discussed in Chapters 3 and 4, an open classroom with clearly developed ground rules which show respect and appreciation for each individual is central to pupils' confidence. The role of a teacher is to support children of all beliefs, theist or atheist, and to encourage each child's contribution.

Experiential learning and spirituality

Experiential learning is central to children's learning in all areas of the curriculum, but has a particular home in RE. Many teachers are concerned about the subject-laden focus of the curriculum and are turning, or in some cases returning, to the ideas of Dewey, Piaget and Vygotsky about the importance of active engagement in learning, and the construction of understanding through collaboration and talk. Activities which encourage reflection on learning as well as acquiring information are important for both RE and CE. In RE much of this reflective learning comes through the Attainment Target 'Learning from Religion'. Make sure that children go beyond learning how religions apply ideas, and have an opportunity to express how they think and feel, and relate the ideas to their own lives.

CE relies on experiential learning to open up empathetic dialogue. Hot-seating (a drama technique outlined in Chapter 4) is an excellent way for children to get to grips with the relationship of religion, motivation and human rights, for example through an 'interview' with Martin Luther King, Mother Teresa, Muhammad Ali, Mahatma Gandhi or Archbishop Desmond Tutu. (See Mackley and Draycott, 2000, for more strategies for active learning in RE.)

The ERA (1988) sets out the aim for the school curriculum to 'promote the spiritual, moral, cultural, mental and physical development of pupils and society' (DfE, 1994, p.9). Defining 'spirituality' and considering its place alongside the development of emotional and moral literacy is part of RE and has led to considerable debate about what constitutes 'spiritual education' for children (see Straughan, 2000). Jane Erricker offers a definition which works for CE as well as RE, if spirituality is seen as about one's essential humanity rather than religion: '[spirituality] can be the nurturing of all children towards a fuller understanding of their own emotional and aesthetic potential and the development of the skills required' (Erricker, 2001, p.200). There are aspects of identity and values which RE is uniquely placed to develop. CE benefits from an holistic approach towards exploring and understanding one's personal identity, creativity and sensitivity which RE encourages. This is relevant to all children irrespective of religious affiliation. Through opportunities to express their feelings and their individual identity through a range of stimuli, whether emotional language, music, art or drama, they can develop greater self-confidence and self-knowledge. They also practise skills needed to discuss social and moral choices, identity and values.

A common pedagogy for RE and CE

RE and CE both require skills of sensitivity and negotiation in teachers. As Chapter 3 emphasised, activities which encourage reflection and emotional expression need an atmosphere which is supportive and non-judgemental. As teachers, we move from instruction towards facilitation, and offer a role model of an active learner, inclusive, enthusiastic and open to new ideas about unfamiliar concepts and practices. An image I often use is that of the teacher walking beside children, rather than leading from the front. We may know more about the theory, details about practice and technical terms, but children bring their own thoughts and experiences. We are not there to teach children our interpretations but rather to develop their own understandings and interpretations.

Identity, culture and religious practice

Identity – developing one's own, and recognising that of others – is central to CE. For many people, their religion is not only inseparable from their identity, but interwoven with their culture, making it impossible to try to understand one without the other. For Christians, Easter and Christmas – sending cards, giving presents, times when the family gets together, special meals eaten – are cultural and not just religious events, which cement a common identity. For Jews, not just the religious festivals of Passover or Chanukah, the Friday night meal, but also the shared history, particularly of the past century, the knowledge of a diaspora, are ineradicable elements of Jewish identity. Many of my Hindu students talk about family relationships and religious obligations as one and the same. Their expression of Hindu beliefs is through their social obligations and they see cultural expression as inseparable from religious expression.

Understanding the relationship of culture and religion for CE

Children often develop a stronger sense of their own identity in relation to ideas from other cultures and beliefs. They clarify their own ideas while they learn about diversity, different religious practices and the reasons for them.

Classroom story

Considering hospitality

Rahel, a Hindu pupil, explained that her mother was always very generous when people came to visit and that she saw it as part of her religious duty to offer what she could. She commented, 'Mum treats them as though Lord Krishna himself was visiting.' The class thought about this idea and discussed different ways of greeting guests. Mary's mother said 'Make yourself at home' and this was seen as an invitation to relax and join the family activity. Tej explained how his father offered fruit juice so as not to offend those who did not drink tea, coffee or alcohol. Other children in the class then talked about friends coming for meals, including those who did not eat meat, who did not eat pork and who had food allergies. Amba explained that her family always ate 'Indian' at home except when she had friends to tea when her mother prepared food which she thought the visitors might prefer. Sanjey explained that his mum read the labels of food packets very carefully whenever his friend Mittel came to a meal because although they were also Hindu, he was a stricter vegetarian than they were. The class ended by agreeing that it was important to try to make people feel welcome by acknowledging their beliefs and customs through giving them appropriate hospitality.

Commentary

The discussion showed that different members of the class had understood the reasons behind their friends' requirements. They could speak confidently about their own cultural and religious traditions but they were also sensitive to the wishes and needs of others. They acknowledged that some members of a religion might be more strict in their observance of food requirements than others, but agreed that it was up to individual families to decide what they wanted to do. This showed a sophisticated understanding about the beliefs of others and the realisation that differences may exist within religions and cultures, as well as between them.

Multiple identities

In Chapter I we considered our multiple identities, with religion, ethnicity and culture contributing in important ways to our sense of who we are. Children may feel they need to negotiate between the different communities they belong to. At school they are members of a class, speak English as the common language and share a common set of values in relationship to school life. At home or in an ethnic community they may speak another language, dress in another way and behave according to another set of values. For some, the negotiation between different aspects of identity can be easier than for others. Teachers are in a position to facilitate this for children through providing opportunities for them to talk about their membership of different groups and communities. This is of course important for CE as well as for RE. Children will see that their experiences are respected, learn to respect others and develop self-confidence through investigating their own multiple identities.

Using artefacts to learn about identity and religious expression

Across the key stages, artefacts are commonly used to encourage discussion of religious concepts. Pupils handle and describe them and consider their purposes. The depth of questioning will relate to the children's experience and their knowledge of the religion at issue. Such work contributes to children's understanding of community values as well as RE in that they are encouraged to consider the symbolism of the artefacts to members of a community. They also think about objects of their own which they value and which contribute to their sense of identity.

Classroom story

Sikh kara – *KS1*

Simon had learned in his PGCE course how artefacts engage children with the details of religious practice and stimulate them to express their own ideas. A concrete object creates a dialogue between an outsider's perception of a religious or cultural practice and an insider's symbolism and perception. He decided to use an artefact to stimulate discussion about what is important to a particular religion. He extended the

discussion to what is important to children in the class. He brought in a Sikh *kara* (a steel band worn on the right wrist which shows the oneness of God and the unity and strength of the Sikh community) hidden in a 'feely' bag. The sense of mystery made the artefact seem 'special'. The children sat on the carpet and passed round the bag, so that everyone had a turn feeling the object, without taking it out and looking at it, and without saying anything out loud. When Simon asked them to describe what they had felt, they quite quickly identified that it was a metal hoop or band. Finally, Simon took out and showed the *kara*. Now they had to think about three questions:

- **What was the *kara* made of and why?**
- **What did they notice about how it was made?**
- **Why might people wear it?**

The children concluded that it was made of metal, which was very strong, that it was the same all the way round and did not have a break in it, and that it might help people to remember something important to them. Using their ideas, Simon explained the significance of the *kara* to members of the Sikh faith and what it suggested about the Sikh community. He also explained that it was one of the *panj kakke* ('five Ks' which are the symbols of faith) of Sikhism.

He asked the children to think about their ideas and decide if they could think of things that people wore to show either that they believed in something or because they wanted to remember something. The children thought of their own individual items, symbols from different religions and badges which showed which groups they belonged to. They also discussed school uniform and other uniforms they knew.

Then Simon drew the conversation back to how a Sikh might feel when wearing the *kara*. Children suggested 'happy, proud, strong, thoughtful, special and belonging'. Simon felt that handling the *kara* deepened the children's understanding because they could feel it, test its strength and see its 'oneness', and that they grasped the abstract ideas which might otherwise have eluded them.

Learning about religions	Learning from religion	CE links
Learning about the *kara* and its role in the five K's of Sikhism.	Exploring the symbolism of the *kara* and that people can wear or carry items which have symbolism for them. Exploring items of significance and identifying why they are significant.	Exploring the significance of community in Sikh teaching. Learning to identify items of particular meaning in a religious context and respecting religious diversity.

Table 8.2 Summary of the RE and CE links in Simon's activity using the Sikh *kara*.

Issues for schools

Handling artefacts in school and storing them are important issues. Religious artefacts need to be treated with respect and stored appropriately. Some artefacts are not appropriate in school and if there is any doubt ask a member of the local religious community. Both Draycott (1997) and Howard (1995) give more information about these issues.

Classroom story

Celebrating *Pesach* – KS2

Biblical references: Slavery in Egypt – Exodus I, 2–22; preparation of the Passover meal – Exodus 12, 2–34; Crossing the Red Sea – Exodus 14, 21–31

Bushra was in Year 6 and decided that for a lesson on the Jewish festival of *Pesach* (Passover) she would bring in a *Seder* plate to remind children of the story of the Passover and Exodus from Egypt which is recorded in the *Torah*. The plate she used was made of metal and had the words of the foods used at the *Seder* meal in Hebrew and in English. The class already knew the story of Moses and the Exodus and they had watched a video of a family celebration of the *Seder* meal in Year 4 and discussed the significance of the shared meal. The purpose of this lesson was to deepen understanding rather than repeat the story.

Bushra's Learning Objectives were:

RE: To extend the pupils' knowledge of the celebration of *Pesach* today.
　　To consider the experience of celebrating the *Seder* meal.
　　To engage with the symbolism of the food and the details of the celebration, and through them to consider one's own attitudes to oppression and freedom.
CE: To consider issues of human rights, exploitation and liberation.

From the point of view of CE, the main focus was to use the items on the *Seder* table to stimulate discussion about slavery and freedom: haroset – paste made of chopped apple, nuts, cinnamon and wine; maror – bitter herbs; karpas – lettuce, parsley or celery; salted water.

Bushra used the *Seder* plate at the beginning of the lesson to introduce the subject of *Pesach*. The children recognised it and recalled the story from their work in Year 4. The plate acted as the prompt because the words in English around the inner ring reminded them of the symbolic nature of the meal. Bushra asked the children to tell the story again, and they reflected on the significance of the celebration of *Pesach* for Jewish people. Then she brought out the *haroset* (after checking for nut allergies) and reminded them that it represented the mortar used in the building projects when the Jews were slaves in Egypt. The class shared their understanding of slavery. Some referred to stories they had been told in history, and others considered the emotional and physical distress people suffered as slaves.

Then Bushra showed the *maror* (grated horseradish), which brings tears to the eye because of its bitter taste, *karpas*, which symbolises new life, and the salted water to represent the tears shed while suffering slavery. She asked the children to think what it might mean to Jewish people to celebrate freedom every year, how they might feel about the meal and the impact of the story itself. The children wanted to talk about current issues which were analogous to 'slavery' or oppression and how people could be 'freed'. They discussed the impact of poverty and war on children and how they could be helped. Bushra felt that the artefacts themselves helped the children interpret and understand the symbolism of the *Pesach* story, reflect on its meaning, make connections for themselves and empathise with those who celebrate *Pesach* today, and those who suffer.

Commentary

Having the artefacts available for children to handle meant that they could touch, see, smell and taste. Many children have little or no personal experience of religious practice and artefacts act as anchors when they encounter new concepts. Handling an object can create links between their own experience and the religion being studied. The activities used artefacts as a starting point for pupils to explore concepts which relate to both religious and secular human experience. The religious experience of one community becomes a springboard to explore other types of community experience, creating bridges of empathy and understanding which fulfil the aims of both RE and CE.

Summary

In this chapter we have considered:

- **How RE is delivered in the primary curriculum through Agreed Syllabuses and through two Attainment Targets – learning *about* religion and learning *through* religion.**
- **How these Attainment Targets provide a context in which RE can address CE.**
- **The similarities between the aims, skills and concepts of RE and CE.**
- **Some areas of difference between RE and CE which affect their learning outcomes.**
- **How the 'Crick strands' of social and moral responsibility and community involvement might be explored through RE.**
- **Areas of RE pedagogy, particularly experiential learning and spirituality, which have value for CE.**
- **Issues of identity and how they can be supported through RE and CE.**
- **Examples of how to use religious artefacts to draw out issues of human as well as religious experience, creating opportunities for work on identity and community.**

Note

1 For discussion about the interpretation and impact of the 1988 Education Reform Act and the Model Syllabuses, see editorials in the *British Journal for Religious Education*, Autumn 1989, Summer 1991, Autumn 1991, Autumn 1994. These are also available in Hull, 1998, *Utopian Whispers*.

PSHE – Personal social and health education

QCA – Qualifications and Curriculum Authority

ITE – Initial teacher education

ITT – Initial teacher training

OFSTED – Office for Standards in Education

INSET – In-service education for teachers

NGO – Non-governmental organisation

DfEE/DfES – Department for Education and Employment; changed to Department for Education and Skills in June 2001

TTA – Teacher Training Agency

EO – Equal opportunities

NC – National Curriculum

PoS – Programmes of study

DfID – Department for International Development

DEA – Development Education Association

LSA – Learning support assistant

NQT – Newly qualified teacher

Categories

1. General
2. Circle time, self-esteem, emotional literacy, collaboration in the classroom
3. Controversial issues
4. Economics: children's attitudes
5. Equal-opportunities policies
6. 'Futures education'
7. Geography and global citizenship
8. History
9. Human rights and anti-racist teaching
10. Philosophy for and with children and communities of enquiry
11. Race and racism
12. Refugees and asylum seekers
13. Religious education
14. School councils and school parliaments
15. Social and moral development, values and whole-school ethos

I. General

Bailey, R. (ed) (2000) *Teaching values and citizenship across the curriculum,* London: Kogan Page. Good chapters on geography, history, English and other subjects.

Brown, M. (ed) (1996) *Our World, Our Rights: Teaching About Rights and Responsibilities in the Primary Classroom*, London: Amnesty International.

Burns, S. and Lamont, G. (1996) *Values and visions: A Handbook for Spiritual Development and Global Awareness*, London: Hodder and Stoughton.

Claire, H. (2001) *Not Aliens: Primary Children and the PSHE/Citizenship Curriculum*, Stoke on Trent: Trentham. Based on qualitative research with primary-age children – reports on their concerns and understanding of a variety of citizenship and PSHE issues.

Clough, N. and Holden, C. (2002) *Education for Citizenship, Ideas into Action*, London: Routledge/Falmer. One of the best available sources for practical activities in primary, across the range of Citizenship Education.

Crick, B. (1998) *Education for citizenship and the teaching of democracy in schools: Final report of the Advisory Group on Citizenship*, QCA.

DfEE/QCA (1999) *The National Curriculum Handbook for primary teachers in England, Key Stages I and 2*.

DfES (2003) *Excellence and Enjoyment: a strategy for primary schools*.

Jerome, L., Hayward, J., Easy, J. and Newman, A. (2004) *The Citizenship Coordinator's Handbook*, Cheltenham: Nelson Thornes.

Klein, R. (2001) *Citizens by Right: Citizenship Education in Primary Schools*, Stoke on Trent: Trentham Books with Save the Children Fund. Based on work with young primary children – excellent and practical.

QCA (2000) *Non-Statutory Guidance on Religious Education*, QCA, London.

QCA (2000) *Personal, social and health education and citizenship at Key Stages 1 and 2: initial guidance for schools.*

QCA (2002) *Citizenship: A Scheme of Work for Key Stages 1 and 2*, QCA, London.

QCA (2003) *Citizenship at Key Stages 1–4. Guidance on assessment, recording and reporting.*

QCA (2004) *A national framework for Religious Education: Draft work in progress – consultation version*, QCA, London.

www.standards.dfes.gov.uk/schemes/cit.info Schemes of work being developed through the QCA.

www.dfes.gov.uk/citizenship News, resources, and other website links related to citizenship.

www.citizen.org.uk Institute for Citizenship site. Mainly KS3, but adaptable for KS2 or 1, and helpful resources for teacher INSET. Useful table from UNICEF about range of active participation, from genuine to tokenism.

www.citfon.org.uk Citizenship foundation site. Independent charity which initiates practical projects with young people to develop skills, knowledge and understanding.

2. Circle time, self-esteem, emotional literacy, collaboration in the classroom

Bliss, T., Maines, B. and Robinson, G. (1995) *Developing Circle Time*, Lucky Duck Publishing. Clearly written activities. Different emphases to Mosley (below) – more concerned with confidentiality and feelings; less about behaviour management.

Borba, M. (1989) *Esteem Builders: a K-8 self-esteem curriculum for improving student achievement, behaviour and school climate*, Jalmar Press: California. American; practical and easy-to-use activities for KS2/3 classrooms.

Burns, S. and Lamont, G. (2000) *Values and Visions: Who are you? Who am I? An anti-racist programme for schools,* Hodder and Stoughton with DEP, Cafod and Christian Aid. Takes on bad feeling between different groups; self-esteem and identity of refugees; why people live in Britain; culture and customs.

Button, K. and Winter, M. (no date) *Pushing back the furniture: practical ways of teaching social skills, developing co-operation and enhancing self-esteem in the primary classroom*, Behaviour Support Service, Kirklees Education Authority.

Goleman, D. (1996) *Emotional Intelligence*, London: Bloomsbury.

Gust, John (1994) *Enhancing self-esteem: a whole language approach*, Good Apple, Paramount Publishing. Activities clearly set out.

Hobbs, N. (2000) *Project Charlie*: PSHE, Drugs Education. Practical activities for work on self-esteem, relationships, decision-making and resisting peer pressure. Order direct from Nancy Hobbs, 102 Buckingham Road, London N1 4JE.

Mosley, J. (1996) *Quality Circle Time*, LDA.

— (1998) *More Quality Circle Time*, LDA.

— (1998) *Turn your school around*, LDA.

Mosley's approach emphasises reward systems and removal of privileges for transgressing rules.

www.jrf.org.uk/knowledge/findings/socialpolicy/n71.asp British review of self-esteem research by Professor Nick Emler from LSE.

www.self-esteem-nase.org Good site for American self-esteem articles, including by Michelle Borba, John Vasconcellos and Robert Reasoner.
www.kidshealth.org American site on self-esteem.
www.antidote.org.uk Manifesto and resources on emotional literacy.
www.dialogueworks.org.uk Emotional literacy.

3. Controversial issues

Claire, H. (2003) *Dealing with controversial issues with primary teacher trainees as part of citizenship education*, **www.citized.info/articles.shtml**. Scroll down till you reach this article, which has very detailed ideas for work with students on thinking logically, and case studies of students' work on controversial issues.
Crick, B. (1998) *Education for citizenship and the teaching of democracy in schools*. Final report of the Advisory Group on Citizenship, QCA, pp.56–61 (also on web).
Onesko, J. (1996) *Exploring the issues with students despite the barriers*, Social Education, Vol. 60, pp.22–27.
QCA/DfES (2001) *Citizenship: a scheme of work for Key Stage 3: Teacher's Guide*, Appendix 9: pp.46–48 (also on web).
Stradling, R. (1984) in Hill, S. and Reid, C., *Teaching Controversial Issues*, London: Edward Arnold.
www.onlineethics.org Good material on teaching about ethics in scientific contexts.
www.globalethics.org Theoretical and practical discussion about values and controversies.
www.flinders.edu.au/teach/teach/inclusive/controversial Excellent on ground rules and strategies with students and children.
www.indiana.edu/%7Essdc Excellent article by Diane Hess, 2001, Teaching students about controversial public issues.
www.nationalmocktrial.org/cases/index This is where I found the mock trial based on Goldilocks v The Three Bears.
www.rethinkingschools.org/ This UK site publishes articles about a variety of topical controversial issues and has a search engine for past articles.

4. Economics: children's attitudes

Claire, H. (2001) *Not Aliens: Primary School Children and the PSHE/Citizenship Curriculum*, Stoke on Trent: Trentham. Chapter 7.

5. Equal-opportunities policies

Jacques, K. and Hyland, R. (eds) 2nd edition (2003) *Professional Studies Primary Phase*, Exeter: Learning Matters. Chapter 11: Equal Opportunities in the School, Meeting the Professional Standards for QTS.
Myers, K. (ed), 2nd edition (1992) *Genderwatch after ERA*, Cambridge University Press.

6. 'Futures education'

Hicks, D. (1994) *Educating for the Future: a practical classroom guide*, Surrey: WWF.

Hicks, D. and Holden, C. (1995) *Visions of the future: why we need to teach for tomorrow*, Stoke on Trent: Trentham.

Holden, C. (2003) 3rd impression, *Keen at 11, cynical at 18?* In C. Holden and N. Clough (eds) *Children as Citizens: education for participation*, London: Jessica Kingsley.

7. Geography and global citizenship

Carter, R. (ed.) (2000) *The Handbook of Primary Geography*, Sheffield: The Geographical Association.

Christian Aid (2000) *Local Citizen; Global Citizen Activities for Teaching Citizenship and Personal Development for Use with 8–12 Year Olds*, London: Christian Aid.

DfID/DfEE/QCA/DEA/The Central Bureau (2000) *Developing a global dimension in the school curriculum*.

DfID/Action Aid (2000) *Learning Global Lessons: 50 Non-Fiction Literacy Hours*.

Fisher, S. (1980) *Ideas into Action: Curriculum for a Changing World*, London: World Studies Project.

Fisher, S. and Hicks, D. (1985) *World Studies 8–13: A Teacher's Handbook*, Edinburgh: Oliver and Boyd.

Grimwade, K. et al. (2000) *Geography and the New Agenda*, Sheffield: The Geographical Association.

Oxfam (1997) *A Curriculum for Global Citizenship*, Oxfam.

— (2001) *Your World, My World: A Wake Up World Photopack for Citizenship, PSE and PSD*, Oxfam.

Pike, G. and Selby, D. (1988) *Global Teacher, Global Learner*, London: Hodder and Stoughton.

Steiner, M. (1993) *Learning from Experience: A World Studies Source Book*, Stoke-on-Trent: Trentham.

Young, M. with Commins, F. (2002) *Global Citizenship: The handbook for primary teaching*, Oxfam.

Organisations and websites

Action Aid provides educational resources and services for schools: Chataway House, Leach Road, Chard TA20 1FR. **www.actionaid.org**

Christian Aid provides materials for literacy, geography and citizenship, and staff who will visit schools. **www.christian-aid.org.uk**

Development Education Association (DEA): national organisation which supports NGOs and local centres providing materials and support for global education. 33 Corsham Street, London N1 6DR. **www.dea.org.uk**

Save the Children (SCF) produces many materials for teachers and children: 17 Grove Lane, London SE5 8RD. **www.savethechildren.org.uk**

Sustrans Safe Routes to Schools provides free project material and support for schools to help make cycling and walking safe. **www.sustrans.org.uk**

www.seizetheday.com gives details about planting trees and other opportunities to counter global warming.

UNICEF provides information, teaching resources and links with children around the world: 55 Lincoln's Inn Fields, London WC2A 3NB. **www.unicef.org.uk**

The Geographical Association champions geography in the school curriculum, provides advice and guidance to teachers, and produces many resources for teaching primary geography: 160, Solly Street, Sheffield S1 4BF. **www.geography.org.uk**

WWF-UK (World Wide Fund for Nature) produces an annual catalogue of resources for teachers and schools: Panda House, Weyside Park, Godalming, Surrey GU7 1XR. **www.wwf-uk.org**

www.eco-schools.org.uk Free materials to enable schools to carry out an environmental review and make an action plan.

www.education.ed.ac.uk/efs Active learning in environmental education.

www.globalfootprints.org Activities for primary children related to sustainability.

www.oxfam.org.uk/coolplanet/ Aimed at children 6–16, it is interactive and has many resources and links to useful sites.

www.wastewatch.org.uk Environmental issues at primary level.

www.wwflearning.co.uk Case studies relating to sustainability and environmental issues.

8. History

Claire, H. (1996) *Reclaiming our Pasts: equality and diversity in the primary history curriculum*, Stoke on Trent: Trentham. Chapters 4 and 12 for significant people.

— (2002) *Why didn't you fight Ruby?* Education 3 – 13, June.

— (forthcoming) *History and Citizenship*, Historical Association.

— (2004) *You did the best you can! Social and moral development through history*, in Osler, A. (ed) *Teachers, Human Rights and Diversity*, Trentham.

Clough, N. and Holden C. (2001) *Education for Citizenship 7–14*, Falmer/Routledge, for case studies on Ancient Greece and Mesopotamia.

PCET Educational Charts (2004) The Pankhursts, Gandhi, Anne Frank.

www.qca.org.uk/ca/inclusion/respect-for-all/ For projects on three significant people in Year 2, KS1, and work on Britain since the 1930s for Year 6.

www.ncaction/creativity

www.irelandinschools.org.uk

9. Human rights and anti-racist teaching

Brown, M. (ed.) (1996) *Our World, Our Rights: teaching about rights and responsibilities in the primary classroom,* London: Amnesty International.

Friedman, E. *et al.* (1999) *Let's make a difference: teaching anti-racism in primary schools, a Jewish perspective,* London: J-CORE.

Osler, A. (2000b) *Citizenship and democracy in schools: diversity, identity, equality,* Stoke on Trent: Trentham. Analytic resource at adult level: good chapters on human rights around the world.

— (ed.) (2004) *Teachers, Human Rights and Diversity,* Stoke on Trent: Trentham.

Save the Children Fund (2000) *Partners in Rights: creative activities exploring rights and citizenship for 7–11 year olds,* SCFUK.

www.runnymedetrust.org/ Current articles about race-related issues.

www.britkid.org British site devoted to dealing with racism among young people – good strategies for working with students.

www.oise.utoronto.ca/orbit/anti-racism_sample.html Site from Toronto, with (in 2004) an excellent summary of strategies to deal with Islamophobia, including 'Reclaiming the Stage' – namely focusing on the aspects of Islam that are peaceful and tolerant, to counter the current stereotypes of terrorism and fundamentalism.

10. Philosophy for and with children and communities of enquiry

Fisher, Robert (1995) *Teaching Children to Learn*, Stanley Thornes.

— (1997) *Games for Thinking*, Nash Pollock.

— (1996) *Stories for Thinking*, Nash Pollock.

Fox, Richard (1996) *Thinking Matters – stories to encourage thinking skills*, Southgate.

Lipman, Mathew (1988) *Philosophy goes to school*, Temple University Press.

— (1994) *The Philosophy of Childhood*, Harvard.

Both readable introductions to Philosophy with Children.

Matthews, G. (1984) *Dialogues with Children*, Harvard.

Murris, Karen and Haynes, Joanna (2000) *Storywise: Thinking through Stories*, 2 vols: Dialogue Works, The Old School Centre, Newport, Pembs. Detailed notes on how to run sessions and examples of dialogue; Teacher's Guidance: similar but extends material in Vol I.

Quinn, Victor (1997) *Critical Thinking in Young Minds*, David Fulton.

www.dialogueworks.co.uk/dw/wr/kmurris/pwcl.doc Explains methods of Philosophy with Children.

www.dialogueworks.co.uk/dw/wr/kmurris/trfl.doc Explains role of facilitator in Philosophy with Children.

www.sapere.net Philosophy with Children.

www.utasedu.audocs.humsoc/philosophy Useful and interesting Australian site.

www.somersetthinkingskills.co.uk Small but informative set of papers about theory and ongoing work.

www.teachingthinking.net. Dr Bob Fisher's *Centre for Thinking Skills* (CRITT) at Brunel University which runs PIPS – Philosophy in Primary Schools.

www.salt.cheshire.gov.uk/mfl/thinking/Document2.PDF. Provides an easy-to-follow algorithm for setting up a community of enquiry.

www.bathnes.gov.uk/psychology/apex/teachersinfo/teachercourseoct03.htm Briefly defines Philosophy for Children.

philip.adey@kcl.ac.uk Professor Adey, Centre for the Advancement of Thinking, at Kings College, London University, has revived and extended much of the material which primary teachers used in the 1970s and 1980s (before the Literacy and Numeracy Strategies) through a research programme on cognitive acceleration to develop logical thought.

11. Race and racism

Bournemouth Borough Council with Christian Aid, Soundstorm and Bournemouth Theatre in Education (2003) *Resource book for teachers: Surya's Story,* contact Bournemouth TiE, **tie@bournemouth.gov.uk**. 'Child of the World' and Teachers' Resource Pack will be available later this year from Bournemouth Borough Council, Inclusion and Achievement (Publications), Dorset House, 20–22 Christchurch Road, Bournemouth, BH1 3NL.

Gaine, C. (1995) *Still no problem here,* Stoke on Trent: Trentham.

Parekh, B. (2000) *The Future of Multi Ethnic Britain: Report of the Commission on the future of Multi-Ethnic Britain*, London: Profile Books with The Runnymede Trust.

Osler, A. (2000a) 'The Crick Report: difference, equality and racial justice', *The Curriculum Journal,* vol. 11, no. 1, Spring 2000, pp. 25–37.

12. Refugees and asylum seekers

Refugee Council (1996) *Refugees: we left because we had to,* London: Refugee Council.

— (1998) *Refugees: a primary school resource*, London: Refugee Council.

Rutter, J. (2003) 2nd edition. *Supporting Refugee children in 21st Century Britain*, Stoke on Trent: Trentham. Information about the main countries that refugees/asylum seekers have come from, and describes good practice in refugee education.

— (2004) *Sold Short: education policy and refugee children*, Buckingham: Open University Press.

www.refugeecouncil.org.uk

www.refugeecouncil.org.uk/news/myths/myth001.htm Useful for teachers and student teachers wanting to get factual information prior to doing work with a class about refugees. It offers statistics about the numbers of refugees accepted into the country, the situation with respect to benefits and the law.

www.savethechildren.org.uk/scuk/jsp/resources/details Gives information about different refugee groups.

www.savethechildren.org.uk/temp/scuk/cache/cmsattach/ 1125.AssembRefugees.pdf Ready-made script for an assembly about refugees, which could be performed by older primary children. Children would gain a fair amount of knowledge just from reading the script.

Books for children about refugees

Hasbudak, Z. and Simons, B. (1989) *Zeynep: That really happened to me,* ALTARF.

Naidoo, B. (2001) *The Other Side of Truth,* London: Puffin.

Zephaniah, Benjamin (2000) *Refugee Boy,* Bloomsbury.

13. Religious education

Broadbent, L. (2000) 'Values Education, citizenship and the contribution of RE' in Bailey, R. (ed) *Teaching Values and Citizenship,* Derby: Kogan Page.

DfE (1994) *Religious Education and Collective Worship: Circular 1/94,* London: DfE.

Draycott, P. (1997) *Religious Artefacts: Why? What? How?*, Derby: CEM.

Erricker, J. (2001) 'Spirituality and the Notion of Citizenship in Education' in Erricker, J., Ota, C. and Erricker, C. (eds) *Spiritual Education, Cultural, Religious and Social Differences, New Perspectives for the 21st Century,* Brighton: Sussex Academic Press.

Howard, C. (1995) *Investigating Artefacts in Religious Education,* Norwich: RMEP.

Hull, J. (1987) Editorial 'Religious Education and Modernity', *British Journal of Religious Education,* Summer 1987.

— (1998) *Utopian Whispers,* Norwich: RMEP.

Jackson, R. (1997) *Religious Education: an Interpretive Approach,* London: Hodder and Stoughton.

Mackley, J. and Draycott, P. (2000) *A to Z Active Learning Strategies to support Spiritual and Moral Development,* Derby: Christian Education Movement.

QCA/SCAA (1994) *Model Syllabus I* and *Model Syllabus 2,* London: SCAA.

Straughan, R. (2000) 'Spiritual Education: what's it all about' in Bailey, R. (ed.) *Teaching Values and Citizenship,* Derby: Kogan Page.

14. School councils and school parliaments

Clough, N. and Holden, C. (2002) *Education for Citizenship: Ideas into Action, A practical guide for teachers of pupils aged 7–14,* Routledge/Falmer, Chapter 2.

John, M. (2000) 'The Children's Parliament in Rajasthan: a model for learning about democracy', in Osler, A. (ed) *Citizenship and democracy in schools,* Trentham.

www.schoolcouncils.org, or contact them on **info@schoolcouncils.org** (phone 020 8349 2459).

www.citizenship-pieces.org.uk/citizen.htm?schools+councils/ wholeschool.htm

www.standards.dfes.gov.uk/schemes2/ksl-2citizenship/ participation_online

www.ccc.govt.nz/ChildrensStrategy/ToolBox/Tools/ChildrensCouncils ParliamentsForums.asp New Zealand site critiquing tokenism of many school parliaments.

www.acwa.asn.au/wf2000/papers/l2flerin.doc Article about children's parliaments which are longstanding in Slovenia, and include primary-aged children.

www.childrens-express.org/dynamic/public/what_do_kids_010602.htm Reported on primary children involved in Schools Parliament for Islington in London, in 2002.

15. Social and moral development, values and whole-school ethos

Claire, H, (2004) 'You did the best you can: history, citizenship and moral dilemmas', in Osler, A. (ed) *Teachers, Human Rights and Diversity,* Stoke on Trent: Trentham.

Halstead, J. M. and Taylor, M. (2000) *The Development of Values, Attitudes and Personal Qualities: a review of recent research,* NFER.

Jackson, P. (1992) 'The enactment of the moral in what teachers do', *Curriculum Inquiry,* 22, 4, pp.401–7.

Midgley, M. (1997) 'Can education be moral?', in Smith and Standish. Discusses pupil participation and whole-school ethos.

Rowe, D. and Newton J. (eds) (1994) *You, Me, Us – A New Approach to Moral and Social Education for Primary Schools*, Citizenship Foundation.

Smith, R. and Standish, P. (eds) (1997) *Teaching Right and Wrong: moral education in the balance*, Stoke on Trent: Trentham.

www.ethosnet.co.uk/casestudies.htm Scottish Schools Ethos Network based at Moray House, Edinburgh. Case studies about pupil participation and the importance of whole school ethos **ssen@education.ed.ac.uk**

www.becal.net/toolkit/acorneres/acorneres.html Reports primary school research project on the relationship between staff values, whole-school ethos and children's values.

Achieving QTS

Our *Achieving QTS* series now includes 20 titles, encompassing *Audit and Test*, *Knowledge and Understanding*, *Teaching Theory and Practice*, and *Skills Tests* titles. As well as covering the core primary subject areas, the series addresses issues of teaching and learning across both primary and secondary phases. The Teacher Training Agency has identified books in this series as high quality resources for trainee teachers. You can find general information on each of these ranges on our website: www.learningmatters.co.uk

Primary English
Audit and Test (second edition)
Doreen Challen
£8 64 pages   ISBN: 1 903300 86 X

Primary Mathematics
Audit and Test (second edition)
Claire Mooney and Mike Fletcher
£8 52 pages ISBN: 1 903300 87 8

Primary Science
Audit and Test (second edition)
John Sharp and Jenny Byrne
£8 80 pages ISBN: 1 903300 88 6

Primary English
Knowledge and Understanding (second edition)
Jane Medwell, George Moore, David Wray, Vivienne Griffiths
£15   224 pages   ISBN: 1 903300 53 3

Primary English
Teaching Theory and Practice (second edition)
Jane Medwell, David Wray, Hilary Minns, Vivienne Griffiths, Elizabeth Coates
£15   192 pages   ISBN: 1 903300 54 1

Primary Mathematics
Knowledge and Understanding (second edition)
Claire Mooney, Lindsey Ferrie, Sue Fox, Alice Hansen, Reg Wrathmell
£15   176 pages   ISBN: 1 903300 55 X

Primary Mathematics
Teaching Theory and Practice (second edition)
Claire Mooney, Mary Briggs, Mike Fletcher, Judith McCullouch
£15   192 pages   ISBN: 1 903300 56 8

Primary Science
Knowledge and Understanding (second edition)
Rob Johnsey, Graham Peacock, John Sharp, Debbie Wright
£15   224 pages   ISBN: 1 903300 57 6

Primary Science
Teaching Theory and Practice (second edition)
John Sharp, Graham Peacock, Rob Johnsey, Shirley Simon, Robin Smith
£15   144 pages   ISBN: 1 903300 58 4

Primary ICT
Knowledge, Understanding and Practice (second edition)
Jane Sharp, John Potter, Jonathan Allen, Avril Loveless
£15   256 pages   ISBN: 1 903300 59 2

Professional Studies
Primary Phase (second edition)
Edited by Kate Jacques and Rob Hyland
£15   224 pages   ISBN: 1 903300 60 6

Assessment for Learning and Teaching in Primary Schools
Mary Briggs, Angela Woodfield, Cynthia Martin, Peter Swatton
£15   176 pages   ISBN: 1 903300 74 6

Teaching Foundation Stage
Edited by Iris Keating
£15   192 pages   ISBN: 1 903300 33 9

Teaching Humanities in Primary Schools
Pat Hoodless, Sue Bermingham, Elaine McReery, Paul Bowen
£15   192 pages   ISBN: 1 903300 36 3

Teaching Arts in Primary Schools
Stephanie Penny, Raywen Ford, Lawry Price, Susan Young
£15   192 pages   ISBN: 1 903300 35 5

Learning and Teaching in Secondary Schools
Edited by Viv Ellis
£15   192 pages   ISBN: 1 903300 38 X

Passing the Numeracy Skills Test (third edition)
Mark Patmore
£8   64 pages   ISBN: 1 903300 94 0

Passing the Literacy Skills Test
Jim Johnson
£6.99   80 pages   ISBN: 1 903300 12 6

Passing the ICT Skills Test
Clive Ferrigan
£6.99   80 pages   ISBN: 1 903300 13 4

Succeeding in the Induction Year (second edition)
Neil Simco
£14   144 pages   ISBN: 1 903300 93 2

To order, please contact our distributor:
BEBC Distribution
Albion Close
Parkstone
Poole BH12 3LL

Tel: 0845 230 9000
Email: learningmatters@bebc.co.uk